HE SPEAKS VOLUMES

HE SPEAKS VOLUMES

A BIOGRAPHY OF
GEORGE BOWERING

Rebecca Wigod

with a foreword by Margaret Atwood

Talonbooks

Talonbooks
278 East First Avenue, Vancouver, British Columbia, Canada V5T 1A6
talonbooks.com

Talonbooks is located on xʷməθkʷəy̓əm, Sḵwx̱wú7mesh, and səl̓ilwətaʔɬ Lands.

First printing: 2018

Typeset in Arno
Printed and bound in Canada on 100% post-consumer recycled paper

Cover design by Typesmith, interior design by andrea bennett

Cover photograph of George Bowering by LaVerne Harrell Clark, courtesy of The University of Arizona Poetry Center. Photograph copyright © 1963 Arizona Board of Regents.

Talonbooks acknowledges the financial support of the Canada Council for the Arts, the Government of Canada through the Canada Book Fund, and the Province of British Columbia through the British Columbia Arts Council and the Book Publishing Tax Credit.

LIBRARY AND ARCHIVES CANADA CATALOGUING IN PUBLICATION

Wigod, Rebecca, 1951–, author
    He speaks volumes : a biography of George Bowering / Rebecca Wigod.

ISBN 978-1-77201-206-4 (SOFTCOVER)

    1. Bowering, George, 1935–. 2. Authors, Canadian (English) – 20th century – Biography. 3. Biographies. I. Title.

PS8503.O875Z94 2018   C811'.54   C2018-904743-7

To the memory of Geoffrey Molyneux

*In 1978, when he was editorial page editor
at Vancouver's* Province,
he gave me my start in newspapers.

Even when the poet seems most himself ... he is never the bundle of accident and incoherence that sits down to breakfast; he has been reborn as an idea, something intended, complete.

—W.B. YEATS, *A General Introduction for My Work* (1937)

CONTENTS

LIST OF IMAGES

All photographs courtesy of George Bowering and Jean Baird except when otherwise noted in the image's caption.

GEORGE BOWERING &
THE GANGS OF KOSMOS

Margaret Atwood

I first met George Bowering and his wife Angela at a writers' party in Montreal in 1967. I was teaching at Sir George Williams (now part of Concordia), and so was he. She was wearing a mini-dress and white knee-high go-go boots, one of the fashions then; he was wearing a Donald Duck tie and doing a silly duck walk, and quacking – he was in the habit of acting up to disguise shyness, I suppose – eliciting from Angela the cry of, "Oh George!" that was familiar to all acquainted with their curious doubles act, in which George would step outside the lines in a deliberately embarrassing manner and Angela would catch him doing it and rebuke him for it. In those early days, she would also giggle delightedly. How could he be so naughty?

The English Canadian writing community was quite small then. Maybe it wasn't a community as such, but a flotsam-jetsam agglomeration of people interested in writing, and a small enough agglomeration so that those individuals tended to clump together for warmth. It was mostly the poets who knew one another, they having drifted hither and thither on buses and other modes of cheap transport and also having read together in various dives and at various universities. (The novelists were mostly holed up in private, bashing out their novels on their typewriters, though I did meet Clark Blaise in Montreal then as we were both teaching at Sir George; and Mordecai Richler wafted through town, and John Glassco was there, and Hugh Hood.) There were not yet any writers' festivals, and Jack McClelland had just started his ambitious and successful cross-country book tours, so you met other writers by happenstance, and through mutual friends. Poets in or around Montreal, or coming through for readings, included F.R. Scott, Gwendolyn MacEwen, and Doug Jones, Al Purdy, Irving Layton, and Leonard Cohen. And George Bowering.

I already knew George's work through *Points on the Grid* (Contact Press, 1964) and *The Man in Yellow Boots* (*El corno emplumado*, 1965), and I knew about the *TISH* group, as I had been in Vancouver in 1964/5. We poets read one another's work in those days; there wasn't so much that you couldn't keep up. At that time I was also working with Anansi in its early days – days in which it published mostly poetry, including my book *The Circle Game* (Contact, 1966), which had won the Governor General's Award but was out of print by that time, having printed the large number of 420 copies.

So I knew George and Angela, and I also knew Anansi, and I ended up putting together a collection of George's poems, *The Gangs of Kosmos*, which came out from Anansi in 1969. The magazine citations for the poems are a trip down memory lane, a trip that sometimes draws blanks: *The Ant's Forefoot*: what was that? *Camel's Coming*? *The Resuscitator*? But there's *Quarry*, and *Poetry* (Chicago), and *The London Magazine*. Not so shabby.

I think it's a pretty good collection. All the strengths. George was already worried about growing old, on page 62 (Haha, we laugh now: we thought *that* was old?) and is already as elegiac as he later became. No silly duck walks in the poems; those were done by his bodyguard, at parties, and for faking his own biography from time to time. All writers keep a double in store so they can save the reality for the art, and George's double was just more obvious than most.

The last poem, "You too," ends with an *envoi* to the reader:

How can I die alone.
Where will I be then who am now alone,
what groans so pathetically
in this room when I am alone?

I do not know, I know
you begin where my eye
leaves off, you too, turning
my pages are alone.

So there you are, George: I just read the poem. Again. Alone.
It all came true.

Note: Margaret Atwood's foreword was originally commissioned by The Capilano
Review *for the "Bowering's Books" issue, TCR 3.24, and is reprinted with her
permission and the kind assistance of* The Capilano Review.

A Note on Spelling

In his early writing, George Bowering used phonetic spelling for past-tense verbs – he'd write "slipt" instead of "slipped," for example, and "popt" instead of "popped," following the practice of California poet Robert Duncan. Also, Bowering routinely omits the apostrophe from contractions, writing "dont" and "cant" – William Faulkner used to do it, he has said. Another of his stylistic eccentricities is the portmanteau term "USAmericans," which he uses so as not to give citizens of the United States more than their due. He reasons that "America" means "everything from Alaska to Tierra del Fuego."

These spellings and related peculiarities appear without the addendum "[*sic*]" when he's quoted in this book.

HE SPEAKS VOLUMES

CHAPTER 1

MR. PROLIFIC

They keep telling me to talk more,
write less –

but I cant figure this out, I
will be doing neither
soon enough.

—"My Family's All in Bed," *Urban Snow* (1992)

The first time I met George Bowering, he was fresh from the two-year round of festival appearances, school visits, media events, and wine-and-cheese receptions that filled his days when he was Canada's first Parliamentary Poet Laureate in the early 2000s. I could have rattled off the titles of some of his books but didn't know his work intimately – far from it. Mostly, I knew him as a much-published writer with a reputation for being generous, even garrulous, when journalists asked for his opinions. I was working at the *Vancouver Sun* and wanted to interview him for a books-section feature about the laureateship; he was game and suggested we meet at Helen's Grill, his unpretentious hangout.

Jean Baird, who would become his second wife – twenty years younger than he, five years younger than I – was at his side during the session. At first, I didn't welcome that. Every reporter would rather be alone with an interview subject than have a minder running interference. But his seventieth birthday was in sight and it was clear she thought the world of him, though she wasn't above taking an occasional shot at his folksy shtick. Once, she referred to him as "His Bubba-ness." Another time, she spoke of a TV camera crew having been alert for the moment when he'd stick a finger up his nose. ("They thought, 'Oh, no! He's going to stick his finger up his nose again and we're going to miss it!'") Bowering was the class clown as a boy in the forties and would still do anything for a laugh.

After I left the newspaper business in 2010, I thought of him – of his giant, varied oeuvre, which has brought him recognition and forever tagged him with the adjective "prolific," and of his capering personality, endearing to some, annoying to others – and wondered if I could write the biography he deserved. The following spring, I sent him an old-fashioned letter making the proposal and seeking his cooperation. Unlike Saul Bellow, who told James Atlas that answering questions for a biography by Atlas felt like "being measured for your coffin," Bowering wanted to be the subject of a book-length profile. Why else would he have kept his voluminous correspondence with other writers, be they famous, like Margaret Atwood, Michael Ondaatje, Margaret Laurence, Al Purdy, and Allen Ginsberg, or more narrowly admired, like Margaret Avison, Robert Kroetsch, John Newlove, and Hugh Hood? Why else would he have kept a diary for decades? Although he's wanted his own record of his life, he's also kept an eye out for posterity. While still in his twenties, he wrote beside some student-newspaper clippings he'd taped into his then quite new series of hardbound journals, "Biographers: Say he was a real sucker for his name in print!"

Since he gave his okay, much of what I've learned from reading his books and diaries, visiting him at his West Point Grey home (notable for its cleanliness and order, even though he and Baird share it with a big furry dog), talking with him more than twenty times, and interviewing his relatives, friends, former colleagues, students, and sandlot baseball buddies, has surprised me. I hadn't known that he reveres the English Romantic poet Percy Bysshe Shelley, especially his *Ode to the West Wind* and *Adonaïs* elegy, or that he considers himself a direct literary descendant of Gertrude Stein, William Carlos Williams, Ezra Pound, and H.D. – all born in the United States in the late 1800s. It has never fazed him that, except perhaps for Williams, they're notoriously hard to read. He likes abstract painting more than representational; he has plenty of time for the composer Arnold Schoenberg and his atonality; he prefers squawky free jazz to the kind that makes good elevator music. He'd rather read novels by John Hawkes and Jerome Charyn than those receiving stamps of approval from Oprah Winfrey and Heather Reisman. In his view, literature should keep breaking new ground. Stein's prescription for writers – "If you can do it then why do it?" – has become his credo.

At home in Vancouver in 1998, a relaxed George Bowering in a rare photo *sans* glasses. *Photograph by Barry Peterson and Blaise Enright.*

Bowering was born in Penticton, British Columbia, in 1935. Growing up in Oliver, a nearby agricultural village, he stood out for his quick wit and creativity. Once, when a geography teacher asked him where Pittsburgh was, he had the presence of mind to reply, "Eighth place," thinking, as he often does, of Major League Baseball. Because he could draw likenesses, a local barber commissioned him, a young teenager, to make caricatures of Oliver's firefighters. Nearly two dozen of his oversized cartoons decorated the community hall for a firemen's ball. (He received a couple of dollars for his work.) He acted in plays, including a school production of Oscar Wilde's *The Importance of Being Earnest*. He wrote songs, which he and his best friend, Will Thornton-Trump, sometimes sang as part of a quartet. The two of them warbled in the high-school choir and played tubas in the band. For a time, they broadcast a kind of lunch-hour radio show from the principal's office, playing jazz records, telling jokes, and performing skits they'd written. George was aiming for fame in adulthood. "I couldn't face the idea of living a lifetime unknown," he says. "Of course I had to get known."

When he began writing poems at nineteen, he soon found a voice and manner that appealed to publishers. It was the fifties. Poetry was becoming popular in North America, and a postwar vogue for "little magazines" was creating ever more outlets to spread it around. In Vancouver, where he started going to university in 1957 to complete his bachelor's degree, George was part of a community of young poets. He has written about walking through Kitsilano then and hearing "all along the summer street the typewriters at the open windows." Later there were plenty of poets – and visual artists, too – in the hippie-era Kosmic League in which he played baseball. In 1974, his two-year-old daughter, Thea, sat on his knee after a game. With them were two artists who'd played on his team: Brian Fisher and, visiting from Ontario, Greg Curnoe. George pointed to Brian and told Thea, "He's a painter." He then pointed to Greg and said, "He's a painter." Thea pointed to him and said, "You're a poet." He loved that.

His early poems – like "Radio Jazz," "Grandfather," and "The House," from the sixties – are remembered and cherished by many. Thea, now in her forties, says the ones she has reread most are from her father's early collections. "From *Another Mouth* [1979] and *In the Flesh* [1974] and *The Silver Wire* [1966], beautiful lyric poems," she says. "I just love them." Erín Moure, a Montreal- and Kelowna-based poet to whom he's been a mentor, remembers being wowed when she came across his 1969 book *Rocky Mountain Foot* at sixteen. "It was such a refreshing approach to the poem," unlike anything else that she, "as a student in the pre-CanLit era," had been able to find. Years later, George would join a group to study *her* challenging poetry with friends.

He started *Imago*, a magazine devoted to the publication of long poems, when he was a rookie English professor in Calgary. He felt that serial poems and book-length poems needed a home, since literary magazines didn't want most or all of their pages taken up by one writer's work. As he moved to London (Ontario) and Montreal, and then back to Vancouver, he kept producing *Imago*. He published twenty issues between 1964 and 1974, and every third one showcased a single writer. *Imago*, which featured Charles Olson, Gerard Malanga, bpNichol, Victor Coleman, David McFadden, and Margaret Randall, among others, achieved two important things: It established a precedent for the long poem as book, and helped to create an international network of poets. George published and corresponded with poets from the United States, the United Kingdom, and Latin America, in some cases translating works from Spanish into English.

Bowering himself has written twelve book-length poems. His *Autobiology* and *Curious* were influential in the seventies, while *Kerrisdale Elegies* (1984) is widely seen as his greatest achievement in poetry. His allusive, way-out *Allophanes* (1976) went into *The Long Poem Anthology*

(1979), where editor Michael Ondaatje gave it such excellent company as Daphne Marlatt's *Steveston* and Robin Blaser's *The Moth Poem*.

By the time Thea was in elementary school, her dad had turned his hand to prose. In the eighties he added novels and criticism to his output. His novel *Burning Water* zeroes in on Captain George Vancouver's activities off Canada's west coast in 1792. Playful and imaginative, it tells the story in a postmodern way. The writer Wayde Compton, once a protégé of Bowering's, calls it "probably the single biggest influence" his mentor has had on his work. Later in the eighties, Penguin Canada published *Caprice*, Bowering's second historical novel. It's set in the British Columbia Interior in the dying days of the Old West; the novel's eponymous heroine is an imposing horse-woman, a whip-cracking Québécoise on a revenge quest. George's essay collections also came thick and fast in the eighties; they range from the conventional (*The Mask in Place: Essays on Fiction in North America*) to the quirky (*Errata*, a name he chose because he wondered if the italics used for a book title and those often used for a Latinism might cancel each other out).

During the nineties, Bowering reinvented himself as a popular historian – Penguin Canada's then editorial director, Cynthia Good, nudged him in that direction after publishing *Caprice*. Her feeling was that if he could do historical fiction, he could do history, period, and make it entertaining. *Bowering's B.C.: A Swashbuckling History* is detailed, confident, and jaunty all at once; even better, Good considered his name recognition great enough to justify the title. The tenor of the response, most of it highly favourable, was, "If more such histories were written, I'd read more history," as John Harris wrote in the *Vancouver Review*. Bowering went on to write a book of irreverent prime ministerial portraits for Penguin and then to tackle the whole of our history in *Stone Country: An Unauthorized History of Canada* (2003).

Bowering in his forties, before the famous Ghiberti bronze doors of Italy's Florence Baptistery.

There are more than a hundred titles in his enviably diverse oeuvre. In old age he's been writing colourfully about sex, using enough Henry Miller–ish detail to raise some readers' eyebrows. *Pinboy* (2012), billed as a memoir on the cover, describes the seduction of a fifteen-year-old boy named George Bowering by a female teacher. Readers could be forgiven for thinking this really happened to the author in high school. It didn't. Marc Côté, publisher at Cormorant Books, told me: "It was sent to me as 'the inside-out autobiography of George Bowering' – those were the exact words used – so we called it a memoir. The problem with George is that you never know if [what he says or writes is] true or not." Côté would still call *Pinboy* a memoir if he had to classify it again. He thinks there's more elasticity in the memoir genre than in autobiography. "It came out of [Bowering's] heart and his memory, as flawed as those two organs are," he says. George views it as a novel, though it was a finalist for British Columbia's National Award for Canadian Non-Fiction. He told me, "I'm not that much interested in categories. Someone would say [about one of my earlier books], 'Is that poetry or prose?' and I'd say, 'Well, you know, some poetry is prose.'"

The book was noticed – not just for the sex scenes but for its poignancy and fine writing. In a review in the *Globe and Mail*, T.F. Rigelhof admitted he'd never before read a Bowering book from cover to cover but had gulped this one down, then reread it slowly; he hadn't been able "to stop thinking and talking about it since. It won't be to everybody's taste, but it makes a perfect gift for any man over sixty-five who loves women and baseball and still reads books …"

On April 21, 2015, Bowering suffered a cardiac arrest a short distance from his home. The quick reactions of a schoolgirl who happened to be near him on the street saved his life. During the three weeks he was in hospital, doctors lowered his body temperature and induced a coma. When George regained consciousness, he had no memory of what he'd been through. His recovery was slow; he was weak and tentative for a good while. And yet his drive to write – and his anticipation of his next book's release, which he'd enjoyed feeling for decades – was as strong as ever. In the year following his close call, at the age of eighty, he published five books.

As George Fetherling and Sharon Thesen have pointed out, he is ludic – playful in his writing, sometimes to a fault. This glibness is what kept Rigelhof from reading his pre-*Pinboy* work. Then there are the antics that have led people to call him a trickster. Throughout his career he has given out false biographical details about himself. The bare bones of his origins are that he was born on December 1, 1935, in Penticton, the son of a science teacher. However, he has given the year of his birth as 1936 and 1939 and has stated that he was born in Oliver, Okanagan Falls, and Osoyoos. His funny "Poem for High School Anthologies" boldly misstates his particulars as "Princeton,

British Columbia, / December 1, 1939, the son of / a high school Latin teacher."

All manner of accolades and awards have come his way, with his appointment as Canada's first Parliamentary Poet Laureate a crowning wreath. Still, there have been disappointments. He would have liked to win a BC Book Prize and doesn't think the Lieutenant Governor's Award for Literary Excellence, given him in 2011 by the same organization, counts. (He would have preferred to win the Dorothy Livesay Poetry Prize, the Ethel Wilson Fiction Prize, or, ideally, both.) And though his books have received thousands of reviews, George noted in his diary in 2010 that the one truly discerning review he'd received was George Woodcock's assessment of his first novel, published in *Canadian Literature* in 1968. He'd been brooding over this for more than forty years!

Nick Mount, an English professor at the University of Toronto, dedicates an entire chapter of *Arrival: The Story of CanLit* to George, calling him the poet most associated with Vancouver. Erín Moure appreciates his generosity and draws attention to George's knowledge and celebration of other writers' work as well as his regular attendance at their readings. Jon Kertzer says this, too, in his long entry on Bowering in the *Encyclopedia of Literature in Canada*. Kertzer goes on to make the trenchant observation that George's writing is "always public, even when it is intimate." And yet I wonder how well today's wider public knows him. When I invited my new neighbours in for pre-Christmas drinks, telling them about the book I was working on, I found differing degrees of knowledge. One man, a senior member of the Victoria bar, had never read him and didn't even know his name. By contrast, a neighbour divulged that she'd been part of his circle in the seventies, when she'd spent a week with Angela, his first wife (and Thea's mother), stripping the kitchen cupboards in the big house they'd bought in Kerrisdale.

In an early talk I had with George and Jean, the prolific poet/ trickster spoke ruefully about how quickly fame had come to him when he was young and how, these days, "nobody knows who I am." Jean joked, "Everybody knows. Nobody cares." Whereupon George intoned, "The next step is: Nobody knows."

There's no reason for such gloom – George has had a terrific run. But he's also more complex than many people realize. He's an intellectual, though he doesn't always give that impression, and has specialized literary interests. As John Bemrose once wrote, his work displays a "rather defiant avant-gardism." Its sly playfulness has long been recognized: With its 1997 review of *Bowering's B.C.*, the magazine *Books in Canada* ran a drawing that caricatured him as a coyote. But there's more to him than that and, having had a brush with death, he's open to having readers see it.

☙ CHAPTER 2 ☙

THE BOY

> I dont recall being hugged
> by either of my parents; I grew that way, food in my
> mouth they gave me, frequent drinks of water,
> exercise in the hills behind the house
> & in the back yard. They made certain I had
> work to do there.

—"West Window," *West Window: The Selected Poetry of George Bowering* (1982)

The day after Christmas 1934, a good man who taught high school in the Canadian West married an athletic young woman in her late teens. Not long before, she'd been one of his students. His name was Ewart and hers was Pearl. This happened in West Summerland, a fruit-growing community in B.C.'s Okanagan Valley.

Ewart Harry Bowering's family had originated in the English counties of Somerset and Berkshire, Pearl Patricia Brinson's in the United States: Michigan and Missouri. Their parents had moved to Alberta and they'd been born there – Ewart in Wetaskiwin, Pearl in Three Hills. But they'd grown up in the Okanagan and met there, and that was where they planned to stay.

Pearl Brinson would marry Ewart Bowering, formerly one of her high-school teachers. They would have four children, of whom George was the eldest.

The valley, far from the bright lights of Vancouver, is blessed in many ways. To the people who live there year-round and the tourists who flock there in summer, it's a place where, as George put it in the epigraph to *Writing the Okanagan*, "God said, 'Finally, I got it right.'" In winter, the swatch of inland semi-desert is neither excessively cold nor cloaked in snow, and in spring, summer, and fall, skies are clear enough to make it a vacation paradise. In summer you can pretty much count on sunshine every day; the bright heat builds steadily until the valley feels like an oven.

The region's Edenic qualities have been evident to new arrivals since the late nineteenth century. In an advertisement inviting Britons to settle in the valley in the first years of the twentieth century, Albert Grey, 4th Earl Grey, Canada's Governor General, recommended fruit growing as an occupation, praising orchardists as, "par excellence, Nature's Gentlemen." He spoke a tiny bit too soon. It wasn't until the late twenties, when there was reliable irrigation and when disease-, pest-, and weather-resistant fruit tree varieties had been developed, that fruit growing became a viable career for people willing to work hard. The desert bloomed and the valley's economy prospered. In the thirties, forties, and fifties, the main activities in the region were growing and packing tree fruit. From June to September, delicate cherries, apricots, peaches, and prune plums – and pears and apples, mercifully hardier – were picked, packed, and shipped. Young people working their way through university could easily find summer work on ladders among the trees or in the cool of a packing house.

Ewart Bowering, born on June 10, 1907, was tall, handsome, principled, and well enough educated to teach teenagers math, physics, and, most often, chemistry. He sat down with a newspaper every day to keep informed and he read popular fiction to relax. Pearl Brinson Bowering, a fit, easygoing brunette born on August 11, 1916, was a reader, too, especially when the household chores were done. She was an energetic homemaker who often baked a panoply of pies or several loaves of bread at a time.

Both spouses revelled in athletics. In fact, Pearl thought that's what drew Ewart to her: "He liked the way I played sports," she told me in 2013, when she was in her late nineties. She bowled and played badminton, tennis, and softball. On the ball field she was tough enough to play catcher, which would lead George, her first-born child, to reflect many years later, "I had no idea that it was an unusual privilege to see one's mother squatting with a metal mask over her face and a chest protector covering the front of her." Ewart played catcher for the Oliver Elks; he played broomball in winter and coached girls' basketball at school. Later in their marriage the couple would take up golf and curling.

In Peachland, where they first lived together, and in their later homes, Pearl always had a pot of coffee going in the kitchen. Before people worried about excess caffeine, it was a way to make a house a welcoming home. In the evenings, the couple liked to socialize over cribbage, bridge, hearts, and other card games, Ewart thriftily rolling everyone's cigarettes from a can of Black Cat tobacco.

During the Great Depression, even people with steady jobs were on the lookout for extra cash. Pearl, who'd worked in a hair salon before she married, went back to doing perms when money was tight; she also sorted fruit in a packing house, her hair wrapped in a bandanna. Ewart supplemented his teacher's salary by joining highway crews (he worked on the Rock Creek Canyon Bridge in the summer of 1951) or doing factory work. In the fall, he came home from work, changed into tougher clothes – "denims," Pearl called them – and went out to pick apples, staying on the ladder as long as the light allowed. He was a ruthlessly efficient picker.

Despite their differing attainments (Bowering has written, "My mother was a schoolgirl athlete from a hillbilly family and she snagged him ... [My father] was the chemistry teacher at Southern Okanagan High School"), a quiet, steadfast love kept husband and wife together. When Pearl reached the late stages of her first pregnancy at nineteen, she went south to Penticton and stayed with her father and stepmother so she could give birth in the hospital there. Labour didn't progress easily. "Pills for pain were keeping me awake," she recalled. "They put me to sleep." The baby, a boy, looked bruised when he finally emerged. Pearl said that "his skull was shattered and there was a big lump at the back." The date was December 1, 1935 – the same day Woody Allen was born in the Bronx.

Pearl's baby boy was whisked from her bedside and placed in the nursery for days. She wanted to see her son but no one would tell her anything. She didn't know whether he'd survive or have full faculties if he did. She said to a nurse, "It's painful. Will you start to take the milk out?" She was relieved to be told, "You might be needing it," and even more thrilled when she learned that the baby had what it took "to make life."

She and Ewart named him George Harry Bowering. "George" sounded sturdy and honest, while Harry was the traditional middle name for first-born Bowering sons – Ewart had it and so did his British-born dad.

Young George was a firecracker of a little boy with big, round, mischievous eyes. Pearl sometimes dressed him in a sailor suit. In 1937, when he was fourteen months old, she went to Kelowna to have her and Ewart's second child. This time, labour was easier. The baby was a girl, and they named her Sally-Ann Patricia. Sally and George, having started their lives in the Depression, would grow up with ingrained tendencies toward grit and thrift.

Georgie in a sailor suit with his mother, Pearl. In his 1972 long poem, *Autobiology*, George Bowering "meets his own three-year-old voice."

The memorable events of George's early life are still very much with him. They're part of what he calls his "biotext," the personal experiences he draws on when he writes. *Autobiology*, his 1972 naive-voiced long poem, has a section in which a child watches, failing to speak up fast enough, as an adult unwittingly closes a door on a kitten's neck. Grimly, Ewart went off to dispose of the kitten's lifeless body, considering himself at fault. But George blamed himself because he hadn't spoken up.

A heart condition kept Ewart out of World War II, but if he was going to keep teaching he wanted to change jobs. So he found a new one in Greenwood, in the Boundary District farther inland. By September 1940 the family had left behind their home in Peachland, the one with the raspberry canes out front and the arch of greenery over the gate.

Greenwood, just west of Grand Forks, had been incorporated as a city in 1897. In the first years of the twentieth century, a mining boom boosted its population to three thousand. Ore coming out of the B.C. Copper Company's Deadwood and Mother Lode deposits made the construction of a smelter necessary, but Greenwood nearly turned into a ghost town after the First World War and the collapse of mining. The unused smelter's smokestack pierced the sky like a mercantile steeple.

Pearl remembered until her last days that the Greenwood she'd encountered had "huge buildings with nothing in them." It was one of several inland places to which the Canadian government began moving twenty thousand coastal British Columbians of Japanese ancestry in 1942, believing them potentially sympathetic to the Axis powers and thus a national security threat. (In 1988, the government acknowledged the unfairness of the internments and accompanying property seizures with an apology and redress payments.) "They went to school, and my husband taught them, too," Pearl remembered. "At nighttime the RCMP looked after them. There were a lot of them, not just a handful, the poor souls!"

In Greenwood, the family's dentist was a Japanese Canadian whose first name happened to be George. Six-year-old George Bowering found it hard to reconcile this quiet, polite man with the propaganda images he saw of "evil Jap fighter plane pilots with ... huge teeth and thick glasses."

The family's brief stay in Greenwood engendered deep-seated memories for George. The Bowerings all knew the white picket fence in front of their house had been moved there from the graveyard. There was a screened veranda where Ewart and Pearl let George sleep on hot summer nights. The family dog lived in the backyard and, on one memorable occasion, a deer carcass hung there. Also behind the house was a shed where the family kept chickens. It was Ewart's chore to wield an axe and unsentimentally kill the hens whose egg-laying days were behind them, while Pearl had the job of plucking, cleaning, and cooking the birds. George watched with queasy fascination as she pulled out the luridly coloured entrails. Decades later he would write a serial poem preserving his observation that "sometimes there would be eggs in there, with no shells on them."

Greenwood held a community sports day at which Pearl – "PB" to her relatives – displayed her limber strength. Men and women alike were invited to try hammering metal spikes into blocks of wood, and for two years in a row she was the women's spike-driving champion.

George and Sally started school in Greenwood. Although George apparently didn't talk much before the age of three, he knew how to read when he was "four going on five." Picking up on his dad's love of newspapers, he'd started puzzling out articles when he was four.

It was in Greenwood, too, that, disregarding adults' admonitions, young George played with matches outdoors, kindling a fire that spread before his astonished eyes. Soon a hillside was ablaze, triggering the arrival of men with hoses and shovels. He was abashed at having caused "such peril while there was a war on." Since his parents didn't find out, he wasn't punished, which only added to his guilt. He was also hugely regretful when he knocked an old raw egg, sitting enigmatically on his father's workbench, to the ground. It broke, raising a sulphurous stink, and he saw that the chick within had started to grow wings. As a young man, he would write in "The Egg," a poem about the guilt he carried for several years:

... as if I
myself smelled, as if I had brought
those tender stinking wings to earth.

The family periodically went to visit Ewart's parents in West Summer-land. Ewart's dad, Jabez Harry Bowering, born in England in 1873, had come to Canada as a teenaged orphan. Harry eventually became a circuit-riding preacher in Manitoba and Alberta. By the time his grand-children got to know him, though, he was a snowy-haired postmaster who walked with a cane. George liked going to church with Harry's second wife, Clara Bowering. There he heard the words "Holy holy holy lord god almighty," which he would put in "Grandfather," his famous early poem. Religion, clearly, was in touch with the ineffable. At five, George fleetingly wondered if *he* could be the second com-ing of Christ he'd heard about. He had a sense of being different, of having a mission in life.

In the early forties, with war news filling the newspapers and radio broadcasts, Ewart and Pearl moved their family again. This time they went west, back to the Okanagan. They chose Oliver, named after John Oliver, a former B.C. premier who'd had an economically important irrigation canal, known locally as The Ditch, built there in the twen-ties. Oliver's high school had offered Ewart a job. The community had about two thousand residents, and it was incorporated as a village in 1945; there were no sidewalks and Highway 97 was its main street. But there was work: Besides the orchards and related enterprises there was a sawmill and some manufacturing. Oliver's every feature, from a lone tree stark on a hilltop to a small figure-eight-shaped lake to its two pool halls, would come to feel elemental to George and would infiltrate his poetry and prose. In his work, he calls the place Lawrence.

George started grade three at Oliver Elementary School. He enjoyed it, since he liked making people laugh and the classroom held a good-sized audience. A classmate named John Boone remembers him repeating jokes he'd heard Bob Hope and Jack Benny make on the radio, adding some of his own to the mix. He also did uncannily accurate imitations of teachers (at which, according to Boone, the girls exclaimed, "Oh, Bowering!").

Boone, who would one day become a Vancouver cardiologist, was a farm kid, and he considered George a town kid. In fact, the Bowerings lived in two houses in orchards before they bought the one that would make George and Sally town kids. That house, conveniently close to the elementary school, cost about $3,200, with an uncle of Pearl's lending money for a down payment. The outside of the house was sheathed in tarpaper and chicken wire when the family moved in. George would write in his twenties that "years and years" went by before the exterior walls saw stucco. Decades later, he'd write in *Pinboy*: "My family was not rich. While my father and I were digging the septic tank out, we all had to shit and piss in a tall bucket with a toilet seat on it."

Their neighbours included a colleague of Ewart's named John Zarelli – "Zeke Zarelli" in student parlance – and a family named Wilkins whose daughter, Carol, accidentally broke George's nose while they and other kids were playing freeze tag.

Oliver was a place where "you didn't necessarily know everybody," George's closest friend from childhood, Will Thornton-Trump, would say late in life, "but you sort of knew *of* everybody." As a boy, his full name was William Walter Hamilton Lyttle and he was called Bill. He remembers the moment in 1946 when he and George first laid eyes on each other. His family had recently moved to the Okanagan from Vancouver and he was sitting in his father's Ford outside their new home. "The Model A had a starter button that was separate from the ignition," he says, summoning the details. "You could sit there if you were a kid, when nobody was around, and poke the starter button and it would go jerk-jerk-jerk and move the car just a little bit. So I was running down my father's battery when this kid came up. He had a bandanna around his head, down to his eyes, and another one around his nose so that only his eyes were showing. He was wearing a toy six-gun, and he said, 'You're the new kid, huh? Wanna come play guns?' I said, 'Nah, I'm busy.' I didn't know it at that time, but that was George."

A week later, the skinny ten-year-old offered Will, who was nine, a carton of his old comic books for "one thin dime." Will took him up on the deal and, before long, they were pals, he spending nearly all his free time at the Bowerings'. "It seems to me, in retrospect, that his parents were always saying, 'Willy, go home.'" He was "sort of like the neighbourhood kid who was always hanging around, like Elmo in *Blondie*."

As best friends in the pre-television age, the two boys found lots to do. They collected tadpoles and either kept them in water, hoping to see them morph into frogs, or let their silvery jelly dry out in the sun. Inspired by Al Capp's *Li'l Abner* comic strip, they mixed up batches of Kickapoo Joy Juice in a washtub. Not being too closely supervised, they went for long walks in the hills, bestowing names on geographical features. They gave the name Blue Mountain to one rocky, tree-clothed eminence. Sometimes they took Sandy, Will's younger brother, with them. He would grow up to be Alexander Thornton-Trump, an engineering professor, but as a lad he had a tendency to wail when thwarted. Once, the three of them, wearing pith-helmet-style hats, were descending a narrow trail into a valley. Will remembers that near the bottom, Sandy "pitched forward onto his face," smashing the brim of his hat. As he collected his breath for an epic tantrum, his face a study in contortion, George quickly dubbed their location Cryhat Valley.

In the forties, boys in Oliver had the run of the village. John Boone recalls that there were acres of open ground beside the elementary school – "native couch grass, desert land, some sagebrush, and cactus." George adored the arid landscape with its airborne scent of sage, its antelope bushes and rattlesnakes. Toward sunset on a summer's day, he loved to place his hands on rocks and feel their store of absorbed heat. In the mid-eighties, when he was tethered to moist Vancouver, he would tell a friend he missed the dry summer weather of his childhood, "the rush of the old familiarity of the summertime smell light, etc., the arm burnt on the car door …"

Back then, the boys of Oliver ran wild across the open land, challenging one another with homemade wooden swords they'd carry in their belts. Once, George hid in The Ditch, which was dry because it was winter, urging Will to "prove [his] manhood" by single-handedly taking on a group of boys they called the Maxwell gang. In Will's memory, "there were maybe four of them. All of us had our swords drawn. I was hard pressed and was obviously going to lose, and then George came dashing out of the irrigation ditch, flailing his sword, running towards us … He took on half of them and I took on half, but there were too many for us and we wound up badly beaten. But I proved my manhood. I remember George saying, 'Willy, that was a magnificent defeat.'"

The minutiae of those days are still vivid for George and Will, who share a trove of memories that a few well-chosen words can instantly retrieve. There was one unforgettable moment when a bull was chasing them across a meadow near Tuc-el-nuit Lake. As they raced across the hummocky grass, bull in hot pursuit, George shouted, "I wish it were tomorrow!" As panicked as they were, it struck Will that his friend was giving himself airs with that meticulous grammar. ("I thought, 'He's trying to show his superiority around this hick town.'") Now that they're old, the sentence "I wish it were tomorrow" springs to their lips whenever they're in a fix. One of them says it and suddenly they're kids again, back in that meadow, running for their lives.

CHAPTER 3

THE YOUTH

I started working in orchards when I was twelve. I knew how to strip suckers ... I knew how to thin apples, stack boxes, prop apple trees, pick cherries, pick apricots, pick peaches, pick pears, pick prunes, and pick all varieties of apples. I knew how to change sprinklers, load trailers, and even drive tractor a little.

—*Pinboy* (2012)

When young George wasn't brandishing a wooden sword among friends and foes, he spent hours on his own, reading. He got a quiet thrill out of inhabiting the real world and a fictional one simultaneously. At thirteen, he began writing down the titles of books after he'd finished reading them. This would become his enduring practice, and the notebooks where he's kept the list – he calls them scribblers – have survived. The first book whose details he wrote down was Archie Joscelyn's *Blue River Riders*. Soon after, he read Jack London's *The Call of the Wild*. He devoured westerns, blasting through the works of Zane Grey, Luke Short, and Max Brand. Following his dad's taste, he read Erle Stanley Gardner's detective novels and, encouraged by best pal Will, he developed an appetite for science fiction.

Reading was an early pastime for George, who at thirteen began noting down the title, author, and publisher of every book he read.

As they wandered the hills or just kicked around together, he and Will had conversations about life that sometimes edged into metaphysics. George wondered whether all the world's people could be aspects of a single self. "I believed it was possible all men share a brain," he would later write, "but nobody gave a sign they would know about this." Certainly, Will recalls that his friend was a smart aleck, prone to tying Pearl up in sophistry. "His mother couldn't out-argue him," he says. "I remember one time George and I were going to go up in the mountains. His mother said, 'Take a jacket. It's nice and warm down here, but it's cold up in the hills.' And George said, 'No, Mum, it's actually warmer up there than it is here. It's closer to the sun,' and she wasn't sure how to counter that."

As for other hazards, George had been warned never to enter the Okanagan River (because "the best swimmer in town drowned in there") and to stay away from motorcycles and rifles. But he indulged in one activity that would have horrified his mum if she'd known. He liked to run down the drifts of loose, sharp shale rocks that covered certain hillsides. It was like skiing, and the required combination of control and letting go would later remind him of what it feels like to write literature. When you're a kid running a rock slide, he says, "you gotta keep movin' or you'll be covered with shale," and when you're an adult at a computer keyboard, you start to create and "you don't know where you're going to wind up."

Pearl and Ewart Bowering had a third child, Roger, in 1946. The first of their two "postwar kids," Roger would spend much of his adult life in Oliver, keeping cool in summer by using his open garage as a kind of outdoor room. Friends called him Dodge. He had a cache of stories about the devilment his big brother and Will got up to as kids – when he was a toddler, for instance, they put him in his high chair and fed him lard. "They told me it was ice cream," Roger said. "The front door opens, I start crying my head off. I figured I could get [George] into trouble for feeding me lard. Will said, 'But, Mrs. Bowering, he was *enjoying* it!'"

As a two-year-old, Roger had a terrible accident. The Bowerings were building an addition to their house, so there was a hole in their yard with a plank over it. "For some reason, I started to walk across the plank," he recalled, "George holding my hand but also jiggling the plank." Roger lost his footing and fell in, landing on his head. He shrieked. George ran into the house, yelling, "Roger's in the excavation!" Pearl, recalling the accident, said George and Will stood about "wringing their hands [and saying], 'What do we do? What do we do?'" Her daughter, Sally, didn't need to ask. She climbed down the ladder and got Roger out of the hole. Roger came home from hospital "with a steel clamp in his skull with a plaster bandage around his head," and George prayed for his recovery.

George and Sally Bowering with their baby brother, Roger. George and his best friend once put Roger in his high chair and fed him lard, telling him it was ice cream.

George turned thirteen at the end of 1948, which he hyperbolically insists was the greatest year in the history of civilization. He was full of wonder at what surrounded him. The Cleveland Indians' pitching rotation was particularly stellar; it was "a marvellous sports year all round." The cultural offerings of the day – DC Comics, *The Treasure of the Sierra Madre*, Spike Jones's zany musical act – were a source of delight to him. And somehow he and other boys his age knew that Christian Dior had upended fashion with the New Look.

Pearl and Ewart's fourth child, Jim, was born in 1949, completing the family. Because of the age gap between the two sets of children, Sally stepped in to help raise her younger brothers. "She was saddled with raising us," Roger recalled. Life was placid. "There was no animosity, no fighting in the family. Everybody pretty much did their own thing." Jim learned more from Pearl, domestically, than any of his siblings did. He learned to cook and even bake bread. "He could look after himself," said Roger, "while the rest of us would make Kraft Dinner."

When George and Will got to Southern Okanagan High School, they carried on like a comedy team, George trying to elicit laughs and Will abetting him like a classic straight man. "Since there was only one high school in the town and his father taught there," Will says, "George had to be the clown, the iconoclast. He had to prove himself with the guys."

Teenaged George developed opinions, which he freely expressed at school. He became an anti-monarchist, objecting to what Britons paid to maintain the Royal Family and heartily resenting that their king was also Canada's king. Gwendolyn "Wendy" Amor, the half-British girl with whom he went steady, starting around age fifteen, took issue with those views (if Bowering's early, unpublished autobiographical novel, *Delsing*, accurately reflects reality). Once, during a class discussion, she leaped up and passionately disagreed with him, declaring, "There was a king long before you were born, and there will be long after you're dead." His sounding off got him into trouble. He was frequently sent from the classroom to stand in the hall. Walking by, the principal – whom the kids called Prune behind his back – would say, "Hmm. Horseplay, my friend?"

Wendy broadened George's knowledge of the world. She'd been born in Canada but had spent part of her childhood in the U.K. When World War II broke out, her father, Leslie, became an air raid warden in London. Her mother, Dorothy, took her and her younger sister, Judy, to stay on a farm in Herefordshire. Wendy, a toddler, wore an evacuee's identification bracelet, inscribed "OGGE 90 5." To keep out of harm's way, Dorothy, Wendy, and Judy lived in B.C. from 1940 to 1945.

In 1949, the Amors moved from England to an orchard south of Oliver that had been in their family since 1933. By then, they also had a son, David. Leslie grew fruit and would, toward the end of his career, manage Oliver's Sun-Rype juice plant. The Amors were active in St. Edward's Anglican Church, whose congregation was tightly knit. There was a social stratum in the village composed of people of British origin with an admixture of anglophile Canadians. Pearl felt some of the Brits gave themselves airs. George, who tended to agree, remembers her saying that many had probably been working-class privates in the war, "but when they came over here they put on a blazer and a regimental tie." As in farming communities the world over, there were some highly prosperous families and some scrabbling to make it, their children, as David Amor puts it, "all cheek by jowl at school together."

As a young teen with an English accent, Wendy seemed geeky when she first appeared at Southern Okanagan High. In *Delsing*, the Frances Sinclair character modelled after her shows up in a Girl Guide uniform, thick stockings, glasses, and pigtails. It doesn't take Frances long, though, to learn to accentuate the positive. That was likely also true of Wendy, who had green eyes and the self-assurance of a first-born child. In Roger Bowering's memory, she was pretty, with curly brown hair. She and George went on their first date on October 10, 1952, and he was soon "wildly, moonlightedly, hit-paradedly" in love with her, to quote his summation in *Delsing*. He came to love everything about her appearance, including her imperfections. As an adult, he would privately thrill to the memory that she'd had "no eyebrows, to speak of, & a crooked canine tooth, ankles a trifle too thick." She gave him her wartime ID bracelet and he dedicated *Delsing* to "OGGE 90 5."

She called him Tigger, after the self-described "bouncy, trouncy, flouncy, pouncy" plush tiger in A.A. Milne's *Winnie-the-Pooh* books, and often reproved him for being immature. (In *Delsing*, the narrator sighs, "If only she could accept me wholly as I am, instead of wanting me to cut my hair or stay quiet at baseball games, or close down my career as village wit.") On visits to the Amors, George played with David, who remembers him as gregarious, "a flamboyant character."

George and Wendy talked about eventually getting married and having a son and a daughter they would name Theodore (a fan of Ted Williams, George wished he'd been given that name) and Dorothy. During their romance he didn't press her for sex, but once, when they were alone in a humble beach cottage Pearl had bought at Tuc-el-nuit Lake, he got to see and touch her naked body.

"Wendy really is a touchstone for George," says David Amor. "It's probably pretty tricky to separate out the historical person from the mythological one."

High school was a satisfying universe for Bowering. His life felt full. He lived in other worlds when he read and he experienced a different reality when he joined the Royal Canadian Air Cadets. In his twenties, he would describe the organization as a parody of the Air Force, "all different shapes and colours of boy in blue uniform and wedge cap." His summer jobs gave him cash but also grief: At fifteen, descending an orchard ladder while heavily laden with apples, he cracked a vertebra; back pain has dogged him ever since. Also when George was fifteen, he and a friend agreed to clear slimy green algae from an outdoor pool for low wages. On a brutally bright, hot day, the friend had the sense to quit while George got sunstroke for his pains. He worked as a pinsetter in a bowling alley that summer, too – an intolerable job, given the blast-furnace heat of the pit.

Sports lifted him up and took him someplace else. Although he didn't play baseball until quite late in his adolescence, he kept score for the Oliver Baseball Club, the OBCs, taking the job away from his dad. He had the thick rule book memorized, and his knowledge of baseball and basketball rules emboldened him to offer sports reports to the *Oliver Chronicle* and the *Penticton Herald*. The *Chronicle* paid him fifteen cents per column-inch while the *Herald* gave him twenty-five. As far as he knew, he – though just a kid – was Oliver's only sportswriter, so he scorned the idea of working on his high school's student newspaper, *The Scroll*.

For a while he thought of following his 1953 graduation with journalism school in the States and going on to work there as a sportswriter – say, at the *St. Louis Post-Dispatch* because one of his idols, Bob Broeg, was there. He wrote to Broeg, who sent back a courteous letter. Broeg suggested that George become not just a sports reporter but an all-rounder, saying, "You've got to generalize, to be a triple threat, before you can specialize." Signing off, he wished George good luck and said, "If you get through St. Louis, look me up."

What happened instead was that, because he was seventeen, short of funds but madly in love with Wendy, he followed her to Vancouver Island, where she was to attend Victoria's Provincial Normal School, a teachers' college. He enrolled at Victoria College (the University of Victoria's precursor) and spent the 1953–54 academic year there. As a kid from sagebrush and rattlesnake country, he found it intriguingly foreign to be on a forested island. He took geography, which he liked, even though one of the classes met at 8 a.m. on Saturdays. He made a poor impression in his history class by writing a paper in red ink, which only profs were allowed to use. He fell behind in French class and quit halfway through. He has two non-academic memories from the brief sojourn: Dean Martin was all over radio, singing "That's Amore," and seven cents would buy a Vic College student not one, but two big sticky doughnuts.

After first year, Wendy broke up with him. He started a summer job with B.C. Topographical Survey, but that "fizzle[d] out immediately." Smarting from his failures in love, school, and work, George sought "a real authentic five-star period of remorse and exile." He had in mind something like the French Foreign Legion but sensibly opted for a domestic equivalent. His years as an air cadet had groomed him for the Royal Canadian Air Force, which had attracted such Canadian writers as Al Purdy, George Johnston, and Raymond Souster. So, at nineteen, he and Fred Miller, a friend from school, joined up together. It was July 10, 1954, a day on which Vancouver was unseasonably lashed by rain. He took shelter in movie houses, watching *Prince Valiant* and two other films, numb from the big step he'd taken.

The fifties were the Air Force's golden years in terms of funding, aircraft, and profile. After basic training in Saint-Jean, Quebec, George was told he might not be suited to the life of an enlisted man because of his high IQ. So he requested training in photography, with which he'd had a bit of work experience. He got it at Canadian Forces Base Borden in Ontario and emerged an aerial photographer. In retrospect, the mathematical tasks he performed while airborne seem extraordinary. He had to calibrate a camera "the size of a washing machine inside the fuselage of a DC3 flying over Lake Simcoe and its surrounding counties." He calculated the plane's airspeed, drift, yaw, and altitude while keeping tabs on the camera settings. He also took still photos, the first step in making aerial maps.

For most of his three-year stint he was assigned to RCAF Station Macdonald in Manitoba. It was a NATO air gunnery training station, so the aerial photographers mostly put 16 mm film into gunsight and wing cameras on Lockheed T-33 jets. They took "little movies" of young NATO pilots shooting at canvas targets that planes towed over Lake Manitoba, and then developed the film.

His starting rank was Aircraftsman Second Class – "acey-deucy," in Air Force slang. "It was a term used to describe anybody who was wet behind the ears," he recalls. He then became an Aircraftsman First Class and, later, a Leading Aircraftsman, or LAC. He was given a patch decorated with propellers to sew onto his uniform but never got around to doing it.

Regimentation didn't sit well with George. He was constitutionally a leader, a joker, and an unapologetic eccentric; he didn't like being told what to do. His apparel, in particular, went wide of the mark. Aircraftsmen were supposed to wear suspenders, but he cut holes in his trousers' waistband so he could use a belt. He also made an alteration, using yellow paint, in order to find his rubber boots. "You'd look in the huge mudroom, going into the cafeteria, and there would be, like, five hundred pairs of boots and one pair with yellow toes on it." And he kept being told, "You've got to go and get a new hat. That hat is just a disgrace."

On the plus side, Macdonald had a surprisingly fine library. The education officer in charge had acquired books by the Americans Kenneth Patchen and Kenneth Rexroth – influential to the Beat Generation and San Francisco Renaissance poets. George would fill a paper bag with carrot sticks and spend his lunch hours there, reading poetry. Also alleviating the drudgery of Air Force routines were the pleasures of his off-hours – "drinks and women," he would write in the early seventies. Pubs in nearby Portage la Prairie "closed the bar at nine forty-five & we arrived at the dance at ten fifteen & the taxi cost fifty cents." It was in the Air Force that he lost his virginity, later than most of his friends. When not on duty, he strove for a cool look by emulating James Dean, slouching around with a cigarette hanging off his bottom lip, sunglasses hiding his eyes.

In the Air Force he made a close friend, Richard Lane, a pale, skinny, red-haired teen who came from Vernon, B.C. Lane's nickname was Red but he would have preferred Rick; to his family, which included a younger brother, Patrick (now a celebrated writer), he was Dick. He and George met during a poker game in barracks at

Macdonald. Since they both aspired to be writers, they encouraged each other. "We shared his little Underwood typewriter," George wrote in "The Memory of Red Lane" (in *A Way With Words*, 1982). Seeing themselves as free spirits, like Jack Kerouac and Neal Cassady, they also played pool and talked all night. At 4 a.m., Red went off to the airmen's mess, where he was a cook's helper. He could crack an egg and drop it into a frying pan with one hand.

The base's newspaper, *The Rocketeer*, printed the funny pieces Bowering wrote about life in the photography section. More daringly, he wrote poems. He sent some out, and *Hockey Pictorial* published one – "The ABCs of the NHL" – in November 1958. Handsomely laid out above an ad for Player's cigarettes, it filled a page. He'd written a hockey-themed rhyming quatrain, simple but true, for each letter of the alphabet. For example,

> *H is for Howe*
> *Need we say more?*
> *His efforts so often*
> *Determine the score*

He also produced some short stories, submitting them to journals like the *Antioch Review* and getting rejection slips. He remembers Wendy, who'd moved on to the University of British Columbia in Vancouver, sending him a published sonnet signed "E.B." On the clipping she'd written, "This is Earle Birney." He didn't recognize the name of the man who was then "the most famous poet in my province," which embarrasses him in retrospect.

Red left the Air Force in the summer of 1956, and on July 9, 1957, George left, too, since Wendy had said she'd have him back. "All my life decisions were based on what my girlfriend did," he told an interviewer in 2011. In 1959 he would reflect on what the stint meant to him, besides giving him Technicolor flying dreams and letting him mention, in author bios, having been an aerial photographer. "What did I get out of my three years?" he asked himself. "Well, I matured some ... I saw people and places all over Western Canada and Ontario and Quebec. That is important."

He expected Red Lane would be a dear friend forever. As he would later write, "We want each other's knowledge, & we freely hand it to each other, dramatizing ourselves to each other always, as fated-to-be-companions always will." They wrote to each other, Red using a juiced-up Kerouac voice and drawing cartoons to amplify his points. He would hint that he had something wrong with him, shouting in a 1962 letter, "OOG AGG, help, I got Tubercollossis, ERG BLAH ..." But no one would worry unduly, and then Red would move to Vancouver to hang out with the writing crowd. They all expected to enjoy his company for years, but it wasn't to be.

❧ CHAPTER 4 ❦

THE DIARIST

By these fruits
we measure our weight & days.

—"Desert Elm," *The Catch* (1976)

George has kept a diary since he was twenty-two. In hardcover note-books, starting on April 10, 1958, he's kept track of his state of mind, health, thoughts, reading, writing, personal life, athletic performance, and sociopolitical milieu. Most people don't have the backbone to start such a project, much less stick with it month after month, year after year.

He does it partly out of a habit of orderly record-keeping, one he developed in high school when he kept score for the Oliver Baseball Club, "high in the chicken wire box / on top of the grandstand ..." And he came to believe, as his dad did, that a mature man handles his affairs neatly and methodically. A second drive behind his diary-keeping is the keen awareness of time passing that he's had since he was young. In 1959 he wrote, "Sometimes this life of mine seems only an inch high, and gathering nothing as it hurtles insidiously along; in 16½ years I'll be 40, and what, where, will I have done?" He felt the same, if not worse, in 1970, when he lamented, "The days click by so

37

fast. I expect that when I'm forty they'll whirr like the ¢ part of the gasoline pump."

His diary is an extraordinary record. He demurred when he first told me about it, saying it mostly contained his bowling scores and, later, his performance in baseball games. But reading its fifty volumes, I saw him morph from a country lad full of inchoate desire, promise, and ambition into an educated urbanite; a professor of Canadian, American, and English literature; a husband and father; a versatile, much-published writer. The entries trace the path by which a bright, curious youth, born in the Great Depression with intellectual and artistic endowments, made his way in the world. Driven by a prodigious work ethic but juggling the responsibilities of salary earner, husband, and parent, he made a habit of sitting down to write, no matter what was going on around him. (He has not only produced a giant oeuvre and kept a record of his life; he also sent mountains of letters to friends and associates – some of the best minds of his generation, to borrow Allen Ginsberg's phrase. He kept carbon copies, and they fill many boxes at Library and Archives Canada.)

When writing an entry, he picks up a fountain pen or a ballpoint and generally fills one lined page. He likes writing to a set length. He enjoys the infinite number of ways the space can be used and, paradoxically, the economy it imposes. Above the lined portion of each page he records the date, time, and place before putting down what's on his mind. And once he's done that, he writes his initials, "GHB," in a monogram-like arrangement in the upper left-hand corner. He's big on rituals and routines of all kinds.

He labelled the first volume "His Impulsive Diary I." (Later volumes give the dates of the first and last entries inside the front cover but aren't titled.) In the first entry, he wrote, "I am reading James T. Farrell's *Bernard Carr*. From this day forth I will guard my private life from Irish-American novelists." (He felt as if Farrell could see into his young male mind.) Three days later, he wrote that he'd been awake at 4 a.m., "reading my life in Farrell."

Half a year later, on October 8, 1958, the twenty-two-year-old raved about having met the American poet Marianne Moore. Just into her seventies, she was visiting UBC, where he was doing a bachelor's in history and English. "Four of us campus poets had this tremendous honor today. We sat with her at a long table, and I was next to Her. And she had nice things to say about [my poem] 'The Intellectual Turned Artist.' What a wonderful woman; so charming, such a wit, a keen observer of life!"

Five years later, the series of thrilling summer workshops and lectures at UBC that would become known as the Vancouver Poetry Conference blew audiences' minds. On August 1, 1963, Bowering wrote in his diary about the most charismatic of the visiting poets: "Last nite in July Allen Ginsberg read his poems in sequence, sometimes beautifully, stepping back from the headlong passion, other times, as in 'Sunflower Sutra,' flying with old-time exciting crack voice. This is the first time I've heard him read in person, and wonderful thing is that after all the identity-personality fixation, he here in flesh, is first of all a *person* and a rather handsomely, earnestly beautiful one – a quiet man who can honestly make loud noises."

In late January 1969, when he and his first wife, Angela, were living in Montreal, they went to a chic party thrown by Mordecai and Florence Richler. Afterwards, he wrote: "At first I was downcast to see the place full of rich-looking middle-age people standing with drinks like pictures in *Toronto Life*. A few writers & other not bad people showed up, tho, and we got to socialize I suppose with [legendary CanLit champion] Bob Weaver. (At one point I heard Richler telling a couple abt the time he was visiting his tailor, an 'east-end boy,' along with 'Terry Stamp' and 'Phil Roth.' I got up out of the couch & fled to the drinking room.)" Winding up his account of the evening, he tutted, "God, the crowd was the kind of people Richler satirizes."

In Montreal in September 1970, he noted, "Helen Hutchinson did a taped interview of me for her TV program called *Life Style*. It came off fairly well, talking away w/ makeup long crusted on the big pimple on side of my nose."

The entry he made on May 23, 1972, shows how frustrated he sometimes got teaching literature at B.C.'s Simon Fraser University, a struggle that would be part of his reality for thirty years. "After I spent 20 hrs on the weekend reading [William] Blake I went to the seminar and found that the people had not read The Marriage of Heaven & Hell, & hadnt even read the Songs of I and E [*Songs of Innocence and of Experience*]. What do they expect? One of them says why cant I just say whether I like it or not without trying to understand it. How fucking depressing!"

His diaries are sprinkled with accounts of his dreams – mostly only fascinating to the dreamer, though it's funny to see that, while in Mexico in June 1964, he had one about teaching the actor Richard Burton to play rock-paper-scissors. Less random is the dream he recorded in September 1971, just before Thea's birth. He dreamt of "the baby being born with its navel in its forearm, not a good situation ..."

Sometimes he alters the diary's narrative flow by inserting a list, since he loves lists, especially alphabetical ones, and often makes them while trying to fall asleep. (Sometimes, the theme is Writers: Adams, Brautigan, Creeley, Duncan, Eigner ... Sometimes, it's Cities: Amsterdam, Beirut, Chicago, Denver, East St. Louis ... Or it may be Baseball Players: Allen, Bosman, Conigliaro, Dean, Ellsworth ...) In the summer of 1978, he regaled future biographers with a list of his favourite things (lightly abridged): "My favourite colour is yellow. My favourite vegetable is onions. My favourite fruit is grapes. My favourite animal is coyote. My favourite bird is swallow. My favourite meat is veal. My favourite sport is baseball. My favourite baseball team in the AL is Boston, in the NL is the Dodgers. My favourite hockey team is Toronto Maple Leafs. My favourite active baseball player is Ferguson Jenkins ... My favourite Canadian poet is Margaret Avison. My favourite cooking is Italian. My favourite drink is bloody Caesars. My favourite city is Trieste. My favourite painter is Rembrandt. My favourite novelist is John Hawkes. My favourite modern poet is H.D. ... My favourite candy bar is Eat-More." He was forty-two at the time.

He would repeat the exercise in March 2016, revealing that as an octogenarian he still roots for coyotes, Trieste, and the Dodgers. But martinis have become his favourite drink and his inventory of favourites has expanded as he's seen more of the world. Feijoas (not widely available) are his favourite fruit, manchego his favourite cheese, and the Alhambra, in Granada, Spain, his favourite building.

He affixes newspaper and magazine clippings to the pages of his diaries, often in lieu of a written entry. They're primarily of two kinds: reviews of his books, both friendly and hostile, and published photos of friends and acquaintances. The clippings alone are a record of his achievements and connections.

Taped-in reviews abound. In 1984 he included a review of his story collection *A Place to Die* in which Alan Twigg, an authority on B.C. literature, called him a "local Edison of postmodernism" and "one of those rare literary gadflies, like Margaret Atwood and George Woodcock, whose versatility invites the slings and arrows of outrageous envy." Bowering commented, "This is surprising" – he didn't have the impression Twigg liked his work.

The published photos George has put in his diary include one of Atwood in September 1968, holding her book of poetry, *The Animals in That Country*. Near it, he wrote, "She has a great sense of line, and a fine ability to externalize strange feelings. So in a minute or two I'm going to write her a note & tell her so." A decade later he taped in a colour magazine photo of Montreal's Irving Layton with his arm around a smiling woman, both holding champagne glasses. Though rarely catty in his diary, he indulged himself that day, writing,

(12:14 pm)

Mon. Oct. 26/09   *Vancouver*

The Box
George Bowering; $19 paper 978-1-55420-045-0, 192 pp., 5½ x 8½, New Star Books, Sept. Reviewed from unbound galleys

Each of the 10 stories in George Bowering's latest collection is prefaced by a photograph. The photos bear some relation to the accompanying stories, but serve more to pique the reader's interest than to illustrate any particular narrative detail.

The stories themselves are varied in genre, but unified by inventiveness, self-referentiality, and wordplay. Bowering's protagonists are frequently writers or intellectuals, and his narrative style is highly self-conscious, as if written for a reader as intimately aware of the form and conventions of the short story as he is. There are recurring literary allusions and references to theories of literature and science.

In "An Experimental Story," these two realms overlap. The narrator introduces the story as an "experiment" meant to determine whether or not a "somewhat corrupted" youth would "revert to a natural innocence upon moving to the sticks." Although the narrator's sensibility is distinctly Victorian, the subject of the story – a contemporary teen who moves with his mother from downtown Vancouver to the Okanagan Valley – is completely up to date. The story is at once a metafictional exercise and a deceptively simple, skilfully executed vignette about adolescence.

"Sworn to Secrecy" and "The Box" play with gumshoe conventions in the same way that "An Experimental Story" plays with scientific objectivity and naturalism. The collection also includes a magic-realist baseball tale involving a leprechaun, two darkly comic short plays, and a probing dialogue between two aging poets.

The Box will appeal to those who enjoy postmodern playfulness. Bowering's prose is polished and his characters are well-drawn, but the overly clever nature of the stories and the frequent authorial intrusiveness becomes tedious. At their best, however, the stories combine inventiveness and humour

NOVEMBER 2009 | QUILL & QUIRE | 23

with finely realized craft. – *Devon Code, a writer in Toronto.*

I can't believe it. Somewhere they found a "critic" who still, in 2009, thinks that an author can "intend" in his text, or is it his story?

Well, I didn't do much else in Toronto but I quite enjoyed the writers conference, I mean. On the way there I read Dashiell Hammett, and on the way back I read Douglas Coupland.

Bowering puts reviews of his books in his diary, occasionally talking back to the critics.

"The visionary rebel poet takes a wife, & she turns out to be a nice plump rich Jewish lady [Harriet Bernstein, his third wife] with lots of rings & face make-up and now they can go to Miami for the winter months." (The official Irving Layton website says, "The short-lived marriage to Harriet caused Layton much grief, the result of which was *The Gucci Bag,* one of Layton's darkest and most bitter books.")

In the mid-eighties George was again mildly catty when recording literary gossip he and writer friend Audrey Thomas had traded over lunch: "… we both dig Paulette Jiles. We both like Sharon Thesen's writing, and we both think that Mavis Gallant is a twit of a person, though we like some of her work."

He also described, as he'd mentioned to me, his performances in the softball games he played with huge enjoyment until he was sixty-six. In spring 1976, when he was on a team called the Granville Grange Zephyrs in Vancouver's Kosmic League, he assessed how he'd acquitted himself: "Sunday we beat old rivals the Ramblers 9–5, how satisfying. I made an error on a hurry double play. I flied to right, lined a single to left, popt to first, grounded sharp to second, driving in a run, and popt to right." In the same spirit, he adored going on road trips to Seattle with friends who shared his enthusiasms. They watched Mariners' games, bought books in the University District, and blissfully washed down Mexican food with beer. His accounts of those odysseys went into the record, too.

He has also preserved his thoughts on operas, art exhibits, concerts, and movies. In 1977 he said *Annie Hall* is "put together like a postmodern novel, lots of cuts out of narrative, a few awkward." He wrote, too, about being a panellist on *Look That Up!*, a quiz show Chuck Davis hosted on CBC Radio for three years in the early eighties. He got to deploy his knowledge and be funny while striving to outscore fellow panellists Mike Absalom, Jean Elder, and Anne Petrie (and later, in her place, Maggie Taylor). Davis's widow, Edna, remembers him having "performed brilliantly." When the show was on the air, he lamented in his diary that Angela cheered for Elder, while Thea liked Absalom. As for him, "I cheer for me."

But his life has primarily been that of a man of letters, and so he records the progress of his writing, which is occasionally fitful. In January 1981, when he'd been working on a long poem (likely *Kerrisdale Elegies*) for thirteen months and had only thirteen pages to show for it, he taunted himself: "Yeah, old GB the prolific poet." A year later, though, he would report having twelve books in the works and in fall 1986 he'd write of working simultaneously on a spy novel, an essay collection, a long poem, and more.

His diaries also contain a wealth of information about the books he has read. In 1982 he pronounced Rudy Wiebe's *The Mad Trapper* cinematic but thought it contained too much explication and stilted dialogue. In 1988, while reading *Various Miracles* by Carol Shields, he liked the stories and said, "In some ways she reminds me of [his Ontario poet friend] David McFadden, with a certain wide-eyed straight account of coincidence and the numinous." He didn't think she was much good at titles, though.

The diaries chronicle his work as an editor of anthologies and of friends' books, his dealings with the editors who were guiding him, his trips to Ottawa to serve on committees of the Canada Council for the Arts, the literary conferences in which he participated, and the many cross-country tours – generally scheduled for the snowiest, iciest days of winter – on which he promoted his books. In May 1982, when he was in Whitehorse, Yukon, with two fellow writers, he summarized: "W.P. Kinsella and I got along fine, though we disagree nearly totally on just about everything, though we both like baseball, write abt Indians, and dig Mexican food. He is one of those conservatives who don't like taxes and metric, etc." George also got along with the late Rosalind MacPhee but disagreed with "everything she says abt poetry & being a poet."

Bowering's politics are also on display in his diaries. He and Angela voted NDP, so elections seldom went their way. They were excited when B.C.'s New Democrats triumphed in 1972, George marvelling, "First time I've ever voted for a winner." The diaries also attest to his interest in history. He thinks of D-Day every time June 6 comes around. On September 11, he thinks not so much of New York's Twin Towers as of the death of Salvador Allende, the Marxist Chilean president felled during the 1973 coup d'état. On November 5 what pops into his mind is Guy Fawkes's foiled plot to blow up the British House of Lords in 1605. He's miffed if the media fail to flag these anniversaries.

Mostly, though, the diaries are rich in the small details that would elude someone passing through life without a pen and notebook. They capture fleeting thoughts. The night of December 14, 1965 – their third anniversary – he and Angela were playing cards with a friend. Who should phone but McClelland & Stewart, saying it would like to publish his first novel. Naturally, he was thrilled, but he had a feeling that others might expect him to greet the news coolly. "Old jaded George," he wrote the next day, is hardly "as blasé in his secret soul as some people believe."

≀ CHAPTER 5 ʃ

THE VARSITY MAN

He loved her grandmother's box at the opera.
He loved appearing first night at the theatre
wearing a thirty-dollar charcoal suit on the society page.

—"Old Standards," *Another Mouth* (1979)

After leaving the Air Force in July 1957, Bowering couldn't wait to start taking classes at UBC in Vancouver. He wanted to absorb as much literature as he could during the day and work on his own poems, stories, and novels at night. He'd always enjoyed school and had done enough manual labour – all those wooden props he'd dragged up under apple trees' laden boughs, all those tractors he'd driven through orchards – to know his best hope for the future was a life of the mind.

In his early twenties, the ex-airman was crazy about Naturalist writers, the early twentieth-century novelists who saw genetics and social conditions as shaping the ways people behaved. James T. Farrell, best known for his Studs Lonigan trilogy of the 1930s, knocked him out. The first time he set foot in the UBC Library's stacks in autumn 1958, the mountains of published writing made him giddy. He homed in on the PS section, American Literature, sensing that this was where he'd lose himself. "Oh, a full shelf of Farrell, a tier of Henry Miller, stacks of John Steinbeck." It was bliss.

The poetry in PS wowed him, too. People familiar with his artistic development know he had an epiphany in the stacks at that time. Coming across a copy of William Carlos Williams's *The Desert Music and Other Poems*, he read the title poem, in which the New Jersey doctor-writer reflects on the seediness, sadness, and mystery of the Mexican border town of Juárez, where he and his wife had gone to have dinner with friends. He also speaks up for the value of a poet's vision in the modern world, declaring, "I *am* a poet! I am. I am …" Bowering was gobsmacked. It was "so hot that the book dropped from my hands …"

Every time young George went outdoors, he registered new sensations – those of the coast, the campus, and the big damp city nearby. Vancouver's rain was an affront to a young man who had only known the aridity of the Okanagan. For a while he went around with wet hair plastered to his skull because, back home, he'd never seen a man carry an umbrella. A February 1959 downpour made him curse the weather gods. In his diary, he used purple prose to inveigh against the "devil-ridden, bone-soddening rain that slashes down cruelly, mercilessly like a liquid Nazi."

And yet the campus and city were verdant places of discovery. The Pacific vistas from Point Grey, where he went to class, were a collage of greens, blues, and greys. He stored up memories of sights he loved for use in poems and prose. Like a latter-day William Wordsworth, he noticed clouds "trembling down Mount Seymour," pigeons "cascading into Victory Square," and "sunsquare shadows chopping up Georgia Street."

In search of urban grit, he and his friends sometimes rode the bus downtown to walk the streets of what was then called Skid Row, now the Downtown Eastside. In places like Jimmy Ling's café, they saw tougher lives than the ones they were leading. The cheap cafés, neon

In the 1950s, Vancouver's cool Pacific vistas were a delight to George, who'd grown up in an inland semi-desert.

signs, and back alleys festooned with telephone wires – captured in Kodachrome by Fred Herzog – had a kind of rough beauty. Bowering, an apparent extrovert who considers himself a loner by nature, was drawn there in the late fifties. "I was gathering material," he would later write, "drowning myself in atmosphere."

As a student in UBC's Faculty of Arts, Bowering was surrounded by people with artistic impulses and interests. Suddenly, it wasn't weird to love Wordsworth or Faulkner, to see plays or act in them, to attend an opera with your girlfriend, or try to write a barnburner of a poem inspired by Ginsberg's *Howl*. In quiet moments he realized how lucky he was. "What a wonderful time of one's life," he rhapsodized. "All this study; all this literature, art! To know that one took the right door sometimes, and now the room is full of what one is looking for …"

As a tall, lanky, bespectacled guy from B.C.'s Interior and an Armed Forces veteran who was older than most other undergraduates, he stood out. Was he an odd duck or a man of mystery? It depends who was doing the looking. Jamie Reid, a fellow student, thought George cut "really a kind of ridiculous-looking figure." Determined to get the remaining wear out of clothes he'd been issued in the Air Force, he sported his old fatigues whose legs ended at mid-calf. A trench coat he'd gotten in the RCAF became his quirky signature garment on campus. In the early seventies, Donald Cameron would tell of having been with him in 1959, "the gangling young would-be writer [loping] down the halls" of UBC's Buchanan Building, his "plastic RCAF raincoat flying behind him." As for the man inside the clothes, Reid saw "a comedian and a buffoon … very quick on the uptake and very funny." George knew he was having an effect on others. One day, in an essay called "Baseball and the Canadian Imagination," he would even admit he'd "had a crush" on himself because he was the "hero of the green room, the newsroom, the muse room, the art gallery, the concert hall and the caf."

The cafeteria the Arts students frequented was a place to get revved up on coffee in the morning and drop into later for gossip or a heated discussion. Fellow student Fred Wah, who came from Nelson, B.C., farther inland than Oliver, remembers Bowering arriving each morning and ordering a cinnamon bun and coffee. "He was smoking cigarettes – you could smoke there – and talking about poetry. George was sort of flashy; he flashed himself around." (Bowering says he only rarely had the money to buy one of the locally famous gooey buns.)

The caf had a cynosure known as the "arty-farty table." Creative types and their hangers-on claimed it. You had to be "a poet or an actor or a good-looking young woman in the Players Club," the campus theatre group, to sit there. On December 2, 1959, the day after his twenty-fourth birthday, George "sat from 12 till 5 in a chair in the cafeteria and gabbed about art and sex and stuff with various dancers, actresses, etc." Mike Matthews, a student actor who worked on the Homerically named campus newspaper, the *Ubyssey*, and on *Raven*, UBC's literary magazine from 1955 to 1962, hung out there. Matthews liked to hold forth, expressing all manner of opinions; Reid, too, was given to impassioned rants.

In the late fifties, UBC's reigning student poets were Desmond Fitz-Gerald and David Bromige. Lionel Kearns, another Arts student from Nelson, remembers that in those days, Bromige was "a very fussy Englishman ... [who] wanted everything written in strict iambs," though he would change significantly later. The dominant voices in the "little tiny world of student writing and publishing at UBC" had ties to Britain. But gusts of American air would soon blow in and knock the old order down.

Maria Hindmarch, who came from Ladysmith on Vancouver Island, was in her first year at UBC in the spring of 1958. She remembers being in the caf and telling a fellow student how much she liked "Summer: Vancouver," a story of Bowering's she'd read in *Raven*. "He's right over there. Why don't you go tell *him*?" came the reply. She did, and was charmed when the budding writer, five years her senior, shook her hand, talked a while, and walked her back toward her dorm.

In the evening, the caf's habitués would head downtown to the pub in the Georgia Hotel, which they called "the G." George and his new friends – including Jamie Reid, who loved the French Symbolist poets, and Lionel Kearns, who had poetic, musical, and athletic leanings, liked to check out recently opened Duthie Books, on Robson Street. Literary magazines made a tempting display on the ground floor while the Paperback Cellar, reached by way of a spiral staircase, gave more shelf space to poetry than fiction. The students sometimes picked up copies of the *Vancouver Sun*, the city's afternoon daily, when they were downtown. George and best buddy Will Thornton-Trump, who were roommates in Vancouver, were dismissive of the journalist/ politician Elmore Philpott. In the innocent days when the newspaper printed letter writers' home addresses, Philpott actually showed up at their door following the publication of a letter in which they'd nominated him for "uncolumnist of the decade," primed to dispute their judgment. Will had to receive him; George was out.

At the end of his first year at UBC, writing was the course in which Bowering had done the best; his lowest mark was in history. English, Spanish, and psychology were his other subjects. On his own time he devoured Ernest Hemingway, F. Scott Fitzgerald, James Joyce, Thomas Wolfe, and Jack Kerouac, and applied himself to Henry James, whose books were more of a struggle. He didn't work during the school year but took upcountry jobs in summer to earn money for tuition. Cheques from his dad carried him through lean patches when classes were underway. His mum sometimes sent care packages containing homemade pie. "I got a check for 150 dollars from Pop, so am solvent for a while more," he noted in February 1959. "Now I owe the folks 369 dollars." That was a goad for him to mail a batch of short stories off to magazines and hope for generous payment.

In the 1958–59 school year, he took an English lit course taught by Clint Burhans Jr., a professor he liked, despite his "loudness and brashness," and a writing course taught by sweet-natured Jacob Zilber. In February 1959, George, who was also taking Spanish, sociology, and Asian studies, predicted "a cool Zilberian reception" for a story he was about to hand in. Later in the month, as his classmates picked the story apart, the session "whirled into a deep discussion of my philosophies of life, time, existence," he wrote in his diary. All the attention may have given him a swelled head.

Rooming together, he and Will lived in starving-student squalor. In his wonderful long poem "Old Standards," George characterizes one of their strikingly minimal living arrangements as a "mushroom earwig cellar room." They had cots, and not much else, in the basement of a house near campus. The bathroom was upstairs and they got to have baths once a week. "It wasn't all that good," George relates. They had a hotplate; not knowing much about cooking and unable to afford fancy ingredients, they often made themselves spaghetti topped with canned tomato sauce or even soup. In his late fifties, Will wrote a story that embellished real-life events: He and George invite two lovely sisters who gave them a lift home from school into their dive. Things seem to be going well until the chocolate pudding George starts to serve turns out to be rancid and their rickety card table collapses, spattering the expensively clad women with curdled glop.

Fortunately, Bowering didn't have to linger in their grungy digs. His thrilling girlfriend of that time, Joan Huberman, welcomed him into her apartment and lent him her car. She was taking theatre courses at UBC and was passionate about painting, photography, literature, and music. She sculpted, played tennis, and belonged to the campus diving club. What's more, she was stunning. Once, as George recounted in his diary, she answered her door wearing a pink evening dress and wowed him with her décolletage. Another time, he jotted down that her "inward beauty today was shining like after-swim water on her face."

Huberman came from a distinguished European musical family. Her paternal grandmother, Elsa Stewart-Galafrés, had been a concert pianist turned Viennese stage and film actress. She was also an authority on ballet. She'd been married to the Polish-born violinist Bronislaw Huberman and then to the Hungarian composer Ernő Dohnányi. Bowering remembers Stewart-Galafrés living in a cottage next to English Bay with her third husband, Cliff Stewart. When guests came to dinner, it was her genteel European habit to put a saltcellar – "a tiny little thing on legs, full of salt, and a tiny little spoon" – at each place setting. Stewart-Galafrés and her partner were opera buffs, attending most productions at the newly opened Queen Elizabeth Theatre. They liked nothing better than to treat Joan and George to excellent seats. The four were at a performance of Puccini's *La Bohème* when a photographer from Vancouver's morning newspaper, the *Province*, snapped their picture. Nicely composed, it ran on November 7, 1960. It showed the older couple in dignified formal dress, Joan adorable in a street-length dress with a corsage and clutch purse, and George with short, neat hair and horn-rims, in a suit and tie.

Joan's parents had divorced and remarried. The second wife of her handsome father, John Hally Huberman, was the composer Barbara Pentland. Her music – "avant-garde, far-out, difficult" – appealed to George, and he loved having a personal connection to such a serious artist. During the time he was with Joan, he bought Pentland a print of Paul Klee's painting, *Fish Magic*, because she'd said she wanted to write music based on it. He was so short of money he sold his bicycle to get the required fifteen dollars.

What with their classes and assignments, George's writing, Joan's hobbies, and the many plays, movies, and concerts they went to, their lives were a hectic whirl. They spent the last day of February 1959, a Saturday, searching for and finding Joan's cat – a tom misleadingly named Cherie-Blanche – and then having a late lunch of steak at her apartment with Verdi's *A Masked Ball* on the radio. Later, they went bowling and shopping for second-hand books, read the *Sun*, and saw Spencer Tracy in *The Last Hurrah*. They were competitive when they bowled. On one occasion, Joan beat him twice but he "managed to out-aggregate her."

In September 1960, they were both cast in a campus production of Bertolt Brecht's *The Good Woman of Setzuan* – George as the policeman, Joan as the First Woman. And they hoovered up serious literature. His diary tells of how they "blitzed a book store previously inviolate, and brought home the swag: James Joyce, Eugène Ionesco, Bernard Shaw, Ezra Pound."

Joan had many admirers and seemed not to want to settle down with one man. Sometimes, when George felt she was treating him badly, he would buy a mickey of brandy for less than a dollar and down it dramatically in the parking lot beside the caf. Not quite a week after the *Province* had published the cute photo of them, Joan told George they were through. Knowing what he was losing, he wrote in sorrow, "I miss so much those things that seemed so natural before – Joan's troubles with school, her new kicks in painting, her arguments about semantics and psychology, together visits to her grandparents, seeing her dashing from bed to bathroom in sweater and bare bottom." They got back together in 1961, split up, and then reunited.

Despite this emotional Sturm und Drang, the Okanagan man in his mid-twenties was growing academically and as a writer. In spring 1960, he received his bachelor's degree. He then spent an unclassified year at UBC, filling the gaps in his knowledge of English literature. "The neatest year I ever spent in school," it was learning of the purest, most curiosity-driven sort. He read Chaucer, Shakespeare, Pope, Fielding, H.G. Wells, Pound, Burroughs, and Williams, earning first-class marks in three out of four courses.

Graduating from the University of British Columbia in 1960, Bowering set his sights on a master's in English.

Bowering entered the English department's master's program in fall 1962, just as Joan was preparing to marry the artist Gordon Payne. (By then, George was dating Angela Luoma.) Being a graduate student brought with it the possibility of working as a teaching assistant and taking charge of a section of English 100. At the time, TAs earned $200 a month for each course they taught. George needed the money badly: He'd been subsisting on sixty-five-cent dinners at the Varsity Grill and wasn't above lifting uneaten sandwich halves from the caf to fill his belly at lunch. Still, he didn't feel qualified to stand in front of a class and hold forth, so he proposed a lesser role marking students' papers. Nonsense, said his professors, assigning him a section with forty or so students. Kearns was also a TA in English, as was Frank Davey, a talented, industrious student who'd grown up in Abbotsford, east of the city. Bill New was another. Later to have a distinguished career as the academic, writer, critic, and editor W.H. New, he was then a young man uncertain about his future. He had an undergraduate degree in geography and was hoping his plan to switch to English lit made sense.

The English department's TAs were given offices in huts – former Army and Air Force structures that the university had moved onto campus after the Second World War to meet the needs of a rapidly expanding enrolment. The humble wooden buildings were meant to be temporary but gave yeoman service for years. Kearns figures it was an advantage that he and the other English TAs weren't in the Buchanan Building, near the professors – the huts gave them their own turf. They also felt quite unencumbered in class. "We had to follow the reading list and our students had to write the department exams," Kearns says, "but other than that we had free rein."

Davey remembers that Hut B-6 was the one in which he, Bowering, and New shared an office. It had earlier been a neurology lab where animal experiments were done, so they called it the monkey hut. Occasionally, they caught a whiff of formaldehyde. Frank and George moved two huge wooden desks to face each other, since they were always dashing off poems – sometimes on the same subject, in the companionable spirit of Wordsworth and Samuel Taylor Coleridge. Joan, who often rode her bicycle to the hut, inspired twin poems by

Davey ("For a Girl") and Bowering ("Motor Age"). Their pushed-together desks and poetry fever made them ready to go in fall 1961, when they and three friends would start *TISH*, a now-legendary mimeographed poetry magazine that would become "required reading for far-out poets all over the country." Not only could Frank and George do their TA work in the hut, they could write poems and plan future *TISH* issues there.

Bill New set himself up in a corner. "I got the sense," he recalls, "that they didn't want anybody else there; they wanted it to be the *TISH* office." He didn't know what *TISH* was all about until, one day, Davey spelled out how he and some fellow students had been drawn into the excitement swirling around certain rising U.S. poetry stars and were launching a magazine for their own work in a similar vein. New remembers Bowering, Davey, and their friends seeming "extremely sure of themselves."

Others had the same feeling. "The [*TISH*] scene was very tight and very closed. The belt was snugged so tight," recalls Robert Hogg, a young poet friend of Davey's who would one day become a professor of literature in Ontario. Hogg was more drawn to what was called the downtown poetry scene – Roy Kiyooka, Curt Lang, Gerry Gilbert, Judith Copithorne, Maxine Gadd, and others, including, for a time, Red Lane.

Pierre Coupey, founding editor of *The Capilano Review* and a founder of the *Georgia Straight*, says, "The *TISH* group was a very tight group, and they've remained a tight group, haven't they? They set out to capture the canon. They wanted to seize it, and they've largely succeeded, and they've supported each other all the way through." Coupey belonged to a group of North Shore poets Bowering dubbed the North Vandals. Coupey remembers the ferocity of allegiances in the sixties: "The Vancouver poetry scene [was] one of the meanest scenes I've ever known in my life. At the time of [John] Newlove and [Gerry] Gilbert and bill bissett, you had the UBC students – anathema! – and then you had the Kitsilano and the east-side, the downtown, and blah blah blah, this, that, and the other. God, there was a lot of competition!"

At the same time, George had another absorbing literary duty. The *Ubyssey* gave him a column on its Critics' Page. It was called "Placebo" and he launched it with a bang. On September 22, 1961, he excoriated campus arts groups for their timidity. The Players Club, he wrote, should be producing students' work or plays by writers like Samuel Beckett. Instead, it "apes the Vancouver little theatre world, turning out 'safe' potboilers ..." He accused *Raven* of resembling "a Georgian cremation urn – overly embellished on the outside, and full of mouldy ashes." He charged student painters, sculptors, and photographers with imitating San Francisco artists and, invoking the university's Latin motto, signed off with the words "Like, *Tuum est* ['It is yours'], sweetheart."

This fiery debut caused the Players Club to put out a call for student-written plays, while *Raven* invited him and Reid to guest-edit the next issue. But a representative of the campus Musical Society bridled at George's put-down of her group and urged him to join, saying, "Perhaps, once unprotected by the sanctity of a desk, your criticism may be worth recognition." In subsequent columns, he had the good grace to applaud the student productions he considered daring and well executed.

Like others who wrote for the Critics' Page, he gave readers credit for being smart and discriminating. He shared his enthusiasms with them, describing Charles Olson, a hugely influential American, as "the poet whose life's work is the paradigm for the art in our time." He also smiled on the poetic ground Irving Layton had broken in Canada, writing, "Wherever he goes in this country the snow melts in his path." Looking back, he rather surprisingly says that "the *Ubyssey* crowd, to me, was really [more] important than *TISH*."

In the fifties and sixties, UBC had a club called the Writers' Workshop in which undergraduate writers appraised one another's work. The students deposited their stories and poems – with their names left off, if they craved anonymity – in a drop box outside a hut on the campus's West Mall. Tony Friedson, the club's faculty sponsor, picked them up, made copies, and distributed them to members. It was mostly fourth-year students who attended, but Frank Davey joined in his first year. Davey, who would go on to write books, teach at universities, and edit *Open Letter*, a long-lived journal of literary criticism, remembers George coming to every second or third Workshop meeting, the others always glad to see him. "He was a very cheerful fellow, a bit of a joker; he liked to tease people."

Jamie Reid joined because he'd written a short story that Jacob Zilber had found too sentimental. The professor suggested that in the Writers' Workshop he'd find out what the modern short story was all about. "George was there," Reid told me, "and he was more or less the hero of it." He was the first person Jamie had met who intended to write for a living.

The Workshop wasn't totally a boys' club. Betty Lambert, a playwright with a social conscience, belonged. So did Copithorne and Carol Johnson. Hindmarch joined, becoming a prime mover. Frank says he and Maria "sort of took over the club," with Friedson arranging the venues and striking just the right note as sponsor. "He was very non-directive," Davey recalls. "Often we disagreed with him, and he was happy to have that." Elaborating, Hindmarch mentions two things that fuelled the Workshop: Davey's homemade *sake* and Friedson's "huge generosity." He asked questions to move the discussion forward, and "we'd all shout at him and say, 'You're fulla shit!'"

Friedson urged a young student named Daphne Marlatt (then Buckle) to join the Workshop, seeing in her a gift for both poetry and prose. She had spent her early years in Australia and Malaysia and had felt like an outsider when she came to Canada at age nine.

At the first meeting she attended, shyness all but paralyzed her. It was winter 1960 and the leaves of the high laurel hedge surrounding the house where the meeting was being held were glazed with rain – a sight so characteristic of Vancouver that Alice Munro put it in one of her early stories. She walked back and forth beside the hedge, gathering the nerve to go in. "Frank and George were pretty dominant in that group," Marlatt remembers. "They were having some kind of an argument about poetry. Frank had been reading [aloud] all these free-verse poems – I knew very little [about form] at this point – about cars, hot rods. I got a little fed up with it, and I said to him, 'I bet you can't even write a sonnet.' Whereupon he then set about writing a series of sonnets, for me." It was no secret that Davey was taken with her.

While this was going on, George worked steadily on the autobiographical coming-of-age novel he'd begun in September 1959, as his last undergraduate year got underway. He stayed up late, thumping on his portable typewriter in his and Will's mushroom earwig cellar digs. He went so far as to cover the windows with cardboard so as not to be distracted by activity on the street. Following a practice of Hemingway's, he produced a page a day.

This unpublished novel, *Delsing*, tells of a youth's never-consummated love for his high school sweetheart. The George Delsing character is based on him, with Frances Sinclair based on Wendy Amor. Like Wendy (who would die of cancer, tragically young, in 1977), Frances is petite, with an English accent, good sense, and an amused tolerance for her adolescent suitor, the class cut-up.

Some of the prose in *Delsing* is callow, imitative of Farrell, Kerouac, and other novelists he read with pleasure. In one machismo-soaked passage, Delsing, the sometime narrator, is a teenager reflecting on Frances's pheromones: "Every woman has a particular odor that comes from her mouth up from her throat and all her woman entrails, and that odor is part of the thing a man falls in love with ... every time he gets a whiff of it, he knows he has a woman (the woman) up against him. His woman."

That kind of writing doesn't dominate, though. More often, Delsing views his own doings from an ironic distance, as when he contemplates the charade of going to work in a photo lab in summer to earn money for university: "I'm supposed to go home and lie horizontal on a bed and quit doing things for six hours or so, and then get up and put food in my mouth and walk down to the studio and put pieces of paper in a dish of liquid ... Why, for instance, does a guy do a thing like that five days a week? So he can have enough pieces of paper with a foreign queen's face on them to go and sit in classrooms all winter." Similarly, Delsing and his friend, Bob Small, are at one point seen from a cosmic remove, as if an aerial photographer were zeroing in on them: "Inside the dwelling were seated two creatures, and they were tilting receptacles half-filled with yellowbrown liquid to their mouths, their tilting actions occurring almost simultaneously."

Like many young people, Bowering thought deeply about life. But, unlike most, he forced himself to sit at a typewriter and wrestle his thoughts onto paper. In August 1961, after he'd finished a second draft of *Delsing*, he told himself, "Now to sort it, bind it, and send it out. And get busy on the next one." He thought he ought to be turning out work in torrents. He sent the manuscript to Macmillan of Canada but got a rejection letter. Realizing that what he'd written was crude, he decided to let it go and concentrate on poetry instead.

CHAPTER 6

THE *TISH* MAN

"He's a good prof, the only man I know who knows how to write about new poetry and all ... So in we go, me first in my usual gangbusters way, grabbing his wife & kissing her forehead ... she's been bending over an oven, so I grab a bunch of her brand new peanut-butter cookies, & I flop in the six-foot couch in the living room, look thru the new records scattered on the floor & coffee tables ... Prof ... has some Bourbon, which is unusual around Vancouver livingrooms, & we quaff away ..."

—"Ebbe & Hattie," *Flycatcher & Other Stories* (1974)

The summer before he turned twenty, Bowering set out to become a poet. He made a pact with himself: Whenever an idea came to him, he would sit down and work out a poem. He figured that if he was serious and put in enough time and effort, his skills were bound to improve. As he would write many years later, "Just about everybody writes poetry. It's just that most people never try to write better poetry."

Whenever he got time off from the Air Force, he holed up in his parents' house in Oliver. As the summer heat intensified and valley farmers sent crates of luscious tree fruit to market, he wrote "Pessimism" in June 1955. The first poem he thought worth keeping, it reeks of youthful Weltschmerz and is bitterly satirical. The "I" of the poem is so jaded that birds' songs sound to him like "horrendous cacophonies"; where others see beauty, he can see only "cysts."

He gave titles like "Waste," "Failure," and "Dismay" to the poems he wrote over the next few months. Anyone who reads his early, unpublished poems – they're in Ottawa among his voluminous papers at Library and Archives Canada – can see he outgrew his youthful nihilism fairly quickly. It's also evident that practice made him an increasingly fluent and versatile poet. He wrote intensively, experimenting with form, rhyme, rhythm, and tone. "Saturday Night," his seventeenth poem, from August 1956, throbs with dangerous energy. Military men and their girlfriends are drinking in a bar when jealousy flares and a fight breaks out. The poem begins,

> *Saturday night*
> *And all the guys are*
> *Yelling and running and belching*
> *Beer runs with blood and lipstick.*

The pact he'd made with himself involved not only perseverance but also careful documentation. His sports statistician's love of order and detail led him to type up, date, and number his handwritten poems. Whenever he had a stack of a hundred, he filed it in a three-ring binder, typing up a single-spaced table of contents for the front. (What a fiddly job that must have been, and how unexpected it is that a man known for his irreverent, joshing looseness should be a meticulous record keeper, at least in his writing life.)

He gave each binder a title. The one holding his first hundred poems he dubbed *The Immaterialist*. He named the second, third, and fourth *The Adventurist*, *The Projectionist*, and *The Psalmodist*. By the end of 1984, he'd filled eighteen binders with seventeen hundred pieces – mostly poems, though in the seventies he began including essays, stories, and book reviews in his filing system. The titles of later binders include *The Haruspex* and *The Duodenum*, since he cherishes words that send most folks running to the dictionary.

Eager to be published, he sent poems to magazines across North America and beyond. His early diaries are peppered with comic groans about the rejections he was racking up. In 1959 he lamented, "It's about time I was published. Hell, I'm 24!" The next year he wryly noted that a rejection letter from *Esquire* began with the words "Sorry, no." But rejection wasn't the norm for long: Soon he began to receive acceptances. On the typed poems in his binders he jotted the details of each publication. "The Intellectual Turned Artist," his twenty-fifth poem, appeared in *Raven* in December 1957, after he'd been out of the Air Force for five months. It's a short poem that mentions both the Jivaro, Amazonian people famous for hunting and head-hunting, and Beelzebub.

Of his first hundred poems, the eighty-seventh, "Soliloquy on the Rocks," from 1957, impressed the most editors. *Raven* published it, according to his pen-and-ink notations; so did two other magazines – *PRISM* and *Canadian Art*. It shows a group of friends at the water's edge, walking across rocks at low tide, crushing mussels underfoot and feeling "crackling, crunching guilt with every step." The speaker of the poem wonders, obscurely, whether the mussels are "seaweed-shawled in effigy of our own waterfowl existence."

As his poems gained strength and clarity, the hurdle of publication became easier to clear. Several poems in his second binder were published. The third contains "Radio Jazz," whose energetic push still conveys the thrill of raw, urgent music pouring from a "shelf radio in a hot night kitchen." That poem was influential for his friend Jamie Reid, who loved how it "doesn't draw conclusions but makes the thing manifest in an important way."

With his 383rd poem, George hit the jackpot. "Grandfather," which he wrote on October 8, 1962, tells his paternal grandfather's life story on one page with idiosyncratic verve. Imbued with all the wisdom he had at twenty-six, it has been his best-known poem ever since – a fact he finds mildly irksome. The circumstances under which he produced it are no secret – he's described them in print more than once. He and his smart, stunning new girlfriend, Angela, went to a party at Reid's place in late September 1962. Reid and the young filmmaker Sam Perry shared an apartment in a house on West Pender Street, perched above the train tracks at Coal Harbour. On that night jazz poured from the record player and the cool young friends listening to it quaffed cheap wine, gossiped, flirted, and waved their cigarettes for emphasis.

In a letter she'd sent him in the spring, Angela had teasingly said, "George Bowering, you'd better marry me or I'll sue for breach of promise." But at the party she suggested it might be better not to wed. She wasn't sure she was ready. Frustration flaring within him, George momentarily felt like striking her. Checking the impulse, he instead punched a length of burlap that hid what he believed was a plaster wall. It turned out to be a concrete wall; when they left the party, his right hand was a bruised mess and by morning it had swollen grotesquely. They went to St. Paul's Hospital, where it was taped and immobilized in a sling.

The September 30 entry in his long-running diary is one of only a couple in someone else's handwriting. "Bill Trump is writing this," it begins, "because old crazy dumb fuckin' ol' George broke his right hand against a hard wall in lieu of a girl's soft jaw early this morning."

A week later, his forearm in a cast, he took Angela to a jazz concert: Cannonball Adderley and Yusef Lateef. After taking her home, he walked quickly toward the "linoleumated False Creek digs" he and Will shared in an old house, dodging raindrops and thinking of how he'd review the concert in the *Ubyssey*. He was carrying a case of Old Style Pilsner and couldn't find his key. Will was asleep, so he set the twelve-pack down and chucked pebbles at a window. Will heard but thought kids were doing it. Maddened, George scaled the ladder that was nailed to an outside wall as a fire escape. "I had to decide what to do with the two bent fingers protruding from the wet and soiled cast around my aching hand. Should I hang the case of beer from them, or use them to support my hundred and eighty pounds (counting the beer)?" Solving the problem somehow, he made it to the second floor and clattered in through the kitchen window.

"I heard George come crashing in," Thornton-Trump remembers. "I said, 'Hey, George, some idiot's throwing stones,' and he shouted, 'Why didn't you get up and open the door, you idiot?' He was really steamed, really mad. He slammed the door, and then I heard the typewriter: *bang-bang-bang-bang.*"

Bowering maintains he wrote "Grandfather" by hand, since that was how he drafted poems. It seems likely, given the cast. Regardless of how it got onto the page, it's a work of tremendous energy. Upset over his shifting status with Angela, he cast his mind back in time. He thought of the tribulations of his father's father, Jabez Harry Bowering, an orphan who'd come to Canada with his brother at a young age.

"Grandfather" begins with powerful verbs. This gutsy forebear made landfall and "strode across the Canadian prairie / hacking down trees." Six years later, he got religion – "his eyes were blinded / with the blast of Christ" – and "wandered west / to Brandon among wheat kings." (You can't help but admire this sly mention of the Manitoba city's junior hockey team.) George ratcheted up the drama by twice inserting "holy holy holy lord god almighty," the incantatory words he used to hear when his grandmother took him to church. The poem ends abruptly: After outliving two wives, the granddad who'd been a doer, a builder, and a fiery orator is reduced to existing as a hobbled widower with a Bible by his bed. The closing lines ring out like a sob:

Till he died the day before his eighty-fifth birthday
in a Catholic hospital of sheets white as his hair.

When Will read "Grandfather" the next morning, he was blown away. But George shrugged off his praise, saying the poem didn't use any of the theories or techniques he'd been cultivating. As it turned out, no one cared. His notes on the archived typescript show it has been published thirty-one times – first in *TISH* and later in such anthologies as *15 Canadian Poets* (1970), edited by Gary Geddes and Phyllis Bruce, and *The New Oxford Book of Canadian Verse in English* (1984), edited by Margaret Atwood. Frank Davey sees it as an eminently teachable poem because it is relatively short, with a clear formal structure and a firm ending that has "portents and implications which students can identify and talk about." Atwood mentions it in her 1972 survey, *Survival: A Thematic Guide to Canadian Literature*.

TISH took off with the help of Warren Tallman, a lean, bespectacled, cigarette-smoking man who'd risen from working-class roots in Washington State. A professor in UBC's English department, Tallman could easily spend a whole class analyzing a few lines in a poem. His wife, Ellen Tallman, who'd grown up in the San Francisco Bay Area and gone to the University of California at Berkeley, also taught at UBC. The Bay Area poet Robert Duncan – a gay anarchist and pacifist, exploding with talk and ideas – was a close friend of hers. Through that relationship, the Tallmans were friends with a coterie of California poets who were producing exciting work. And through them they knew Charles Olson, a strapping son of New England who had taught at – and personified – North Carolina's Black Mountain College in the fifties and led the so-called Black Mountain poets. His wide knowledge and limber imagination produced poems with openings like "The lordly and isolate Satyrs – look at them come in / on the left side of the beach / like a motorcycle club!"

Professor Warren Tallman, right, introduced young George Bowering, left, to exciting poets from California and other parts of the U.S.

Another American poet Warren introduced to his students was Robert Creeley. Born in Massachusetts, Creeley had lived on the Spanish island of Majorca, as well as in Guatemala and New Mexico. A childhood accident had caused him to lose an eye, so he had a glass eye and sometimes wore an eye patch. While at Harvard University, he started to translate Rainer Maria Rilke's *Sonnets to Orpheus* and steeped himself in the work of Williams, Pound, and D.H. Lawrence. According to his biographer, Ekbert Faas, Creeley "emulated in verse the kind of whimsy Miles Davis achieved in bebop ..." He is known for two- to four-line stanzas, a simple vocabulary, strong enjambment, and sparse use of metaphor. Warren considered him brilliant and persuaded the department to hire him in 1962. (He stayed for only a year.) George, on meeting him, thought he was hugely knowledgeable and "a perfect no bullshit man."

The Tallmans had relaxed boundaries. Students they found simpatico got invited to their house at 2527 West 37th Avenue. Maria Hindmarch, a student then called Gladys or, affectionately, Glad or Glad Eyes, lived there for a time and helped look after their children, Karen and Ken. The experience was "a joy," she recalls. The Tallmans cared about her so much that once, when Warren was driving her,

Ellen, and the kids to a restaurant for hamburgers, she announced she'd won second prize in *Mademoiselle* magazine's 1959 writing contest. "He almost went into the ditch," he was so thrilled, Hindmarch says. Another time, she and her older student friends Bowering and Kearns took the Tallman children on an outing to UBC. During the drive, they spotted a bald eagle gliding on an air current. The young men began reciting, "My heart in hiding / Stirred for a bird, – the achieve of, the mastery of the thing!" – lines in Gerard Manley Hopkins's sonnet "The Windhover," which Warren had been teaching. Kearns brought up Hopkins's notion of inscape – the individual character and beauty of everything in God's creation – and, from the back seat, little Kenny sang out, "Holy Moses, what an inscape!" Weeks later, he was still saying it.

At the Tallmans' legendary parties, guests stayed up half the night riffing on books, art, and culture. Warren's favourite beer, Carling Black Label, flowed freely. Karen had two single beds in her room and occasionally awoke the next morning to find a visiting Allen Ginsberg sleeping in the spare one.

In 1960, New York's Grove Press published *The New American Poetry, 1945–1960*, edited by Donald Allen – an anthology of the avant-garde work Warren was passionate about. His students, who didn't have money to spare, fell over themselves trying to get hold of copies. Fred Wah, who would later become Canada's fifth Parliamentary Poet Laureate, lifted a copy from the UBC Bookstore and gave it to his girlfriend, Pauline Butling, inscribing it "From Lucky Luciano."

The New American Poetry presented work by the Beat Generation (Ginsberg, Kerouac, and others), the San Francisco Renaissance (Robert Duncan, Robin Blaser, Lawrence Ferlinghetti, Jack Spicer), the Black Mountain poets (Olson, Creeley, Ed Dorn), and the New York Poets (John Ashbery, Kenneth Koch, Frank O'Hara). They bared their philosophies at the back in a section called "Statements on Poetics." Denise Levertov, soon to become a feminist star of the sixties' avant-garde, wrote, "I believe every space and comma is a living part of the poem and has its function, just as every muscle and pore of the body has its function." Robert Duncan, whose poetry is full of myth, erudition, and magic, ended his statement with a flourish, saying, "I make poetry as other men make war or make love or make states or revolutions: to exercise my faculties at large."

George, Frank, Fred, Pauline, and their friends craved an insider's explanation of *The New American Poetry*. Ever since they'd started reading it, around Christmas 1960, they'd been gathering at the Tall-mans' on Sundays to wrestle with one section in particular: "Projective Verse," Charles Olson's thorny but crucial essay on his theories of poetry. Warren suggested they each kick in five dollars to bring Duncan up from the Bay Area to aid their process of discovery. To their delight, he agreed to come. He boarded a Greyhound, stayed with the Tallmans and, on three consecutive evenings in July 1961, gave riveting talks.

Like Bob Creeley, Duncan had had a mishap as a boy that damaged his vision: His eyes seemed to operate independently of each other. His voice was high-pitched and he "never stopped talking," Lionel Kearns recalls. "He was just a motormouth. Everybody picked up different things from him. He said almost everything, so you could [fasten on something and] say, 'This is what Duncan says.'"

Bowering, who was spending that summer in Oliver, travelled to Vancouver to hear Duncan's lectures. On August 2, 1961, when he'd returned to his hometown, he wrote in his diary, "Apparently Duncan has agreed that we should have a little mimeo-mag of our brand of poetry. The ed. board is tentatively me, Frank Davey, Dave Dawson, Fred Wah, and J. Reid." Before heading home, Duncan gave the magazine a name. He'd been discussing with the students the fact that anthropologists aren't above examining fossilized dung to find out what the people of ancient civilizations ate. He suggested that poets, too, should abandon squeamishness and examine every facet of human existence. The students thought about calling their magazine *Shit*, for the shock value. (The following year, in New York City, Ed Sanders would inaugurate one called *Fuck You*.) Duncan proposed lightly scrambling the letters.

George was the oldest of *TISH*'s four contributing editors but Frank – as its editor, plain and simple – stood at the helm. Not in the wheelhouse but somewhere on deck were Kearns and some talented young women, including Butling, Hindmarch, and Marlatt. (The last two would become contributing editors later in the decade.) Fred, adept with tools and machinery, ran the hand-cranked mimeograph machine Frank had picked up second-hand for fifteen dollars, earning the nickname Inky.

The idea, with *TISH* and other little magazines, was for creative people to circulate their own work without interference or delay. Little magazines, which had a long history, really took off in the sixties. Amiri Baraka (then known as LeRoi Jones) and Diane di Prima, who edited the *Floating Bear*, a new magazine in New York City, offered their mailing list to the young Vancouver poets. This gave *TISH* a U.S. readership right out of the gate. The first issue, with twelve legal-size pages, went out to about 350 people in September 1961. A two-cent stamp did the job. In a manifesto-like editorial, Davey wrote that what readers held in their hands was "a moving and vocal mag ... *TISH* is not timid; it is what must come and what does." His certainty was appealing: Readers wanted to hear more.

On the Critics' Page in the *Ubyssey*, David Bromige twitted *TISH* for being American-influenced, calling it "the Black Mountaineers' party-line pamphlet." Lines of thinking from the United States did fuel it. Pound's "Make it new," a challenge to render phenomena clearly so they could be seen afresh, resonated with the *TISH* group. So did Williams's dictum, "No ideas but in things," which helped to clear away nineteenth-century fustian and encourage poems in touch with real life. The *TISH* gang also subscribed to Olson's belief in poetry as a vocal art, its measures based on breaths, and his call for poems reflecting their locus, or place of origin. Also attractive was Duncan and Spicer's mystical idea that poets don't so much produce great work as transmit what they pick up from the world around them. (Bowering agrees. He dismisses notions of poets expressing themselves and being in control of their materials; he sees them more as transmitters than creators.)

Taken together, these principles generated a fresh, accessible poetry that rang with plangent vowels, bold images, local detail, and the rhythms of spoken English.

TISH 2 carried the first part of Bowering's poem, "The Meatgrinder," its opening image one of a "big fat old man" flipping burgers in a café and "watchin the front door for more police." The editors announced they would be printing further sections but then changed their minds. Hindmarch remembers an editorial meeting in which objectors cried, "Pee-yew!" Davey says the poem struck most of the group as "a straight rip-off of Allen Ginsberg ... we didn't think that, even if he was learning from imitation, we should be publishing it."

The third issue of *TISH* contained thoughtful letters from readers, including one from John Robert Colombo. A Toronto poet who would later be called "the master gatherer" because of his many compilations of Canadian facts, quotations, proverbs, ghost stories, and more, Colombo wrote, "I liked particularly your policy of publishing a *group* of poems and the poet's artistic credo."

In December 1961, *TISH* 4 was the first issue to use the tagline "A Poetry Newsletter," emphasizing the product was hot off the presses. A provocative issue, it carried four poems by Kearns, who'd declined a place on the masthead because he found the editors too doctrinaire. His poem "Residue" pulled readers in with its first lines: "He was flying / DH9As then / rickety land-planes over the Channel ..."

In January 1962, *TISH* 5 printed Frank Davey's "Bridge Poem," which still conjures up Vancouver: "City of greasy bridges / I am always going over them ..." Kearns's "Contra Diction," short and delightful, appeared on Valentine's Day in *TISH* 6:

> At worst I think
> poetry only a hobby, an
> activity similar to
>
> the youthful assembly
> of silent model planes
> – my mother commenting "So
> constructive and it teaches something
> too." My father at his guns,
> clearing his throat in reply.

The editorial that opened the seventh issue announced that David McFadden, the Ontario poet whose sensibility George would one day compare with Carol Shields's, was starting a poetry magazine, *Mountain*. As well, the American poet Cid Corman was moving his magazine, *Origin*, from Boston to Kyoto. Like-minded artists were at work all over the world, but the poetry in that issue of *TISH* was saturated with references to Point Grey, the North Shore, Lynn Canyon, bridges, rain, seagulls, and the salt tang of fish. What Olson, Creeley, and Duncan were saying about the importance of one's home place had clearly registered with the *TISH* poets.

TISH 8 carried a rare poem by a woman. "The Dog Transformed," by Seattle's Ann O'Loughlin, was homey and straightforward: A black dog goes out in the cold, comes back ice-crusted, and later, enjoying the stove's warmth, melts "back to black." Today Bowering acknowledges that *TISH* didn't publish many women poets in the beginning. "It wasn't 'cause we didn't want to. [It was more a case of] 'Where were they?'" he says. "I don't know if it's because women writers hadn't yet got hooked into feminism or whether it was because they weren't interested in the avant-garde, or what." Marlatt remembers that it was common for young women to feel overpowered by young men in those days. Once, when she was to be part of a group reading by UBC students, she asked a man to read her poem for her and then was disappointed by the way he'd done it. "I realized, 'Okay, I have to do this from now on. I have to read my own work.'"

By the sixteenth and seventeenth issues of *TISH*, women's voices had become a more robust part of the mix.

At the end of May, the *TISH* poets tried to publish *Sticks & Stones*, a book of Bowering's poetry, but their press acted up, some pages emerged blotchy, and, worse luck, they ran out of money for paper and cover stock. Few copies were collated and not one was conventionally distributed. The poems in the stillborn collection included "Radio Jazz" and "Eyes That Open," a subtle but simple poem George wrote out of love for Angela, his "green eyed girl."

In mid-June, the tenth issue of *TISH* contained a long essay on Olson by Sam Perry. It became so popular that the *TISH* group later reprinted it as a pamphlet. Bowering had a poem about an urgent sexual encounter in *TISH* 11 (dated July 14, 1962). It began, "Putting it in neatly / for only a second," and then went on to describe "the smooth and easy insistence" of the coupling. He'd gained confidence, clearly.

In the summer of 1962, a brief visit to San Francisco brought George into the orbit of poets he admired. (The Tallmans were in the Bay Area at the time and helped him find places to stay, since he had little money for the trip.) He went to call on Michael McClure at his place near Golden Gate Park, but the photogenic, well-connected poet was away in Mexico. George did get to socialize with others, though: The elegant Robin Blaser, who would move to Vancouver in 1966, asked him to a dinner party.

The appearance of *TISH* 12 on August 14, 1962, meant the newsletter had completed a year of monthly publication. It was a place, Davey wrote, where new Vancouver poets could publish first. And so

Daphne Marlatt made an appearance. McClure was in the issue, too. The September 1962 issue contained articles by Creeley and Duncan marking *TISH*'s first anniversary. In "For the Novices of Vancouver," Duncan showed he'd been reading *TISH* with affectionate attention. He responded to many of the poems, quoting liberally from David Dawson's "Tentative Coastlines" series, which conjures up early explorers with scarlet Maltese crosses on the sails of their ships.

TISH 14 was stuffed with good poetry. Bowering's "Grandfather" appeared, along with the sixth section of "Tentative Coastlines." Jamie Reid's "So Long, Mungo" was a tribute to the Kwakwa̱ka̱'wakw carver Mungo Martin, who had recently died.

The fifteenth *TISH* appeared on November 14. John Newlove, a contemporary for whom the *TISH* gang had enormous respect, had two taut poems in it. The contents of *TISH* 16, published on December 14, 1962, included three poems by Luella Booth, a Canadian, and two by Paul Blackburn, an American who was a contributing editor to the *Black Mountain Review*. Bowering's poem "Points on the Grid" slithered down the page, its lines indented to varying depths.

The seventeenth *TISH* was one of the best the first set of editors produced, Bowering thought. It showcased women poets in a way no previous number had. The Americans Diane Wakoski and Carol Bergé appeared. Wakoski's "Apricot Poem," in particular, brings women's experience to the fore. It begins with a jam-making session in which an "old wooden spoon gets shiny & sticky as it stirs" and "hornets hang about the back-porch screen trying to get in."

In 1963, the scene in developed nations was beginning to bloom with psychedelic art and light shows, but for UBC's student poets, the year opened on a queasy note. On January 31, the *Ubyssey* carried an article titled "Clap Hands for George Bowering." The reporter, Suzanne Mowat, praised him as a creator of poetry and fiction, mentioning his work for *TISH*, the various magazines that were printing his poems, and his radio appearances. His friends thought he must have suggested she write the piece and were appalled. In the *Ubyssey*, David Bromige called the article "the most shameless and shameful self-advertisement since [Norman] Mailer, with considerably more justification, beat his breast in [1959's] *Advertisements for Myself*." George took the criticism to heart and regretted having sought publicity.

Less than two weeks later, he found himself in a confrontation with Creeley, who was not only his master's thesis advisor but also a famous poet he looked up to. The mildly horrifying set-to took place in the same atmospheric downtown house where George had punched the concrete wall and hurt his hand. In Reid's recollection, a group of arty friends had congregated as a "really grey, nasty sort of day" edged into evening, talking as they drank cheap beer and smoked pot and cigarettes. Creeley and Warren Tallman were there, well lit, and Al Purdy, out west to give his first Vancouver poetry reading, stopped by. Creeley had been nursing a grudge against Purdy because of a disparaging comment he'd made about Olson, yet George sensed no animosity when he introduced the two. Later, though, Creeley aimed his displeasure at George, calling him a fink and telling him to take off his glasses, "all the while making futile weak gestures of slugging," as George put it in his diary. In *Robert Creeley: A Biography*, the confrontation is described in a condensed but piquant manner. Skinny young George Bowering aroused a "special antipathy" in Creeley because his "manner – the incongruous combination of towering ambition and self-stated shyness – reminded Creeley of his own."

On Valentine's Day, 1963, *TISH* 18 ran an announcement titled "Poetry Offerings." It told readers that over three weeks in July and August, UBC would offer a credit course on poetry writing, English 410. "Limited to 45 students, the course will be conducted by ROBERT CREELEY, ALLEN GINSBERG, & CHARLES OLSON with MARGARET AVISON, ROBERT DUNCAN, & DENISE LEVERTOV contributing." These starry role models – five Americans and Avison, from Toronto – would also be available to people auditing the course or just attending readings and non-credit sessions. The event, later to be called the Vancouver Poetry Conference, would go down in literary history. *TISH* 19, which included "A Hard Time for All of Us," a Reid poem dedicated to Creeley, was the last issue he, Davey, Dawson, Bowering, and Wah produced together. Those issues, collected in *TISH: No. 1–19*, still make lively reading.

Fred Wah, George Bowering, bpNichol, Daphne Marlatt, Frank Davey, and bill bissett come together in 1981, having spent two decades writing poems and producing magazines for poetry and criticism. *Material republished with the express permission of* Vancouver Province, *a division of Postmedia Network Inc.*

A spate of gorgeous days materialized in Vancouver just in time for English 410. Reid's widow, Carol, who was there, remembers it as a blissful time, with "heat and sandals and drugs and wine and poets – everything you could possibly ask for." Ginsberg, who'd been travelling in India, came to help lead the course, which started on Wednesday, July 24. He and the other poets on the faculty weren't as established as, say, Robert Lowell, John Berryman, or Elizabeth Bishop. But looking back after half a century in an essay, "Poetry Summer," Bowering sees them as having shaken up poetry the way bebop had awakened music. Their minds were fecund and their talk was a non-stop flow of ideas.

Never having been together before, they fed on one another's energy. Olson, in particular, set the bar for discourse high. He was always mentioning the ancient Greeks – not just the well-known ones, like Hesiod, Herodotus, Socrates, and Aristotle, but also more obscure figures such as the lyric poet Alcaeus of Mytilene and the geographer Pausanias. Warren Tallman later wrote that during Olson's afternoon workshops "the chalk seemed to leap across blackboards that seemed to swim and shimmer in its wake."

Forty-eight students had registered for the credit course, paying sixty-six dollars for three weeks of lectures on weekday mornings and for afternoon workshops. George and many of his friends were among them; Clark Coolidge and Michael Palmer came up from the United States. In *The Line Has Shattered*, a 2013 documentary by Robert McTavish, they reminisce about the heady interlude, a high-water mark for avant-garde writing. Coolidge says that being among such lively and committed writers made him feel it would be all right to lead the life of a poet, a plan at which even his parents, who were "university people," looked askance.

Nine students paid thirty-three dollars to audit just the morning lectures, while 118 people heard four Friday-night readings by the visiting poets, paying five dollars per session. And seventy or so people paid the university's Extension Department twelve dollars to hear eleven evening discussions.

On the first morning, Ginsberg and Creeley had the floor. Ginsberg asked Creeley brief leading questions about his writing methods and Creeley gave long, ruminative answers. On Monday, July 29, Philip Whalen, the American poet who would later become famous for describing poems as "graph[s] of a mind moving," arrived to join the faculty. He took part in a panel discussion with Creeley, Olson, Ginsberg, and Duncan that ranged across human experience, touching on what one audience member catalogued as "anthropology, metaphysics, literature, economics, politics, religion, philosophy, art, drugs, geography, sexual conduct, history, language, mythology, systems of education, ethics, astronomy, mathematics, speech, biology, physics ..."

Bowering got to meet Olson that day. The man was so big and tall that George had the impression of seeing mostly his belt buckle as he came toward him down a flight of stairs.

Ginsberg was the only Beat poet on the faculty and the one guaranteed to generate headlines. So remarkable was his charisma that whenever he appeared in public, everyone wanted a piece of him. Dan McLeod, the UBC math student and poet who would later be known for publishing Vancouver's alternative newspaper the *Georgia Straight*, remembers him being somewhat like the actor Robin Williams: He was "always spinning out positive stuff." In *The Line Has Shattered*, Daphne Marlatt recalls how a steady stream of seekers took Ginsberg aside during lunch breaks to ask his advice on personal matters. Hearing the beatific, bearded American recite Shelley's *Ode to the West Wind* and *Adonaïs* from memory touched something off in Bowering. "Ginsberg got me interested in the Romantics," he says. The *Vancouver Sun* sent Mike Grenby, a former *Ubyssey* staffer who would later distinguish himself as a personal finance columnist, to cover Ginsberg's evening reading on Friday, August 2. His report described a sweltering night, a crowd of 350 and "a disjointed harangue laced with obscenity." Ginsberg sometimes stopped in the middle of a poem to ask, "Is it interesting, or not?"

Levertov and Avison stayed only a week, and in McTavish's documentary Pauline Butling recalls that the whole event was "pretty boys-y." But Levertov's evident belief in herself and her art set a shining example for Marlatt, who says in *The Line* that it shaped her whole writing life to see a woman "hold a whole audience with the magic of her voice." Two smart women who were comfortable in their skins – Ellen Tallman and Creeley's then-wife, Bobbie Louise Hawkins – lent strength and sanity to what, for many, became a round-the-clock

talkfest. The Tallman family put Olson up at their house. Karen Tallman, then ten years old, remembers him sitting at their kitchen table,
which would jiggle and rattle when a large group crowded around.
Everyone wanted to talk to him, "and he could talk day and night."
Acting on a wise impulse, she ran around taking snapshots of the
grown-ups with her Brownie camera.

On Monday, August 5, Robert Duncan spoke at length about his
life in poetry and about his unusual childhood – his adoptive parents
had thought he was an emissary who'd been sent to them from the
lost world of Atlantis.

George remembers Charles Olson's then-unpublished poem,
"Maximus to Gloucester, Letter 27," being the focus of intense curi-
osity. In Vancouver he was repeatedly asked to read it. (Today, Olson
can be seen doing so on YouTube, declaiming softly in a Massachusetts
accent, gesturing broadly in a stained shirt, his eyebrows bushy atop
his glasses' frames. In the most arresting image, the "I" of the poem
recalls having seen his father come charging at a druggist who he
believed had made a pass at his wife, a bread knife gripped between
his teeth.) On Friday, Wah and Butling (by then husband and wife)
hosted a party that brought eighty people to their tiny campus apartment. Everyone who was present retains a mental image of Olson
recumbent on their bed, surrounded by women.

Vancouver's summer of poetry was no flash in the pan. Instead,
it's legendary for poetry the way Woodstock is for music. Everyone
involved – the faculty, as well as the students – found it mind-blow-
ing. Bob Hogg, who had a full-time job that summer but caught as
much of it as he could, recalls that he and the other Vancouver students had been thinking hard about Olson's "Projective Verse" and
the other Statements on Poetics in *The New American Poetry*. "So
we were pretty well imbued with the poetics and the poetry of [the
speakers]. In fact, one of the comments they made afterwards was
that they couldn't believe the reception they got in Vancouver by all

these young writers. [We] knew their work inside out, probably better than lots of the American students they came across. We were very hungry and curious to know more about them – what they were doing, where their thoughts had come from … Just to be in their company was a fantastic experience."

THE HUSBAND

... Two heads

on a pillow faces to-
gether eyes closed or
open in the dark

Time is on our side
now ...

—"Rime of Our Time," *The Silver Wire* (1966)

Angela May Luoma, the young woman George fell for at the end of 1961, was from small-town British Columbia, as were he and his best friends at university. She came from Courtenay, on Vancouver Island, having spent her early childhood on Quadra Island. Her eyes were a startling green and, thanks to her Finnish forebears (she also had English and Scottish ones), she had wheat-blond hair. When she pinned it up in a French roll she became femininity incarnate, her swan neck exposed. After their first date, on November 17, George wrote in his diary that he'd gone out with "beautiful, blonde, tall neurotic Angela Luoma." The following week he again described her as "a beautiful & neurotic & exciting girl."

Angela liked to analyze people's motives and natures, including her own; she admitted to being "temperamental" and "bossy." According to George's brother Roger, "If you were stringing her a line, she would tell you to your face to cut the BS." She was ruled by strong passions; she made dramatic declarations and threw gauntlets down. She valued authenticity and urged friends and family members to act in ways reflecting their "true selves." She loved the telephone. As George has affectionately written, she thought any call that "came in under an hour was kind of abrupt."

In the spring and summer of 1962, after classes had ended and she and George had gone back to their hometowns to earn money for the next year's tuition, Angela sent him a flood of multi-page letters in her rounded handwriting. One said, "I love you Darling if you make love with anyone this summer, dont tell me … I'll club you to death if you do anyway." In another, she anticipated their eventual reunion, warning that she would be "quite delirious when I see you again – be prepared for anything – hysteria, tears, wild uncontrolled laughter, a fainting spell – anything." Though barely into her twenties, she became protective and motherly when George told her he wasn't feeling well. She commanded him, "Go & see about your chest IMMEDIATELY!!!"

Angela was a Catholic – skittish about birth control, premarital sex, and abortion. When she found out George had had a "pack of safes" with him on their first date, she was genuinely shocked. Also, she warned him she had what we'd today call baggage: There was mental illness in her family and she feared she wouldn't be able to escape it. (She would one day create a fictional character who has an illiterate Finnish grandfather and a "schizoid" father with a grade eight education.) Bowering distinctly remembers this serious conversation taking place in his first car, a black 1942 Chevrolet with a spotlight on top, parked near Broadway and Granville in Vancouver. Angela also told him she had "a record of letting people down & being a drag on them." He didn't care; he loved her. He found her extremely know-ledgeable and perceptive – in fact, "the best appreciator and knower of literature I've ever met, bar no one, including myself" – and her delicate beauty melted him. In her eyes he saw the promise that, for him, she would "ever remain softly loving."

That's not what happened, not by a long shot. Through most of their marriage, solemnized on December 14, 1962, they would make each other miserable, leading their writer friend Brian Fawcett to say they'd had "the worst marriage I'd ever even heard of ... Their emotional energies were utterly different."

But that lay in the future and the present was challenging enough. George was twenty-seven: the age of his father and his father's father when they'd married. Angela was twenty-two. George had recently waited anxiously for McClelland & Stewart to pay him the fifteen dollars it owed him for the two poems he'd contributed to *Love Where the Nights Are Long*, an anthology Irving Layton was editing. He was so short of funds that when a pay phone ate his dime it was cause for despair. George and Angela were both in debt and knew they'd have to live on love for quite a while.

The wedding, a civil ceremony at Vancouver City Hall, felt aus-picious, even though Angela, detained at the hairdresser's, made them fifteen minutes late. George's "Poem for My Wife Angela," first published in 1965, memorializes the gardenia corsage she wore and captures the emotion that shone in their faces. It concludes,

> *The gold ring*
> *minted for your finger*
>
> *is fitted there now*
> *as part of your*
> > *household hours*

George and Angela early in their relationship. He considered her "the best appreciator and knower of literature I've ever met."

and your eyes
of light tears
when you looked at me
your husband

are part of me too

Afterwards, the bride and groom and the four friends who'd witnessed the ceremony had dinner at the China Kitchen. Will Thornton-Trump, George's childhood friend and roommate, was one of them. At first, he remained a roommate, since they were all students and needed to economize. In the morning, it delighted Bowering to see the new Mrs. Bowering's "lovely tousled blonde head" on the pillow next to his. But, more prosaically, it dawned on him that with a woman in the apartment he wouldn't be able to fart as freely as before.

Having a mother-in-law was a new development, too, a sign of maturity and settling down. George liked Lillian Luoma, an elementary school teacher. Once, when she expressed a desire to read William Faulkner, he gave her a list of "the order to read the books in." (He'd read twenty-one of Faulkner's books by June 1960, according to his diary.) An unfortunate bit of timing had her moving to Vancouver around the time he and Angela decamped for Calgary – in September 1963 he was to start teaching at its University of Alberta campus.

Angela, the first of Lillian's three daughters, had been at high school with Jack Hodgins, the future novelist. She had a strong intellect and expected to become well educated and perhaps write, too. But domesticity was expected of brides. Two days into their marriage she concocted "a lovely great supper" and then cleaned up the kitchen while George typed fifteen letters, presumably to the many literary people he kept in touch with, continent-wide. George got into a routine of sending out several letters a day, managing also to teach full-time and write copious amounts of publishable work.

Angela wasn't that organized. Assigned an essay at UBC (or, later, at the University of Alberta), she would start the task too late, write too much, and then, while pruning her rough draft, begin doubting her abilities and sinking into despair. It didn't help that she had a husband who was disciplined about his writing, confident enough not to revise endlessly, and a bit of a comedian, to boot. Inequities accrued in their marriage, and the fact that it had begun in the anything-goes sixties only made matters worse. The Okanagan poet Sharon Thesen, who became one of Angela's closest friends, says that "so many marriages fell apart in those years, where suddenly it was okay to do what you wanted with whom you wanted and everybody was available for this, that, and the other. It wreaked havoc."

In *Piccolo Mondo*, an unusual collaborative novel in which the Bowerings and their friends David Bromige and Mike Matthews revisit their lives in the early sixties, there's a passage in which the character

G disappears, leaving his young wife, A, home alone with no money. The next day, when G hasn't shown up, A gets frantic. Finding out that he's at the home of friends, "stoned on peyote," she goes there in curlers and housecoat, and weeps with relief. G "smiled and smiled and said over and over again, Don't hassle, baby. Don't hassle." It was the sixties, all right.

Bob Hogg remembers Angela's additional difficulty: "She was a knockout beauty. Everyone just swooned over her … I'm sure she was treated as a sexualized object by most of the men she encountered." Gillian Collins, a friend who saw a lot of the Bowerings in the seventies and subsequent decades, remembers Angela's "fabulous hair – heavy blond hair, that kind of Scandinavian hair." In Calgary she got a gig as a stylist's model and received dramatic new cuts and colours "several times a week for free."

The beauty that dazzled men wasn't a kind of armour that gave her confidence. Asked, years later, if her mother was drop-dead gorgeous, Thea would say, "She didn't think she was. She did and she didn't. She knew she was, but she also, like any woman, had anxiety about her looks." In Margaret Atwood's second novel, *Surfacing*, the Anna character – based at least partly on Angela – is constantly applying makeup in hopes that her husband, David, will never see her without it. More worryingly, David (who resembles Bowering as he then was) often treats Anna with casual cruelty, at one point bullying her into stripping off her bikini because he and the narrator's boyfriend "need a naked lady" in a film they're shooting. The dialogue in that passage semaphores a troubled marriage.

In *Surfacing*, Anna goes through a lot of cigarettes, just as young Angela did – she became so dependent on nicotine that she sometimes got up in the night to smoke. Although half of all Canadians smoked in 1965, a dawning understanding of tobacco's destructiveness eventually reduced the percentage of smokers over time. But Angela's addiction was fierce: She smoked three to five packs a day.

The Bowerings in London, Ontario, in the 1960s. A friend who met them a few years later couldn't say "which was the more powerful personality of the two."

When Angela and George lived in Calgary, from 1963 to 1966, their wit and glamour created a buzz on campus. As a long-time friend remembers, "Angela was a Zelda Fitzgerald kind of figure, and both of them liked attention, and they both got it."

Still, this was a young couple struggling to make the rent and find kindred spirits in a place much less hip than the West Coast. In those days, George has written, "[t]here wasnt any jazz in Calgary ... No record stores. No art either." But then they started socializing with three other young professors and their wives, and life got better. One of those women, Lynn Spink (then Cox), remembers a 1966 house party at which she and Angela talked intensely on the hosts' back stairs. "Subsequently, Angela told me she suddenly realized in that conversation that, 'Lynn, you were more than just a housewife.'" The two became close friends, though they would always live far apart. Of the four couples, only the Bowerings would stay together – though many who knew them thought splitting up would have been healthier.

George and Angela's first months together felt enchanted. In bed at night, she read him *Winnie-the-Pooh*, since he'd somehow missed encountering it in childhood. He started a tradition, random but sweet, of giving her a book he thought she'd like on the twenty-sixth of every month. She made meals and did housework. When she was still working on her bachelor's degree, he was exulting over the publication of *Points on the Grid*, his first book of poems. As a result, the emotional climate at home fluctuated. To him it just seemed that *la donna è mobile*, for she loved him one moment and cursed him the next. He decided he had a "collapsing" nature, since he would rather let her have her way than argue. Taking stock on their first anniversary, he judged that even though they often clashed and didn't have the deep literary discussions they'd expected they would, they enjoyed "great sexual honesties and delights of growing frankness." His upbeat conclusion was, "I am extremely happy I have a girl I like and love, both."

A year later, an unforeseen event shattered their contentment. On his twenty-ninth birthday, George received a pre-dawn telegram saying that Red Lane, a year younger than he, had died of a brain tumour. (Two days later, Red's brother, Patrick, sent a clarifying wire: It had been a cerebral hemorrhage.) The hard-partying bon vivant George had met in the Air Force nine years earlier had had talent: George had persuaded his *TISH* friends to publish Red's poems. In his diary, he wrote that he loved Red, who had "never had enough moments of happiness." Red had suffered because of poverty and family tragedies.

George fell into a depression and pretty much stopped talking, except when spoken to. Angela was stunned, too. Red had idolized her; he'd called her "Mother Goddess." He'd started his letters to the two of them with zany salutations: "Big Boom Boom and Bum Bum,"

"Big Bowler & Ball." His early death spread sorrow among Canada's young writers. He was the first of the new generation of poets to die.

In summer 1966, George and Angela's friend Tony Bellette – an Australian who'd been an English department teaching assistant at UBC along with Bowering – asked George, then aged thirty, to accompany him on a trip to Europe. George jumped at the chance: It would be an overpowering new experience. He packed his typewriter so he could register every impression.

Angela stayed in Calgary, alone but for their chihuahuas, Frank and Small. During the six-week foreign foray, she and George wrote to each other constantly, she sending her letters to *poste restante* along his and Tony's route. In one rather alarming aerogram, she said she'd been feeling wretched and so had seen a psychiatrist who was considering giving her Sodium Pentothal, the barbiturate anaesthetic popularly known as "truth serum." She mentioned, "I am going to be a whore in [a campus production of Brendan Behan's] *The Hostage* … So you see, I am not being a vegetable, I am doing things." Also, she'd lost fourteen pounds on the diet drink Metrecal. "I want to be all skinny and brown for you when you come back."

Meanwhile, Tony had bought a new Volkswagen Beetle in Düsseldorf, and he and George had set off on their grand tour. Bellette, who would one day specialize in teaching seventeenth-century English poetry, did the driving and most of the conversing with locals. George looked, thought, and wrote. In Chamonix, he realized they were exclaiming over the grandeur of the French Alps a tidy century and a half after Shelley had in his poem "Mont Blanc." The two stopped in Aosta to cash traveller's cheques, receiving a profusion of Italian lire. Continuing their descent, they rolled slowly through villages, agog at how much was happening on the street. It looked to

George as if people were "killing pigs, spanking babies, balancing hats, painting wheelchairs, throwing pies, kicking grandmothers, carving crutches, laying landmines, digging bomb shelters, removing corsets."

Their adventures in Europe opened their eyes. While there, George composed a travelogue, "Eye-Kicks in Europe," on his portable typewriter. (The title's first word was slang for "something exciting to see.") Toward the end of his life, Bellette would say, "It pleased me to think that I was able to make possible [Bowering's] first exposure to European life and culture as a living reality, though I would never put it like that to him!"

Once he was back in Canada, George, who thought he might end up doing more teaching at the university level, decided to pursue a Ph.D. In those days, educated men on that path could look forward to becoming professors. (Educated women, not so much.) When the English department at the University of Western Ontario accepted him as a doctoral student, he and Angela prepared to pull up stakes and move to London, Ontario, in fall 1966. His last academic act in Calgary was to teach a summer course at what had by then become the University of Calgary. As a valediction, an article in the *Albertan* praised his achievements in poetry. He told the reporter he'd been writing more politically than before, saying that a poem probably couldn't stop a single bullet from being shot in Vietnam. "But on the other hand, not writing that poem is definitely not going to stop that bullet from being shot. If it's one chance in a million, it's the best thing a person can do."

London, a mid-size city of pale yellow-brick heritage houses and streets lined with silver maples, had more history and culture than Calgary but still felt foreign to the young couple. Then they found a house to rent at 650 Ayreswood Avenue that had an outsize living room, three bedrooms, a full basement, and a generously proportioned yard, and the air of strangeness began to dissipate.

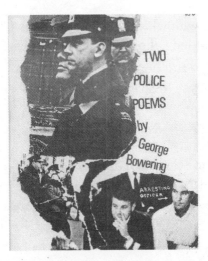

Attuned to the 1960s zeitgeist, a politicized George Bowering wrote "Support Your Local Police" and "American Cops." Talonbooks put them together in a chapbook, publishing five hundred copies in 1969.

Before long, George and Angela tapped into the bohemian stratum below the straitlaced surface. London turned out to be an arts town popping with activity, and they had the good fortune to get to know the painter Greg Curnoe. Tall and lean, with straight hair and a moustache, he was practically a George lookalike, and his wife, Sheila, was a welcome friend for Angela. Busy on many fronts, Greg edited a magazine called *Region* and kept a cluttered studio on King Street where he did wild, zingy, crowd-pleasing things with paint, paste, found materials, and rubber stamps. George loved how Greg walked around with a pencil behind his ear, the better to capture ideas when they struck. Greg's mania for colour made the interior of the Curnoe house kindergarten-bright: Each of their wooden chairs was painted a different colour and even the door frames were striped in vibrant hues.

Angela found a job at an off-campus laboratory belonging to Western's psychology department. She earned eighteen dollars a day and, by and large, enjoyed the work. On their fourth anniversary she presented George with a London Fog topcoat. She loved having her own money with which to buy him things. This comfortable groove didn't last long, though. Sir George Williams University in Montreal offered Bowering the position of writer-in-residence, for which he'd receive $11,000, and he cheerfully accepted. He shelved his Ph.D. studies because Montreal promised excitement. As Canada's centennial celebrations got underway, he and Angela would be able to visit Expo 67 easily.

Because of the influx of tourists coming to the world's fair, apartments in Montreal were scarce. The one they preferred, and moved into in September 1967, was a second-storey suite at 439 Grosvenor Avenue, off Sherbrooke Street in Westmount. It had hardwood floors and was a classic railroad flat, its seven and a half rooms strung along a corridor. The rent was $185 a month. George thought of it as "our poor wooden apartment"; money was in such short supply that he had to raid their penny jar to buy dog food. Still, it became a place where visiting poets and their fans could party after readings. Sir George had a superb reading series, thanks to organizers Roy Kiyooka, Stanton Hoffman, and Howard Fink, and Bowering began helping them. In 1970, one visiting poet – Ted Berrigan, an American – stopped by the Bowerings' place the day after his reading. George was "pleasantly surprised by how much I liked him. Maybe not as much as he & Angela dug each other in their various ways."

It was during the 1967–68 school year that Margaret Atwood, briefly teaching at Sir George, got to know the couple. In a whimsical piece called "Bowering Pie … Some Recollections," she later recalled the impression they made. Angela was gorgeous and fearless in conversation, while George gave "a genial imitation of a man acting like a nincompoop," hiding his real self behind a goofy act. Eventually, she would get used to this and view it with affection. In the 2000s, contributing to a seventieth-birthday Festschrift for George, she drew a cartoon of him wearing a Donald Duck tie and quacking.

A thought bubble coming from him says, "This is just an act – really I'm quite profound."

When his term as writer-in-residence ended, Sir George's English department invited him to stay on as a junior faculty member. He and Angela settled in, remaining in their Grosvenor Avenue place for a total of four years. There were plenty of smart, congenial people to hang out with, including such literary couples as Clark Blaise and Bharati Mukherjee, and D.G. "Doug" Jones and Sheila Fischman. They also socialized with older anglophone poets such as F.R. "Frank" Scott and John "Buffy" Glassco. The latter, an eccentric gay man who'd become known for *Memoirs of Montparnasse*, about his time in Paris in the twenties and thirties, took Atwood and Angela to lunch and had a ball flirting with them, "mak[ing] naughty jokes and tell[ing] scandalous stories."

George and Angela also spent time with their B.C. friends Mike and Carol Matthews, then living in Montreal. Carol remembers Angela's flair for drama. Once, she glimpsed her from a window, walking along Sherbrooke Street "with her long black Russian overcoat and her blond hair, looking like somebody in a Dostoevsky novel and probably imagining herself as somebody in a Dostoevsky novel." Sharon Thesen remembers her friend's "almost mystical, wizardy sense of the underlife of things … She was very talented, but plutonic, underworldly."

In early 1970, Angela dressed all in black for a noticeably long period. Frank Davey, the new writer-in-residence at Sir George, heard that wearing "widow's weeds" constituted her response to the news her husband was having an affair. That was true: George had become romantically involved with Eveline Meyer, the English department's pretty Swiss-born receptionist. Meyer was smart and multilingual, and she fell hard for him. When Angela learned of the liaison, she became practically suicidal. She and George went to the Royal Victoria Hospital's emergency room, waiting for hours among the gashed and bashed so she could see a psychiatrist and be prescribed tranquilizers. George recognized that no matter how he handled the situation, he was bound to end up hurting both women.

The blow to Angela's pride made her want to get her own back. When Stanley Fish, a high-profile American academic, came to Sir George for a brief stint as a visiting professor, she perked up. Davey writes that George baited her in front of their friends, asking, "Couldn't you find someone intelligent?" Thesen says there was a strong mutual attraction but doesn't know if an affair ensued. However, for years afterwards, Angela would dream about fish. Thesen writes in "Weeping Willow," a poem that pays tribute to her intelligent, stylish, often very frustrated friend: "Angela'd had another dream / in which a school of fish ... // & how she should have run off / with the visiting professor ... // Dear reader, / shouldn't we all have run off with someone."

Tony Bellette, the friend with whom George had toured Europe, spent a couple of days with the Bowerings in Britain in June 1970. He came away convinced that their marriage was hooped. In a letter to his parents, he told of "constant nagging, recrimination, [and an] utter inability to share the other person's feelings ... I doubt whether I'll ever do another trip with them. I dont blame either of them, yet I blame both of them." Atwood tried to help them heal their marriage. Bowering's *His Life: A Poem* (2000), in which he reconstructs his life story (in the third person) through old diary entries, says, "Of their marriage / she is always ready to talk." It also contains a line beginning, "They exhaust her ..."

Early in 1971, when they'd been married for eight years, Angela found out she was pregnant. Her often-fraught domestic life with George now held the promise of positive change. It was too late to split up over sexual jealousy and differing attitudes toward money. He approved of her "taking a snooze, dear pregnant lady," when she napped. Pregnancy didn't quash her feistiness, though. When Kenneth

Koch – later to become famous for getting New York City schoolchildren excited about writing poems – came to read at Sir George, Angela "gave him the business," her husband observed, "busting pomposity etc., as she usually does with the poets."

The Bowerings could have stayed in Montreal, but the polluted air bothered them, and they had other options. It seemed George might get a job at Simon Fraser University, which had opened in the Vancouver suburb of Burnaby in 1965 with twenty-five hundred students and the promise of being an innovative, unstuffy institution. The couple began to think about starting their lives as parents with a return to the West Coast, where they'd be closer to family.

📖

The Bowerings started their Vancouver years in a Kitsilano commune. George was, by then, publishing frequently. *Al Purdy*, his pithy book of literary criticism, came out in March 1971 and drew compliments. "It seems," he observed, "as if just about everybody likes it." Two months later, Coach House brought out *Genève*, his trippy long poem based on the tarot. McClelland & Stewart published his first selected-poems book, *Touch*, that September.

The zeitgeist pushed Angela toward a women's consciousness-raising group – and that spurred the women's partners to launch Traditional Pub Night, or TPN, a weekly confab at Vancouver's Cecil Hotel. Male bonding was also available to George through Vancouver's Kosmic League, which formed in June 1971. His baseball mania, which included watching minor- and major-league games, in ballparks and on TV, took him away from Angela. She resented those absences and described them with words like "desertion" and "abandonment." It seemed to Sharon Thesen that she saw "pretty much everything George did along those lines as trying to escape mortality." Was he a perennial boy on the diamond, just a grown-up kid with a smart mouth? Some would say so, but according to a ball-playing friend, the loud heckling he did at ballparks was first-class: "People just loved listening to him."

Others in their circle loved Angela's intensity. Smaro Kamboureli, an expert on Canadian literature, says, "There was something about the passion with which she articulated her emotions and intellect that I found absolutely exhilarating and moving." To Jamie Reid, "she was magnificent."

Out-of-town writers often came to stay with the Bowerings in the big, old Kerrisdale house they bought in 1973. Their dinner parties were wondrous affairs. While the guests talked, gossiped, and flirted, George spun records from their huge collection and the writers' children roared around outside or upstairs. "It would go on for hours," Thea recalls. "My mum would not let anyone in the kitchen and then she'd show up with duck *à l'orange* or baked Alaska – it would always be a really big deal." Thesen's poem "Weeping Willow" mentions these soirées. Angela presided over "ten million calorie dinner parties – // Oysters Rockefeller, Angel-Tit pie, / & much between that was / silky and rich."

But once she began studying for her master's degree at SFU, she stopped doing everyday cooking. "She was being a student," recalls Carol Matthews, "and all she wanted to do was read and study and write stuff and work on her book about [the novelist] Sheila Watson, which is a wonderful book." It fell to George to put dinner on the table – meat loaf, a stir-fry, whatever – and get the right groceries into the house beforehand. This was unfair, he thought, given his arduous workdays and long commute. The spouses stopped looking to each other for love and companionship. Angela found other men, some of them gay, with whom she had more fun. In his diary, George petulantly called one such companion The Magic Fruit.

Angela often said, "George, you fucking asshole," in front of friends and Thea. This made everyone cringe, recalls Lionel Kearns, who says,

"It was a mystery why George put up with that kind of behaviour." Angela used to speak of "The George and Angela Bowering Show," meaning the arguments they had in public. These made people think of the movie *Who's Afraid of Virginia Woolf?*

George wrote a *roman à clef* about his sorry home life – *The Letters of Dido: A Bitter Fantasy* – but withdrew it from publication, realizing it would be hurtful. He believes the story, which he wrote in longhand, has an intriguing structure. However, its words are bitter, including snide veiled references to Dr. William Brown (husband of the activist/politician Rosemary Brown), Angela's psychiatrist for many years. When Bowering sent the manuscript to his literary agent, Denise Bukowski, she saw defences and evasions in it and said, "I would dearly love to see this book delivered straight up."

In company, Angela and George were sophisticated and witty, but sometimes she lambasted him in a way that made their friends cringe.

People who knew what was going on at home could discern George's sadness in his poems. When Bob Hogg taught Bowering's *Kerrisdale Elegies* (1984) at Carleton University, he felt that while "you couldn't know everything … you could read between the lines. There's a lot of feeling in that book about lost love and hurt." Eva-Marie Kröller, a scholar at UBC, had sensed a "pervasive tone of disillusionment and a feeling of isolation" much earlier, in his 1969 book, *The Gangs of Kosmos.*

Thesen believes Angela spent money extravagantly on their house and garden because she was lonely in the marriage. She didn't call George out on his philandering, and that filled her with self-disgust. In long, tortuous conversations with Sharon, she frequently asked, "What sort of person am I who will put up with this behaviour and never leave?" In 1985, a great year for George – he'd been invited to lecture on Canadian literature in Rome and West Berlin, and would also spend time in Australia – Angela took a $75,000 cheque that had arrived for him and spent it on home improvement without consulting him. When he returned and was furious, she levelly told him, "Sorry, I just haven't got it to give you."

The mid-eighties were a truly terrible time in their marriage. On Halloween 1986 she raged at him while he talked on the phone with his Toronto editor about his fourth novel. Privately, he lamented, "If only I had a companion I could talk with, who would love me." In 1987 he thought, "I've tried everything … to make her love me. She just won't do it."

He could have tried harder. By then he had admitted to Angela that he'd fallen in love with Constance Rooke – a married intellectual who was beautiful and universally liked, and who therefore posed a real threat. Teenaged Thea found out and was instantly alienated from him, and of course Angela felt as if she'd been knifed. In the end, George decided not to leave, and he and Angela went on with their lives, trying not to pick at their emotional scars. Their friends hated seeing them torture each other. As Kearns puts it, "We always worried about George and his relationship and wished that he would get a better one."

CHAPTER 8

THE PROFESSOR

"I was certainly gifted with speech – I could hold [the attention of students], thirty at a time ... Meek and mild George Delsing puts on his magic necktie, mutters the ancient words of the scroll, and becomes: ProfessorMan!"

—"The Elevator," *Flycatcher & Other Stories* (1974)

Ryan Knighton, now a writer and cultural commentator in Vancouver, was starting to go blind in the early nineties when he was an undergraduate at Simon Fraser University. He didn't want people to know, so he didn't carry a white cane. "I just had this slightly cautious shuffle," he recalls.

When he was twenty, Knighton took a course taught by Bowering. One day, during a break in class, he stepped outside and picked his way past George, who was having a smoke. Quietly, his prof asked him, "Do you have RP?" He meant retinitis pigmentosa, a genetic disorder that causes progressive vision loss.

Spooked, Knighton asked, "How do you even *know* about RP?"

Bowering knew because his childhood friend, Will Thornton-Trump, had gone blind due to the same rare condition, though more slowly and at a later age. "I could tell," George explains, by the way Ryan "walked and held his head." George invited Knighton to join him and Thornton-Trump at a Canadian Legion pub one night. It ended up being an unforgettable evening, hugely reassuring. Knighton appreciated that Thornton-Trump was not a "woebegotten, beaten-down blind guy" but, rather, one who could keep up with his old buddy's non-stop banter. Knighton felt less scared about his future.

Bowering was a model for his student in other ways. Knighton, who'd grown up a "TV kid" in a blue-collar household, liked how George always carried a book bag so he could read on buses or when standing in lines. Ryan hadn't thought of becoming a writer, but two classes and a directed-studies course with George when he was in fourth year sent him in that direction. "My mind's eye was so much busier in his class than it was listening to the other professors," he says. "He really spoke for your ear." Knighton aims to be similarly colourful and colloquial on the page and believes that his memoirs, *Cockeyed* and *C'mon Papa: Dispatches from a Dad in the Dark*, bear Bowering's thumbprint.

Teaching was never a passion with George; he would have liked to be able to write full-time. But if he had to have a day job, he wanted one that trafficked in ideas, words, and books. He could have gone into journalism or publishing but, having had a father who taught and having had some practice teaching in grad school, he went in that direction.

As a professor, he took some stylistic cues from Warren Tallman, who'd inspired him at UBC. Like Tallman, he shared his favourite poems with students, examining them line by line. "He just has one speed – that's teaching what he knows," says Wayde Compton, who, like Knighton, studied with George in the nineties. As another student put it in 2001, when Bowering was set to retire from SFU after twenty-nine years, he could "pull a fascinating two-hour lecture out of just half a stanza." Like Tallman, too, George socialized with the students whose company he enjoyed. One student, Roger Farr, took from this that George was saying, "This is a writing community we're part of here. It's not just that you do your exercise [in class] and you go home."

Bowering had begun teaching literature to university students in September 1963 at the University of Alberta (Calgary). At first, his annual salary was $5,400. His diary shows he felt excitement, pleasure, disappointment, rage – every emotion the job can awaken in people – early on. Turning kids on to the bawdy humour of Chaucer's *Canterbury Tales* was fun, whereas pulling them through Milton's *Paradise Lost* was "an odious job." In John Updike's novel, *Bech Is Back*, protagonist Henry Bech, teaching at a Pennsylvania college, encounters "starch-fed students blinking like pupfish after their recent emergence from fundamentalism." That probably applied to George, too, when he was closing in on age thirty. Although *Wuthering Heights* was his favourite nineteenth-century novel, the prospect of trying to get a hall full of engineering students to love it seemed laughable.

He soon began to question the merits of teaching the greats of English lit in chronological order: Chaucer, Shakespeare, Milton, Pope, Wordsworth, Tennyson, Yeats, Eliot. He reasoned that if someone like his poet friend John Newlove were reading Eliot and a reference to Baudelaire cropped up, Newlove would go check out Baudelaire. That, he felt, was how literature survey courses should work. Instead of being yoked to chronology, "the instructor shd be told to teach the lyric, the narrative poem, the epic, etc." In January 1964 he thought that teaching wasn't bad, but it was disheartening to see "the miserable mess [students] make of their exams, the disinterest in poetry, the way they refuse to do the reading ..." And plagiarism irked him: Some kids resorted to copying out "a bland 1000 words from the intro in the text or the most obvious secondary sources." He failed twenty-two of the forty-two students in his English 250 class that year.

Bowering had his eye on the world beyond the classroom. In 1965, when an editorial in the *Calgary Herald* declared student demonstrations in sympathy with the Selma-to-Montgomery civil rights march in Alabama to be "blots on the landscape of any organized society" and an "ugly fad" when taken up in Canada, George and a half-dozen other UAC profs disagreed. In a letter to the editor, from which Britain's *Manchester Guardian* would later quote, they wrote, "You keep saying that the race problem in the U.S. is the business of the U.S. It is not. It is a human problem."

George remained engaged with the teaching of great books until the end of his time in Calgary. In early 1966 he reread Faulkner's *As I Lay Dying* "because I have to teach it at my engineers. Sure is a good book. Shows what can be done in six weeks." In the spring, by which time he'd published two books of poetry and had a third, *The Silver Wire*, in production, his employer – reborn as the University of Calgary – promoted him to assistant professor and raised his salary. He taught that summer, but he and Angela left Alberta in the fall.

Meanwhile, in April 1967, his first novel, *Mirror on the Floor*, came out. He was that rare person who has the discipline to write creatively while teaching a full course load, marking essays and exams, and sitting on departmental committees. When he got to SFU in the seventies, his colleague Kathy Mezei was bowled over. She asked him how he found time for it all, and he replied, "I get up every morning and, before I come to the university, I write."

Teaching at Sir George Williams University, in Montreal, he met a student named Artie Gold. This young man had a true poetic gift, and George loved the enthusiasm he brought to learning about the avant-garde. A year or so later, Dwight Gardiner turned up in his poetry class. Originally from Calgary, Gardiner wanted to be a writer but, as he admits now, he had little sense of how to go about it. "It was just going to happen for me magically, or something." Gold and Gardiner found each other and became close friends. Artie got Dwight excited about Jack Spicer and Frank O'Hara, poets from California and New York – sadly, both recently dead. The two were crazy about

writing and books. Bowering became their mentor. He and Gardiner –
who would become a linguist, an authority on the Secwepemctsín
(Shuswap) language spoken by the Secwépemc First Nation in British
Columbia – had two other things in common that cemented their
friendship: Neither could get enough jazz or baseball.

As a junior professor at Montreal's Sir George Williams University,
Bowering revelled in literature. At one moment in 1970 he felt he was "at
the narrow end of a mile-wide funnel," since he knew "so much" and his
students "so little."

At Sir George in 1968, Bowering heard a reading by the American poet
George Oppen, who would win a Pulitzer Prize the following year.
It was "one of the best & most moving readings I have ever heard."
When Oppen read his poem "The Route," Bowering was in tears
and Gold was "completely knockt out." Gardiner recalls that such
readings gave fans "a really lovely time [and there were] great parties
afterwards." The day after one such alcohol-fuelled night in the fall
of 1968, Bowering, hampered by a lack of sleep, taught Faulkner to

a large class. Afterwards, a student came up to him and asked, "Sir, are you stoned?"

Preparing to teach a course on Canadian poetry in the summer of 1969 (just as *Rocky Mountain Foot*, his new book of Alberta poems, was garnering reviews), Bowering wondered if he'd be able to do justice to the work of Al Purdy, Margaret Avison, Victor Coleman, and ten other favourite poets. In the fall, he had to teach seven hundred engineering students a number of short stories he thought difficult to grasp. His committee work was rewarding, though: With colleagues Howard Fink, Roy Kiyooka, and Stan Hoffman, he was helping to organize more readings in the university's deluxe series. The 1969–70 lineup included Purdy and former *TISH* editors Frank Davey and Robert Hogg, plus such Americans as Diane Wakoski, Joel Oppenheimer, and Allen Ginsberg – "a pretty good schedule, if I do say so myself."

The year 1970 brought Bowering attention – and notoriety, too. In April he learned he and Toronto's Gwendolyn MacEwen had jointly won the 1969 Governor General's Literary Award for Poetry in English – Bowering for *Rocky Mountain Foot* and *The Gangs of Kosmos* and MacEwen for *The Shadow-Maker*. This touched off a major flap, since a number of prominent Canadian poets thought Bowering's half of the prize should have gone to the Maritime-born Milton Acorn for his *I've Tasted My Blood: Poems, 1956–1968*.

That fall, George taught a fourth-year English course whose reading list featured works he loved by Stein, Beckett, Olson, Creeley, Williams, and Hawkes. "Gertrude Stein has been getting more & more important to me over the last year," he wrote in his diary on October 1, "& now I'm getting ready to try doing *Three Lives* with my 437 class." Two weeks later he served up James Joyce's *Exiles*, which he expected would be "a relief for them after Gertrude S." Teaching William Carlos Williams in November, he felt as if he were "at the narrow end of a mile-wide funnel, I know so much & they so little ..." The students seemed receptive, but most of their essays let him down.

Bowering admires Gertrude Stein and imitated her writing style early in his career. Later, visiting Père Lachaise Cemetery in Paris, he sought out her grave.

He and Angela could have stayed on in Montreal, as the institution that would become Concordia University in 1974 had the welcome mat out for him. But he had secured a Canada Council writer's grant that enabled him to take a year off teaching. His friends in other English departments – Hogg at Ottawa's Carleton, Davey at Toronto's York, and Kearns at Greater Vancouver's SFU – were trying to convince their schools to hire him. In the summer of 1971 he taught a class and gave a paper at SFU so its English department could get a look at him. He didn't sense much warmth there, and it bothered him that "nobody except Lionel and maybe a couple others seems to speak plainly & directly." Though he did eventually get hired, to hear him tell it, it was a close-run thing.

Canadian nationalism was flowering in the early seventies, but a university that had opened its doors in 1965 couldn't immediately boast an all-Canadian, or even a mostly Canadian, faculty. There just weren't enough Canadian candidates for the jobs, since Canadian universities were then graduating only about seventy-five people a year with doctorates in the humanities and social sciences. It was common for British and American profs to outnumber the homegrown ones in English departments, a situation that outraged nationalists but couldn't be rectified overnight.

Bowering is Canadian, of course, but most of his key influences have been American; he loves baseball, and his candour sometimes makes people think he has an American personality. Another strike against him was that while he taught energetically and had recently won a Governor General's Award, he lacked a doctorate and didn't publish academic work in the standard way. On top of that, some members of the English department thought its greatest need was for a Canadianist, a specialist in Canadian literature. Bowering recalls having been "hired by one vote." Gerald Newman, formerly of the CBC, was the department chair. Creative writing was what Newman cared about most, recalls Sandra Djwa, an SFU professor emerita. She says that there, "as at no other university in the country, your creative work counted on a par with your academic work."

Simon Fraser University, which crowns Burnaby Mountain east of Vancouver, had been built in just two and a half years, its creation such a headlong rush that one journalist dubbed it an instant university. Clint Burnham has written that its architect, Arthur Erickson, could make concrete transcend its original purposes by designing buildings that "straddle the ugly and the sublime, the ponderous and the ethereal, the transitory and the monumental." In keeping with the bold architectural statement it makes, SFU wanted to be more open and democratic than older schools. It was Canada's first university to elect students to its senate and the first to have a woman president (Pauline Jewett, 1974–78).

In the classroom, a teacher is essentially on stage, performing, and Bowering knew that. "He put on a good show," recalls Miriam Nichols, his student in 1980 and now an academic herself. He made a lot of jokes in class, she remembers. "I was always amused, though not everybody was."

The writer Roger Farr, his student in the nineties, will never forget how George started a class. Dressed for the job in a tie and blazer, his hair slicked back, "he would come in and just *slam* the door behind him. We all thought it was hilarious, but I remember a few people thought he was hamming it up too much. He would make a big production of it. He would take his coat off and click open his briefcase," a hard-sided one plastered with stickers, including one of those oval GB stickers used to indicate that a vehicle had come from Great Britain.

George could be outrageous in his lectures. Farr remembers him pretending to gag as he referred to Northrop Frye as "Nor-throw-up Frye." (Part of Bowering's quarrel with Frye was that Frye's notion of Canada focused on central Canada, on "Protestant enclaves in the landscape deep freeze," and didn't encompass the West.)

Christina "Chris" Turnbull, also a student of his in the nineties, recalls another of his "performative tricks." Sometimes he'd enter the classroom as if he'd been talking all the way down the hall, keeping up one side of a conversation as he came in. She describes his teaching style as "not the usual." Bolder class members "could heckle George. He would respond to it in a way that was fun." And "if you were interested in poetry and language and communication, he would have all the time in the world for you." The Ottawa poet and publisher rob mclennan says, "I wouldn't be surprised if he taught a third of the poets in Vancouver." He's been influential in modelling the way living and writing can coexist. Stephen Collis, a Vancouver-area poet who once took a directed-studies course from him, sees him as the kind of poet where "life and art blur together." He's also a "process poet," which means he generally uses a particular method or approach with each book. Collis sees him as having had "a fairly broad, diffuse, indirect influence." Even younger people who don't write like him have probably picked up ideas from him.

His theatrics in class didn't mean his teaching lacked substance. He once told Pauline Butling he'd spent thirty-six hours preparing a class on one of the modernist writers. She was floored: "I never imagined him being so diligent."

Kathy Mezei affirms that he was "an entertaining speaker, funny and articulate," but says he was also "a hard marker," rigorous about spelling and grammar. Those traits came up for discussion on an autumn day in 1973 when Newman told Bowering he'd received complaints about his being colloquial in class but, at the same time, pedantic, curt, and a hard marker. George's view, his diary reveals, was that the complainers were "illiterates who are used at this place to getting a B for proving that they can hold a pen with the ink end on the paper."

Students accustomed to earning high grades in, say, their Chaucer and Milton courses could get a rude shock when he handed their essays back. Knighton remembers hearing about a Bowering-marked essay being used to show teaching assistants how *not* to mark. "There was one page, and the only comment in the margin was, 'This is not proper English.' And on the next page it said, 'This is still improper English.' And the third page said, 'This is not English.'" There's another story floating around – that of a student getting an essay back with a "W" on it. When she asked what the weird letter grade meant, he told her, "Well, if an A is outstanding and an F is a failure, X would be really bad. You got a W, so you're not really bad, but you're a long way even from F."

"He wasn't the coddling type of teacher," Compton recalls. Once, in the nineties, when Angela was ill, George had given a lecture and was in a hurry to get home. A student came up and asked him to explain something. He said, "I don't have time for that now." When the young person objected, "But you're here to teach us," he replied, "No, I'm here to weed you out." He was convinced, throughout his teaching career, that grading standards were too low, but sometimes the chemistry between him and a class was thrilling. At the end of 1973 he regretted that his seminar course was nearly over because the students "really seem to like me, & I feel affection ... for them." He cursed the semester system, which gave professors only thirteen weeks in which to put a course across.

He was open to letting students help shape courses. In the late seventies, he was teaching grad students *A Book* and *Turn of a Pang*, translated works by Nicole Brossard, an avant-garde Quebec writer he champions. Colin Browne, a student who had good French, thought the class should read them in the original. "George was excited by that idea. He said, 'Yeah, let's do it,'" says Browne, who found the seminar to be "a class of discovery, rather than lecturing. We were all discovering together." Now a poet and documentary filmmaker, he still marvels at how, when SFU accepted him as a Ph.D. student, Bowering had heard of Granny Soot Press, his tiny poetry-publishing outfit. Granny Soot is a character in a novel by Guatemalan writer Miguel Ángel Asturias, and Browne's enterprise was definitely "niche." But George instantly said, "Granny Soot – yes, I know your books."

Students who were on his wavelength had it made. As Compton puts it, "You were expected to read the writers he mentioned and then you were in the conversation." On the other hand, Reg Johanson, a poet, essayist, and teacher of literature who once hung out with Bowering and his friends, says that if students didn't already have some notion of contemporary writing, they might have found him "crotchety and impossible, eccentric and rude."

In 1980, when Bowering was being considered for tenure at SFU, he had to fight for it – the English department's tenure committee was disinclined to grant it to him. Miriam Nichols has a memory that would delight David Lodge, Richard Russo, and every other novelist who has written satirically about academia: His colleague Rob Dunham, disgusted that anyone would question George's fitness to be a permanent, tenured faculty member, threw his beloved copy of

David Perkins's *English Romantic Writers* down the hall. Robin Blaser, by then George's colleague, went to bat for him. In late May, the university tenure committee reversed the department's decision and recommended to the president that he be promoted to full professor.

From around 1993 into the early 2000s, George brought literary youngsters and oldsters together in a group he called Dads and Tads. It was a kind of low-rent weekly salon. Some writers who went were in their twenties while others were in their fifties and sixties. On Friday afternoons they met for talk and drinks at Shenanigans pub in the Blue Horizon Hotel on Robson Street. To Reg Johanson, one of the Tads, "having it at Shenanigans and not some other, more twee sort of place says something about the spirit of the thing."

The contingent of Dads included Jamie Reid; George Stanley, a San Francisco poet who'd been teaching at B.C. colleges since the early seventies; Renee Rodin, a writer, artist, and bookseller; Will Thornton-Trump; and sometimes other friends of Bowering's who taught and wrote, like Maria Hindmarch, Judith Copithorne, and Frank Davey, when he was in town. George invited the students in whom he saw writing talent. Chris Turnbull remembers him casually telling her, "A bunch of us meet on Fridays." Besides her and Johanson, the Tads included Knighton, Compton, Anne Stone, Jason Le Heup, Karina Vernon, Cath MacLaren Morris, and Thea Bowering.

In Johanson's memory, "you never had the feeling that you were gathered around the feet of the Great Man." Yet he admits to having attended closely to George's judgments about poetry. "He'd say, 'Oh, I don't like that person,'" meaning his or her writing, "and then I'd be, like, 'Okay, I'd better remove all this guy's books [from my shelves].'" Knighton contends that "there was no mentoring going on whatsoever" on those Fridays. He says, "We were gleaning it from [the Dads]. They weren't offering it, but we were gleaning it." He was flattered to be hanging out with older writers he admired and says, "If I had not done Tads, I don't think I would ever have carried on [writing]. You're at the big-boy table, so you try and keep up." Reid spoke of "a fair amount of foolishness and drinking and clowning on the part of the two Georges" and Johanson recalls that "people got really loaded." In short, the gatherings were for initiates. Carl Peters, a Ph.D. student who idolized Bowering and has since published several scholarly books, was invited but went just once. "I was intimidated by the banter, by the quickness," he says. "I know this sounds sophomoric, but I didn't want to look bad in front of my hero."

The group produced *Tads*, a poetry zine. Copies were circulated among members, passed from hand to hand like *samizdat*. Each of the six issues had a different editor, who wrote and collected poems and then edited the issue, laid it out, and got it printed. *Tads* didn't have the kind of impact on Canadian literature that *TISH* had had, but producing it was good for the mind and soul.

In March 2001, with George's retirement from SFU approaching, the student newspaper, *The Peak*, published a cartoon by Kristjan Arnason. It shows Bowering standing in front of a class, looking intense. (Arnason drew him with an arrow through his head.) He's letting loose a fusillade of utterances, such as, "We're in Yeats country now," "Hardy wants to blow all that to smithereens," "Any real Mexican-style Catholics around here?" and "One good thing about being the Poet Laureate of England is that you get to park on a double line" – all from a page of notes Arnason had made in a Bowering class.

George knew many of the writers whose work he taught. Roger Farr did directed studies with him on Phyllis Webb's poetry. After some preliminaries, his prof said, "Here's her phone number. I'll let her know you'll be calling." It helps when a professor is casual, generous, and part of a network of working writers. On August 27, 2001, though, it all came to an end. With no regrets, he emptied out his campus office and handed back the key.

CHAPTER 9

THE POET

This writing, it is a life done in secret, that
is its charm. It's charm, the stolen (yeah, trickster)
moments, stolen E motion. Nobody but nobody can
stop you at that moment & say hey you're holding
that wrong let me show you.

—"E," *Another Mouth* (1979)

The Black Mountain poets were Bowering's early heroes, and one of them, Charles Olson, famously wrote that of the whole flock of rhetorical devices, simile is "one bird who comes down, too easily." Agreeing with this, George has avoided putting similes in his poems.

Some things came down easily for him, though. In the sixties and seventies, he was a creative powerhouse, turning out stacks of poems. He sent them out widely and, partly because of the name and contacts he'd made through *TISH*, they were often accepted. Montreal's Contact Press published *Points on the Grid*, his first book of poems, in 1964. In it were "Radio Jazz" and "Grandfather," as well as "The Hockey Hero," boyish with its capitalized shouts, "HE MUST BANG THE THING IN" and "BANGING REBOUND!" Contact was a serious publisher of poetry, a real writers' press. George, then twenty-eight, exulted, "I've been looking forward to this many years – my first book – my work between boards, and disseminated – however limited an edition."

His second collection came out in October 1965 and was actually a special issue of a Spanish/English magazine. *El corno emplumado / The Plumed Horn* was a literary quarterly out of Mexico City. Its editors – feisty young Margaret "Meg" Randall, who'd grown up in the American Southwest, and her gentle Mexican husband, Sergio Mondragón – were poets who published work from clear across the Western Hemisphere. Left-wing idealists, they wanted North American and Latin American poets to get to know one another. For George, that really happened. He and Angela visited the couple and their growing family in the summers of 1964 and 1965. One of his affectionate letters to them began, "Hi, Mon Dragons."

The issue devoted to him was titled *The Man in Yellow Boots / El hombre de las botas amarillas*, a reference to the time he painted the toes of his regulation RCAF boots yellow so as to find them easily. Modestly, his name appeared only on the back cover. In the middle, a set of photocollages by Roy Kiyooka, his artist/writer friend, added power, depth – every kind of enhancement.

The poem "The Descent" is one of the book's lyric masterpieces. The poet is studying an old photo of his father, plucked from a box in the attic, and noting the resemblance:

> *it is me in*
>> *outlandish clothes, long wool*
>> *bathing suits, plus-fours, white*
>> *shoes, holding tennis raquet*
>
> *me staring fixedly at the invisible*
>> *rigid camera*

Conjuring up the home in which his dad was raised, Bowering memorably writes, "There were many verbs around that house, and the chief among them was Give Thanks."

He was teaching literature in Calgary when he wrote the resonant poem "Moon Shadow." One day in late October 1964, as he crunched across packed snow after a long day on campus, he caught sight of the moon with a halo around it. He quotes from a seventeenth-century sonnet he'd been teaching, Sir Philip Sidney's "With how sad steps, o moon, thou climb'st the skies," from the sequence *Astrophel and Stella*. In "Moon Shadow" George samples only the words "with how sad steps" and, for a substantial part of the poem, gives the moon a voice. It says, in part:

> I show one face
> to the world,
> immaculate still,
> inscrutable female
> male animal ball
> of rock
> shining with borrowed light

The poem ends wistfully. Its main speaker is walking home, "rainbow round my heart, / wondering where in the universe I am." While discussing Sidney's sonnet in class, George had lightly mocked it. But then, when he stepped outside around 6:30 p.m., he glanced up at the full moon and "saw what Sidney saw." For years, editors compiling poetry anthologies have found a lot to like in "Moon Shadow," which predates the Cat Stevens song, "Moonshadow."

In the summer of 1965, he worked on two exceptional long poems, so different one from the other that they hardly seem to have come from the same brain. "Hamatsa" is a bloodcurdling epic about cannibalism inspired by a Kwakwaka'wakw myth. By contrast, the long poem *Baseball: A Poem in the Magic Number 9* is playful in tone. It's been said that *Baseball* uses his love for the sport as a disguise to talk about his love for poetry.

In those days, George couldn't help but see Calgary as a dusty, backward, redneck town. He had the guts to corral his impressions – he'd noticed Christianity, right-wing politics, "a profusion of chiropractors, and distrust of foreign ideas" – in a magazine article. *Saturday Night* published it in October 1965, soon after *The Man in Yellow Boots*. In *Saturday Night* George made his polemical points coolly, sometimes garnishing them with a twist of dry wit. Referring to the censor board that reviewed all movies shown in Alberta, he noted that its head was a retired military man, this background presumably giving him "the strength to watch anything." The magazine gave the piece an attention-grabbing title, "Alberta's War on Intellect," and waited for the letters to flood in. Although most western readers must have been twitching, if not fulminating, the first response the editors printed was sympathetic. An Alberta clergyman assured the rest of the country that "[w]e have some exceptionally fine people here who, believe it or not, are trying to check the Bible Belt reflex of rearing back in horror and apprehension at the new and unfamiliar." Meanwhile in Toronto, the newspaper columnist Robert Fulford drew his readers' attention to the article, having earlier given *The Man in Yellow Boots* some flattering ink. It was a heady time for a man not yet thirty.

In September 1966, the Quarry Press, a new outfit in Kingston, Ontario, published his poetry collection *The Silver Wire*. The title comes from "To Summer," a lush, joyous poem by William Blake. "Our bards are fam'd who strike the silver wire," Blake wrote, the wire being an imaginary line connecting them with heaven. On the cover, a drawing of a nude woman hints at something intimate, but the book also offers poems that show his interest in politics and history. "News" is about the horrors contained in a stack of newspapers: airplane crashes, an earthquake in Alaska, "seventeen American soldiers face down in Asian mud." The poet pictures the world's violence erupting in front of him:

> A plane could crash into the kitchen –
> a fissure could jag the floor open –
> some olive faced paratrooper bash
> his rifle butt thru the window –

In "East to West," he gives names to some of the six thousand Chinese labourers who built the B.C. section of the Canadian Pacific Railway in the 1880s: Ho Ling, Old Chang, Ho Chin, Ho Lem. He imagines what the life of one of them might have been like fifty years on. By 1931, Ho Chin might have had his queue cut off, become a Christian, and been making a living by selling vegetables from a cart.

As for the promised intimacy, "A Bedroom Sound" shows a man and a woman making love and speaks of "the bounding shiver of skin." The pleasures of melding and merging are undercut, though, by three crisp, bathetic lines reporting on the poet's erection: "up! / it! / comes!" One reviewer chided, "He is here to tell us all, and by heaven he is going to. So we just have to take him, sex and all." The Montreal poet and publisher Louis Dudek huffed, "This is merely brutal, not imaginative, or erotic, or affectionate." But another critic praised his terse, clean style and "sense of wonder in the commonplace."

In London, Ontario, where the Bowerings went next, George couldn't immediately relate to the landscape. Southwestern Ontario, a long-settled place where there were woodlots instead of forests, didn't enthrall him. So, in his mind, he went back to the West Coast. In a library he came across the journal of a Scottish botanist who had gone there with Captain George Vancouver in the eighteenth century. He started writing the long poem *George, Vancouver*, which would be published in 1970.

In London he also wrote "The House," a poem that would become well known. It begins,

If I describe my house
I may at last describe my self

but I will surely lie
about the house.

In the late eighties, Angela would have lines from the poem applied in gold leaf around the tops of the living room walls in their Kerrisdale house. Their marriage was in an uproar, so daughter Thea considers the act a "gesture of love." But George remembers bursting out laughing when he first saw the decoration on returning from a trip.

Just as his year of doctoral studies at the University of Western Ontario was ending, his novel *Mirror on the Floor* hit bookstores. He'd set the story in Vancouver decades before this was considered a wise commercial decision, and McClelland & Stewart had taken the risk. Newspapers, magazines, and journals reviewed it and *The Silver Wire* in 1967. Family friend Tony Bellette declared in a letter, "Goddam, every time I turn the radio on you're talking on it, George." In this swirl of attention, George and Angela took an opportunity in Montreal that had been offered him. They packed up their possessions, selling their kitchen appliances for as little as five dollars each, and again turned their move into a road trip. In the hubbub, one of their two chihuahuas broke a leg.

Montreal's wealth of history, art, and architecture is a visual feast. They fell in love with the Notre-Dame Basilica and were soon showing it off to friends visiting from the West Coast. George liked the fact that his new academic home had a diversity of students and expected them to give some thought to things other than scholarship. He could see, too, that its English department cared about poetry. Besides getting to rub shoulders with the poetry stars who were invited to town to give readings, the Bowerings met local literary lions. F.R. "Frank" Scott, a senior lawyer as well as a poet, wrote them an affectionate, clever poem, "For G. and A.B." It reads, "Never before in the world was so much / loving flowering. // Everytime I look in a bower I see an / Angela and a George bowering."

In November 1967, Toronto's recently founded Coach House Press published George's long poem, *Baseball*, as a booklet. The designer, Gar Smith, made it distinctive. It was triangular, with a flocked green cover, and looked like the sports teams' pennants that kids used to pin to their bedroom walls. (Coach House would print a second edition in 2003, by which time the technology to create the snazzy look had totally changed.)

Fuzzy to the touch because of its flocked green cover and challenging to shelve because of its shape, *Baseball* is a long poem in a league of its own.

Bowering stayed on to teach at Sir George after his writer-in-residence appointment ended. The cataclysm now known as the Computer Centre Riot put the university in the national spotlight early in 1969. Six students of Caribbean descent brought a complaint of racism against a biology lecturer who, they said, treated them differently and graded them more harshly than the white students in the class. They succeeded in getting hearings into the matter set up, but when the hearing process seemed to be going nowhere, two hundred students went to occupy the university's computer centre on the ninth floor of the Henry F. Hall Building. The occupation stretched out over days as an agreement to resolve the issue was hammered out. The students were on the verge of agreeing to it, and were dispersing, when a riot broke out on February 11. The hundred or so protesters left in the building threw computer punch cards and student records out the windows and started a fire that damaged the mainframe computers. City police made ninety-seven arrests. One of the most troubling things about the riot – "a turning point in race relations in Canada," according to *Ninth Floor*, Mina Shum's 2015 documentary film – was what some brain-dead bystanders shouted when they saw the Hall Building ablaze: "Burn, nigger, burn!"

The CBC commissioned Bowering to write a poem about the riot. He did, but "Sir George Computer University" is surprisingly light in tone. Two of its lines do touch on the geopolitical context: "Ah, violence, ah violence, ah viet cong / infiltrating the faculty club."

📖

On March 1, 1969, George again went public with impressions of Alberta he'd gathered earlier in the decade. *Rocky Mountain Foot*, from McClelland & Stewart, is an artistic triumph, with its remarkable use of word collage. Bowering amplified many of the poems with bits of found material that appear in sans serif type. Some are quotations from

Premier Ernest Manning and other public figures whose old-school utterances irked him. He also sampled such Chamber of Commerce–style materials as *Our Alberta* and *The Badlands of the Red Deer River.* This was a technique of Ezra Pound's and also one William Carlos Williams used to good effect in his epic poem, *Paterson.*

In *Rocky Mountain Foot,* seven poems in a row have stark titles: "The Oil," "The Plain," "The Grass," "The Blue," "The Frost," The Snow," and "The Dust." After "The Dust" comes this extraneous but brilliant bit of found history: "Moira O'Neill said (1898): 'A log or lumber house is built, then simply furnished. There are no elaborate meals or superfluous furniture. I like the endless riding over the prairie, the wind sweeping the grass, the herds moving from water to water, the fun of coyote hunting. I like the monotony and the change, the flannel shirt, the liberty.'" And prefacing his poem "The Streets of Calgary" is a brief, eyebrow-raising historical note: "An enterprising man, Kamoose Taylor posted a set of rules, one of which read, 'All guests requested to rise at 6 a.m. as sheets may be needed for tablecloths.'"

Reviews of the book were gratifyingly positive. "We live in Alberta and we see it every day," Lynne Van Luven wrote in the *Red Deer Advocate.* "Bowering has done what we fail to do in our daily pattern of routines – he has captured the essence of the province." And George Fetherling began his assessment by saying, "A genius in part might be a person who thinks of things you should have thought of years ago."

Another strong book of Bowering's verse appeared later in 1969. Toronto's new House of Anansi Press published *The Gangs of Kosmos.* In it are some of the poems by which readers know him best: "The Egg," "The House," and "Dobbin," the last telling painfully of an unloved horse, tied to a fence and left to starve to death. (He'd seen it up in the southern Okanagan hills when he was twelve.) When George asked Margaret Atwood if she'd edit the book, she agreed, saying "Wow" in response to "Dobbin." At the same time, she warned him against sending everything he wrote out into the public realm. "You should do yrself justice & only publish yr best things," she advised.

Captured by a camera in the 1970s: Margaret Atwood, right; Quebec poet D.G. Jones, left; George Bowering and daughter Thea.

"Hamatsa," about a cannibalistic ogre, and "Windigo," another foray into Indigenous legend, are two challenging poems in *Gangs*. But the collection is leavened by lighter ones that raise a smile, like "Grandmother." It tells of an old woman in a "frocky" dress, beating a bowl of icing with a wooden spoon. She asks her young grandson whether he had a bowel movement and he, unfamiliar with the expression, plays it safe and says yes. Some of the poems have irresistible titles, like "After My Rose Period," but the book's title, *The Gangs of Kosmos*, was obscure. Bowering would wait until 2015 to explain succinctly that it's Walt Whitman's characterization of "the poets who would follow in his future." The cover art is by Charles Pachter, a friend of Atwood's since their teenage years. Surprisingly, she's the woman in sunglasses on the front. The author photo at the back is something of a puzzler, too: It shows George with a friend's little girl, but there is no elucidating caption.

George thought well of his skills. In October, he wrote in his diary, "I'm one of the 5 best poets in the country: VC, MA, MA, GB, JN" – Coleman, Atwood, Avison, Bowering, and Newlove.

In his thirties, George began moving away from the lyric poem ("any short poem presenting a single speaker [not necessarily the poet himself] who expresses a state of mind involving thought and feeling") and embraced the long poem. He was, he has sometimes joked, entering his symphonic period.

CHAPTER 10

THE LIGHTNING ROD

> I had to reject my early design to be an American in order to become a Canadian. Like a recent convert or immigrant, I am pretty strong about Canadianism, a lot stronger than those folks from Ontario and Quebec who run the show in Ottawa.
>
> —"Confessions of a Failed American," *Maclean's* (November 1972)

Bowering got word from the Canada Council early in 1970 that he was a finalist for a Governor General's Award for Poetry. He'd been hoping to win one by 1971 but had thought the 1969 prize would have Ralph Gustafson's name on it.

What happened, come spring, was that the judges – one being Warren Tallman – gave it jointly to him and Gwendolyn MacEwen. The makeup of the judging panel, as well as its decision, touched off a nationalism-tinged row. Irving Layton questioned Tallman's right to be on the jury, protesting that he was "an American who though he has lived in Canada for something like 10 years, has refused to become a citizen. He has no interest in Canadian poetry except insofar as it can be considered an extension of the faddish American style of Williams-Olson-Creeley, which ... has no relevancy to our native literary traditions and sensibility." Layton thought that Milton

Acorn, a rough-hewn poet with a working-class persona, deserved the prize for *I've Tasted My Blood*. "There's more poetry in the dirty little fingernail of Milton Acorn," he declared, "than there is in all the collected poetry of George Bowering." But Al Purdy, who'd edited Acorn's book, sensibly told George at a party in Montreal that "you don't have to use one poet to put another down."

Acorn had been briefly married to MacEwen, nearly twenty years his junior. They'd been spectacularly mismatched and their breakup had left him bitter. Knowing this, MacEwen had asked chief juror Robert Weaver to remove her book from the shortlist. But she eventually decided to leave well enough alone, says one of Acorn's biographers. "She couldn't spend her life hiding from Milt, afraid that her successes would only cause him anger."

I've Tasted My Blood was widely considered impressive. In fact, George had written two reviews lauding it. In a *Salon des Refusés* kind of move, Layton suggested that Acorn receive an alternative prize for his writing and political activism. Other prominent literary figures who helped to create the Canadian Poets' Award and dub Acorn the People's Poet at a Toronto ceremony in May 1970 included Margaret Atwood, Mordecai Richler, Patrick Lane, Joe Rosenblatt, and Eli Mandel. They raised $1,000 for the prize – "a substantial sum in those days (the Governor General's Award was $2,500)" – and had a medal struck for him. The Bowerings were in England at the time. In October, George and Gwen received their Governor General's Awards in Ottawa. Having chosen to wear a green velvet suit, George made quite an impression.

The debate over whether Canadian writers should work strictly within their own country's tradition (the argument, that is, over cultural nationalism) burned brightly and destructively for years. Bob Hogg, who attended the Ottawa ceremony, says that in some people's eyes, Acorn "wasn't 'colonized' by the American scene. [But] the whole breadth of literature has been about influence. We [Canadian

poets] would never have got off the ground without Wordsworth."
Gary Geddes and Phyllis Bruce allude to the American-influence brou-
haha in their 1970 anthology, *15 Canadian Poets*. In the biographical
note on Bowering they say "a good deal of nonsense, most of it propaganda masquerading as aesthetics, has been written and spoken" about
his poetry, "especially his association with Charles Olson and other
poets of Black Mountain College." They say he legitimately learned
from earlier writers in figuring out how to get his voice on the page.

Bowering got to spend a few moments with Allen Ginsberg when he
was in Vancouver for an event in November 1978. Promoters of cultural
nationalism were suspicious of George's affinity for U.S. literary figures.

In 1970, he was reading Gertrude Stein obsessively. He loved the
plainness of her language. Explaining the attraction, he now says, "She
was an example of somebody who did not write with the stuff they
told us in high school that fiction demanded – i.e., setting, character,
theme, plot, and so forth ... She's easy to read but you sometimes
wonder what she's saying." Her stubborn individuality appealed not
only to him but also to bpNichol and bill bissett.

In the summer of 1970 he decided to imitate Stein in a forty-
eight-part project, the long poem *Autobiology*. He started writing it
in Montreal, but by the time it appeared as a *Georgia Straight* Writing

Supplement in February 1972, he and Angela had moved back to the West Coast. He's always been upfront about learning from Stein. He asks, "If a writer works all her life to find a way of writing, why should we followers be advised to avoid using what she has given us? Who asks present-day physicists to ignore the work of Niels Bohr?"

Autobiology mostly gives us slices of his early life. Meredith and Peter Quartermain, a Vancouver literary couple, have said it "presents the puzzling and curious George Bowering meeting and hearing his own three-year-old voice." In "The Back Yard," Pearl Bowering eviscerates a freshly killed chicken:

> *... my mother tore its colours from its hole & they*
> *were yellow & purple they were clean & circles*
> *tumbling over circles.*

The poem also brings up the time five-year-old George played with matches and set the foliage on a hillside on fire. "Later I visited [the spot] & the mountain was green & it was not a mountain."

"The First City" is about Victoria, the first larger place where he lived after having grown up in Interior towns. In cryptic Steinian fashion, he writes of having left "a village with a man's name because of a premier [John Oliver; and having gone] to a city with a woman's name because of a queen." Other parts of *Autobiology* zero in on his teenage self. "Come" is about discovering semen, "this white stuff."

The book is strong and memorable, a strange creation. Later in the seventies, he would allude to his circle's irritation with his Stein phase: "... people say why are you doing archaic avant-garde writing. This is warmed over Gertrude Stein there I said her name why are you doing it." Later still, he would cite Stein's rationale: "New writing is ugly at first, then becomes consumable, then becomes the standard."

Coach House published his *Curious*, another long poem in forty-eight sections, the following year. George has said he chose the word "curious" mostly for a meaning it had centuries ago, when it was a synonym for "careful." In composing the sections – each a word portrait of a poet whose writing spoke to him – he was doing careful work. Of course, he was also sticking his neck out, as people don't always take kindly to the way others describe them in public. Some of the poets portrayed, like Kearns, Marlatt, Wah, Margaret Randall, and Brian Fawcett, were his friends and contemporaries. Others were older poets in central Canada: Louis Dudek, Layton, Raymond Souster. He wrote portraits of American poets he admired, including Olson, Williams, Ginsberg, Marianne Moore, and Denise Levertov. And there's one of Stephen Spender, a Briton he'd heard read at UBC, which contains a slighting reference to W.H. Auden. ("I hated him that no talent / easy work soft life faggot with his / witty insults.")

"Irving Layton" is the book's most distinctive portrait. The Montrealer, a mentor to Leonard Cohen, had won a Governor General's Award for Poetry with *A Red Carpet for the Sun* back in 1959. But his flamboyant alpha-dog personality and the pride he took in his virility distracted from his talent. In the portrait, Bowering wonders if the great man could get it up, self-censoring his crude word choices by putting sixteen thick black lines through them.

A stanza of his "Daphne Marlatt" begins,

> *In 1960 she had black pedal-pushers & she*
> *looked so brittle I thought how does she move her*
> *knees, is it painful ...*

Marlatt remembers not liking that. The reference to how she dressed made her think, "Okay, I'm supposed to be a groupie. Well, I don't want to be a groupie – I want to be a poet."

With Daphne Marlatt, a fellow Vancouver poet he has long admired and
written about.

In a review, the Edmonton poet and critic Douglas Barbour wrote that
Curious owed much to "Gertrude Stein's famous portraits of Picasso
and other artists," but other readers felt that only an in-group could
enjoy them. In 1982, when the portraits reappeared in a selected-poems
volume, one reviewer would object that the "man on the street could
care less about where Spender kept his handkerchief or what kind of
beer Raymond Souster prefers." George put the clipping in his diary,
writing beside it that the man on the street "isn't reading poems."

Curious had, and still has, eloquent defenders. Robert Fulford, of
the *Toronto Star*, memorably opined that there was room for it because
Canadian poetry was like a family, with Earle Birney as Gramps, Layton the randy uncle, Atwood as brilliant young Sis, and Dennis Lee
the family's solemn young man. Sheila Watson later stated that the
portraits "describe nothing, explain nothing; they present and evoke.
Above all they respect the intelligence which they confront." Colin
Browne remembers thinking, when he first read *Curious*, "Well, this
is a small circle writing about itself." But now he looks back at it and
thinks, "I'm glad this was written."

Bowering's long poem *Allophanes* is even more obscure. Its first
line floated into his consciousness in September 1974 when he was at

his mother-in-law Lillian Luoma's place on the west side of Vancouver. Standing alone in her living room, looking out at the yard, he heard, "The snowball appears in Hell every morning at seven," in the voice of the late San Francisco poet Jack Spicer. It was as if the line were being dictated to him – Spicer had believed in such dictation – and he decided to start a book with it.

It helps to know one more bit of background. George was teaching at SFU and, that fall, Robin Blaser was teaching an undergraduate course on W.B. Yeats and James Joyce. George sat in on it and wrote the work by hand while his erudite older colleague lectured. The class met twenty-six times, and so *Allophanes* has twenty-six sections. With Blaser talking more about Yeats than Joyce, a number of Yeatsian allusions – to the Order of the Alchemical Rose, for example, and Red Hanrahan – inevitably sifted in. Bowering also dropped in references to Spicer, Edgar Allan Poe, the French anthropologist Claude Lévi-Strauss, the German philosopher Edmund Husserl, and others. Intellectuals have had a field day chasing them down.

Bowering composed his long poem *Allophanes* during lectures his older colleague Robin Blaser, left, gave on Yeats and Joyce.

Allo-, from the ancient Greek adjective *allos*, means "other," and *-phanes*, derived from the Greek verb *phanein* ("to show, bring to light"), means "appearances." To George, who considers this his best long poem, the title means "those things which are other than what they at first appear to be, all taken together." Coach House styled the title in pseudo-Greek letters when it published the slim blue volume in 1976.

Wordplay abounds in the poem. Sophocles's title, *Oedipus at Colonus*, becomes "Oedipus at Kelowna." You come across a fragment from Mother Goose: "To try to drown poor pussy cat." Phrases like "a phonebook of the damned" show an appealing wit. The epigraph atop Section XI comes from an old song: "Run for the roundhouse, Nellie, he cant corner you there." A big bold Hebrew letter, *aleph* (א), appears in Section XVI after the line "Morphemes fall in flames from the tree."

For the average reader, the poem is a word salad. One reviewer found it "virtually incoherent, with the exception of a single moderately lucid section on history." But another deemed it an attractive, intelligent poem that inquires about "the nature of reality in this world without gods." When Michael Ondaatje put it in *The Long Poem Anthology*, a 1979 book he edited for Coach House, Bowering's statement about it said, in part: "As I get older, I come more to realize that my activity as a poet composing is an extension of my desirous childhood Christianity. I want like crazy to get here alone and hear God's voice, I mean it." If writing *Allophanes* was spiritual for him, no wonder he was annoyed when, after he'd read it aloud at a university in central Canada, the main question from the audience was why it alludes to such writers as Dante and T.S. Eliot but not to any in the Canadian tradition.

His more accessible poetic voice didn't disappear in the seventies but continued to be heard intermittently. His 1974 book, *In the Flesh*, contains a mixture of styles, with McClelland & Stewart billing him on the back cover as a "master of lyric verse" who "transform[s] speech into a delicate, sonorous music."

"First Night of Fall, Grosvenor Ave," which he wrote in Montreal, is a tiny, spare masterpiece:

> *In the blue lamplight*
> *the leaf falls*
>
> *on its shadow.*

It probably reminds many readers of Ezra Pound's "In a Station of the Metro." In the same book, but utterly different, is "Stab," a long, Whitmanesque poem that deals with procreation, growing up, and growing old. It begins,

> *I am the empty belly*
> *of my father as he lay*
> *exhausted on my mother.*

It continues, "I am all the lies ever told about me." And it ends with a grandiloquent statement:

> *... I am my own empty belly*
> *exhausted on the belly of my woman.*
>
> *I am the lord God that is Adam & us all.*

Nearing age forty, he had the courage to write what came to him, even if it might evoke scorn or ridicule. He'd been uneasy about putting "Stab" in the book, but it turned out to be "the one *everyone* liked."

The Catch, which McClelland & Stewart published in 1976, contains two stunning lyrical poems that are soulful and mature, weighty and complex. Written in the early seventies, they are just as rewarding to read now.

In "Summer Solstice," the poet is a young father who lifts his daughter out of her crib when she wakes, spoons baby food into her mouth, and deals with what comes out the other end. All around him, gardens are in bloom and Vancouver's North Shore mountains are a thrilling sight, yet he is burdened by a feeling of dread tinged with ennui. "How long life is," he reflects, "how many more of these seasons must I see, hydrangea & the fat rhododendron sullen on the neighbour's lawn." He's aware of his mortality, realizing he is "slowly dying, water evaporating / from a saucer." The poem is suffused with tenderness and fear for the future. If it seems to owe a lot to Keats and Shelley, it's because he wrote it that way; each stanza imitates a different Romantic poet. Only an English professor could match the eleven sections with their Romantic models – the late Rob Dunham used to delight in doing so when he taught it – but parts of Wordsworth's "Lines Composed a Few Miles Above Tintern Abbey" and Coleridge's "Frost at Midnight" have similar cadences and concerns. Gary Geddes, an accomplished B.C. poet of the same generation but with a different aesthetic, said in a review, "I know no other poem of Bowering's in which the language has such a feeling of rightness, where the rhetoric ... creates such a profound ache in me, a feeling of desperate and beautiful poignancy."

In "Desert Elm," George was writing about his father (as he had in "The Descent"). At the time, Ewart was recovering from a heart attack. The ten-section poem bears the stamp of H.D., who, he would later say, is "the best model of how to make verses." The poem also limns the sere beauty of the south Okanagan Valley. It homes in on the region's Siberian, or desert, elms and its abundance of round rocks. "Desert Elm" is conspicuously different from other Bowering poems in that it mentions colours. Someone had noticed that he seldom names colours in his poetry, so, as an exercise, he made himself do it. He tells of his dad's easy command of tools and tasks but cites one occasion when Ewart showed strain: In a ballpark, rounding the bases to make a home run, his eyes bulged and his neck was "red as a turkey's." In the final stanza, the paterfamilias is supine, the blue of his eyes washed out in "the ocean light of the ward window." He died of cancer in 1974, before *The Catch* appeared – a huge loss to his family, former students, and community, where he'd been so civic-minded. George had hated seeing his capable father – his hero for so long – reduced by illness. Seeing Ewart in hospital, puffy from steroids and wearing a "silly accommodating smile," had amazed and repelled him, and of course he felt like a wretch for having that reaction.

Finely wrought, "Summer Solstice" and "Desert Elm" have always resonated with readers. In a newspaper review, Mary Novik pronounced them fluid, moving, and musical, while *The Fiddlehead* hailed the whole book as "a landmark in Canadian poetry."

The pattern set in the late sixties was that McClelland & Stewart published George's mainstream poetry roughly every two years while his more experimental work went to smaller literary presses. By now he has produced so many poems of so many kinds that it's perfectly okay, as one former student says, to read "the ones you love" and ignore "the ones you don't care too much about … You wind up being able to pick and choose your George Bowering."

CHAPTER 11

THE FATHER

"Is this the woods?" she asked.

"Yes, hon. Here's a path, see?"

They went in and after a few minutes he let go of her hand and walked slowly in front of her, once in a while holding a blackberry shoot away from her face ... She trusts me, he thought, and then suddenly he realized that he was exactly ten times her age ... She was his only child.

—"Protective Footwear," *Protective Footwear: Stories and Fables* (1978)

When they married, in December 1962, the Bowerings agreed to wait five years before having a baby. But when five years had passed they put parenthood off again because their plans for their education and careers hadn't solidified. By then, they weren't as tight a couple as they might have been. A symptom of this was the affair George had with Eveline Meyer in late-sixties Montreal.

At the time, it was natural for wayward sparks to fly. He and Angela were smart, good-looking, go-ahead people who were making names for themselves. George had published a novel and was known for his poetry, plus he was producing his little magazine, *Imago*. In 1967, their dear friend Tony Bellette sent them a letter in which he spoke of their attractiveness. He reminded them he'd once seen them in a bedroom at a house party, Angela sprawled on the bed, sexy in a black dress, George airily flicking ash from a cigarette, and their friend Jamie Reid standing "by the fireplace saying fuck & shit & piss ..." The hosts' stereo was playing the slow movement of Franz Schubert's *Death and the Maiden* string quartet. Tony told the Bowerings that in his mind that piece of music was "always mixed up with you two as I'll always think of you – sort of archetypal sexiness and detachment."

By the spring of 1971, they were back in B.C., where people their age could revel in the bohemian life if they chose to. Five years earlier, George had told their Mexico City friends in a letter that Vancouver was "a tremendous turn-on town, everywhere you go there are acid-heads leaning on bridge rails looking at the ocean."

He and Angela – pregnant, eight years into their marriage – moved into a commune on York Street in Vancouver's Kitsilano neighbourhood. Its members included another pregnant woman – their friend Gladys Hindmarch – and her then husband, Cliff Andstein (later to become prominent in the Canadian labour movement). The commune was alive with youthful zeal aimed at making the world a better place. Stan Persky, active on the political and literary fronts, was helping to get the *Georgia Straight* Writing Series off the ground, among many other projects. Brian DeBeck, then his partner, was great at getting all kinds of things done. Persky, recalling how DeBeck hosted huge summer barbecues and energetically diapered babies, says he was "a natural at dealing with everything. He was the most competent person among us." Commune member Lanny Beckman had helped to found the Mental Patients' Association, trying to get the patients' perspective into care for the mentally ill. The house was a meeting place for doers with high ideals, Hindmarch recalls. "There was almost never a day or evening that there wasn't a group of people there. Lanny said, 'The women are uniting, the gays are uniting – what about the mental patients?' They had T-shirts made saying 'NUTS TO YOU.'"

It was an artsy neighbourhood, though less colourful than it had been a few years earlier. "The ostentatious counterculture noise is gone from here," George wrote to his poet friend John Newlove in Toronto. To his eye, the area was "all ugly apartments and communes, longhairs walking around quietly with their dogs."

Members of the commune were principled about everything, including where they bought groceries. Their canned goods came in case lots from a local no-name store, and they cared a great deal about where they shopped for the rest. With amusement, Bowering remembers meetings over "whether or not we could buy things from certain stores if we knew, absolutely for certain, that the owner of the place was a sexist." Each of the seven commune members made dinner one day a week, even if he or she produced only simple dishes like hot dog casseroles and mac and cheese. Beckman's culinary skills were unimpressive but, says George, "he tried, and we ate it." In a poem he would write years later, he says (referring to himself in the third person),

> He stokes the stove,
> he averts the gaze,
> he takes his turn
> on cooking days.

He and Angela didn't join their housemates in going out for gestalt therapy and so got teased for acting like a separate nuclear family. Angela sensed sloppiness in the whole peace-and-love thing and held herself apart. "She didn't like the loosey-goosey stuff," their friend Jamie Reid would recall. Another friend, David Bromige, would briefly take her point of view in a collaborative novel, giving examples of the imprecise hippie sentiments that made her skin crawl: "Beautiful. Don't hassle. Ballin' my old man. My old lady. All ya need is love."

The communards who had writing projects on the go worked on them in shifts. George wrote at night, finishing his long poem *Autobiology* on June 12, 1971. Persky started his writing shift immediately after, at 5 a.m. He and George always talked for ten or fifteen minutes before he hit the typewriter and George hit the sack. When Stan read the *Autobiology* manuscript, he saw that George was "turning what he had learned from [Gertrude] Stein to autobiographical purposes. I decided, 'This is really a book, so what we ought to do is run it off on real cardboard-y paper and then take it to a binder,' and that's what we did." When it came out as the seventh volume of the *Georgia Straight* Writing Supplement's Vancouver Series in February 1972, a note on the last page said, "Five hundred copies printed at the York Street Commune with assistance from the Canada Council."

George remembers having a brain wave, after one 4:45 a.m. chat with Stan, about his future child's name. He and Angela were planning to name a boy Aaron Riel but were still tossing around girls' names: Amanda? Madeleine? Naomi? Simone? "I was sittin' there all alone. I was the only one awake. There were seven of us living there, plus two babies *in utero*. I was thinking of Althea Gibson, the great Black tennis player. I thought 'Althea,' and then I thought, 'If you took the "Al–" off, you'd have "Thea."' I think I left a note for Angela to read when she got up, because I'd be sleeping ... When I woke up, she said she agreed."

That summer, their housemates bought a place a few blocks away on York Street and moved there. George and Angela stayed behind, turning the commune back into a single-family dwelling. The poet George Stanley, just up from San Francisco, slept upstairs and helped them with the rent. Stanley remembers that, on meeting George and Angela for the first time, it was "hard to say which was the more powerful personality of the two." The members of this household, too, took turns making dinner, now concocting more sophisticated dishes, like chicken cacciatore. When a young woman came to interview George Bowering for an article, he and his surroundings impressed her mightily. Beth Jankola wrote in the *Georgia Straight* about seeing wineglasses set out on a table of polished wood and conversing with a "charming, exciting, generous" man who "turned me on to a TV program called [*Monty Python's*] *Flying Circus*, gave me coffee."

In late July, after the Bowerings had become used to feeling their unborn child move in Angela's womb, George wrote to Newlove, "Angela, if I didnt mention it, is expected to whelp in the latter part of Sept. ... If it happens during the world serious I dont know who is going to go up to the Vancouver General & hold her hand. Some non-fan, I suppose." That sounds blasé but, in the event, he wasn't. The baby came on October 6, two weeks past the due date. He went to the hospital, all right, and coached a panting, pushing Angela – "the dear woman," he would call her in his diary – as he'd learned in the Lamaze birth classes they'd gone to in West Vancouver. His excited diary entry describing the birth can be read in *The Dad Dialogues*, his and Charles Demers's epistolary book on fatherhood. He pronounced it "the most emotional moment I can remember" and wrote, "I've got love blazing out of all my senses, to Angela & Thea ... I was laughing, laughing, with love ..."

When newborn Thea Claire Bowering left Vancouver General Hospital with her parents, she entered a home where words, books, and literature mattered more than anything else. And most of the people who came to visit shared that fixation. She grew up, as Fred Wah later wrote in a blurb for her first book, "in the midst of an intense literary household." Her father mentioned her in his poems – "Summer Solstice" and several others – and his prodigious output would intimidate her when *she* started to write. (In her early forties, she would say, "I used to envy people who were artists who had parents who weren't ... I feel for people like Julian Lennon or Bob Dylan's

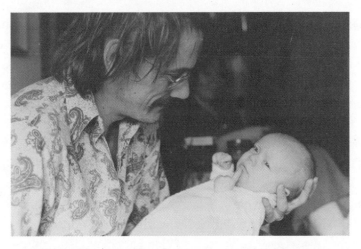

With baby Thea, a description of whose early care and feeding appears in the poem "Summer Solstice."

son [Jakob]. If you know that art is what you want to do, then how do you possibly start?")

When she was an infant, her dad nicknamed her The Gump, after the hockey goalie Lorne "Gump" Worsley, because her baby fat made it look as if she didn't have a neck. To him and Angela, she was Gumpy. In line with their new responsibilities, they became property owners early in 1972, paying $28,000 for a place at 2521 Balaclava Street, near West Broadway.

When Thea was only a month old, a woeful pattern asserted itself in their marriage. George thought he could see Angela's "bloom of motherhood" falling away. It was he who was doing the bulk of the baby care, cooking, cleaning, and home maintenance, he felt, wasting the writing year a senior arts grant from the Canada Council was supposed to afford him before he started teaching at Simon Fraser University in summer 1972. All the while, his wife, he sadly observed, "never says anything to me … except to scream at me & make false accusations …" Two years later, he recorded similar complaints, noting that Angela seemed to be "doing some sort of psychological thing, seeing how vicious one can be to someone else."

This sorry dynamic became an undertow in Thea's childhood, if Bowering's diaries are to be believed. Fortunately, she doesn't remember it that way. She felt loved and cherished by both parents and by their wide circle of friends, many of whom were known names in CanLit, as she was growing up. "Dad was the fun guy," she recalls, because he was always "on" when he stepped out in public. When he wasn't teaching, he made her his sidekick, taking her with him as he went around to bookstores, poetry readings, and art exhibits. He was a riot in the car, a kind of gamemaster who awarded her points when she exclaimed over spotting a Volkswagen bug, a double-decker bus, a monkey-puzzle tree, or the slant-roofed, mid-century modern Kitsilano dwelling they called "the cut-in-half house." When he was at the wheel, there was a rule against playing music by white people: They listened to jazz, Motown, gospel, and the blues.

George was away a lot, though. Constantly publishing poetry, fiction, and books of essays, he was sent out on book tours and, as a professor, he attended meetings of the Learned Societies – "the Stupids," he once called them – and far-flung literary gatherings. Thea stayed home with Angela, whom she remembers as the parent who was good at "practical stuff," for considerable stretches of time. Angela helped her with art projects, corrected the grammar in her schoolwork and later helped her put together a résumé and used her intuition to come pluck her out of dodgy social situations. "If I was involved with sketchy people, if I was at a party, she'd come and get me," says Thea. "I don't know how she found me. It happened a few times." George may not have been aware of that. When Thea was a preteen, he worried about the fact that when he wasn't home to make dinner, Angela just let Thea root through the kitchen cupboards and throw something together herself. His wife, by then an instructor at a suburban college, refused "to entertain the idea that that is not normal."

The family didn't stay in Kitsilano for long. Angela, who had an eye for real estate and, due to poverty in childhood, a yen for gracious living, found a big, venerable old house for sale at 2499 West 37th Avenue, two houses east of Warren and Ellen Tallman's place. They bought it in 1973 for $68,000. George would have preferred to continue living modestly in a neighbourhood funkier than Kerrisdale, but he was overruled. In October, he slid this sardonic line into a letter to Margaret Atwood: "Now here's the news all about the big new house: blah blah blah blah dark wood blah blah blah 10 rooms, and growing blah blah stone foundation, come and see us ..." Other friends teased him, with Newlove starting one of his letters, "How's yer hundred thousand dollar house or whatever. I hear tell the bottom's gonna drop out. Of the market. Probably of the house too."

Thea was a toddler when they moved in. George's long poem, *At War With the U.S.*, published in January 1974, contains a dovish letter to then U.S. President Richard Nixon and these lines about the poet's small daughter:

> *Her first black eye*
> *just when Nixon is getting his*
>
> *Who hit her they ask on the street*
> *The world came by & did it*

Angela set about furnishing and decorating the house to a high standard. Continual expensive renovations would become a bone of contention in the marriage. Karl Siegler, one of George's publishers, recalls that "she was constantly redecorating the house with William Morris [touches] and reflecting pools – top-quality stuff. It was one of her social showcases. George had a study right in the middle of that house. It was as messy and stacked up with stuff as the rest of the house was immaculate. Once, sitting in that study, I thought, 'This is a great visual metaphor of their relationship.'" The study had a window facing west onto Larch Street and Thea had a playroom across from it. In the seventies, before her dad started using a computer, the little girl enjoyed the tap-tap-tap-ding sound of him hitting typewriter keys and throwing the carriage. "You could hear it through the house."

She went to Quilchena Elementary School, across West and East Boulevards and up the hill. When she walked there, George followed at a discreet distance to make sure she arrived unharmed. Though an only child, Thea had lots of friends. At Quilchena, "not by design, a lot of the kids ended up in the arts. It was very tribe-like," she recalls. Aaron Chapman, later a writer and musician, was the boy next door. From his bedroom window, he could see George in his study, frequently hard at work.

The Kerrisdale house, built around 1915 on a sixty-four-foot-wide corner lot, was, with its dark wainscoting and walls lined with bookshelves, suited to dark imaginings. Thea's parents told her "stories of killers, thieves, and martyrs – a telltale heart, a snow queen, a little mermaid." Angela, who had a silvery voice, sang ballads with gruesome Gothic storylines. When Thea was about eight, her father introduced her to "Memory," a bloodcurdling poem by the Scottish-born San Francisco poet Helen Adam. In Thea's memory it's about "a tree that, basically, encourages this child's father to kill the mother, and then the child to kill the father." She lapped it up because, like many young readers of fairy tales, she was fascinated by the macabre. She has a clear memory of her dad sitting on a chair against the bathroom wall, reading "Memory" aloud as she sat in her bath. The water cooled, "but I wouldn't want to get out because I'd want to hear the whole story." The Bowerings did, though, realize that some tales are too scary, especially before bed. When four-year-old Thea sat before the TV, absorbed in the 1948 ballet movie *The Red Shoes*, Angela reminded

George that it "gets ghastly at the end," so maybe they should divert the little girl into doing something else.

Growing up, Thea sampled the pursuits generally offered to upper-middle-class Canadian girls. She became a Brownie and, later, a Girl Guide, going to Brownie meetings at St. Mary's Church across the street. She took gymnastics and figure skating and, eventually, riding lessons, which she liked best of all. After her dad put some of the prize money from his second Governor General's Award toward a baby grand piano for her in August 1981, she started learning to play. In a letter, he sighed, "Thea is playing Mozart on the piano. Who cd ask for anything more?" Her graduation from grade seven involved a potluck dinner with parents contributing dishes. Bowering made a giant bowl of guacamole and noted that "all the mothers and some fathers expostulated on how good it was, what varied talents I had."

The non-standard thing about her childhood was the large number of poetry readings she went to with her dad in bookstores and venues such as the Western Front artists' space. (Occasionally, they ran into Marilyn Bowering, the Vancouver Island poet and novelist. She and George may share some British ancestors but, if so, the link is a long way back. In the mid-eighties, Marilyn gave him a twig from Bourynge Wood in England's West Country.) Thea began to realize that going to readings was "part of being a generous writer"; it was important to be "seen in public spaces with other writers." She picked up behavioural cues from the adults. "You have to look deep in thought when you're listening to poetry," she says. "You have to gaze at the floor and nod your head. I saw a lot of that as a kid and I thought, 'That's what you do.'"

Books were a great source of entertainment and learning for Thea, as they were for both her parents. When she was Brownie-age, she read the Nancy Drew books (written by several authors under the pseudonym Carolyn Keene) and Enid Blyton's *The Mountain of Adventure* and related titles. Once, it took her a week to notice the TV was

"Dad was the fun guy," Thea Bowering says of the parent who took her out to the ball game.

broken. George wrote proudly to a friend, "She sits and reads all day long, reads while she is walking, reads at meals, reads late into the night and before breakfast." In her teen years, he left paperbacks he thought she'd enjoy in her room. The titles that spring to her mind are Ernest Hemingway's *The Nick Adams Stories* and Carson McCullers's *The Member of the Wedding*. When she was at university, her dad went out of his way to introduce her to the work of Montrealer Gail Scott and other women writers. He also arranged for her to have a year abroad at a European university, a life-changing experience he paid for using his advance for writing a history of British Columbia.

In the eighties, the family was part of a circle of friends who staged impromptu backyard productions of Shakespeare's *A Midsummer Night's Dream*. On the 1986 summer solstice, Thea played Puck. Karl Siegler remembers her standing, costumed, on a birdbath, speaking her lines from memory while the grown-up cast members read theirs from books. "It was a spectacular performance," he says. "She was the golden child; she was everybody's hope."

Among George's poems, often highly personal, is the lovely "Thea Bowering in Oliver," which appears in *Delayed Mercy and Other Poems* (1987) and *Urban Snow* (1992). It captures his feelings on seeing her scampering like "a brownish butterfly in the sun" through the landscape in which he'd grown up. In its last words – which may make some readers think of Anne Sexton's "Little Girl, My String Bean, My Lovely Woman" – he catalogues how he saw her: "A daughter, a metaphor, a sister to my first years."

When she was nineteen and no longer in need of his gamemaster antics or guacamole, he envied the dads he saw out walking with their little daughters. He wished it wasn't the case that Thea's childhood had gone by "in a wink, certainly a lot faster than my own."

Thea graduates from Simon Fraser University, making her faculty-member dad proud.

CHAPTER 12

MR. BASEBALL

A baseball park is supposed to be a refuge ... a place where time
and death and disease and duty are forgotten. It is the field for play,
a funny sort of place that is at once free from all the constrictions
and dangers of life, and bound perfectly to rules that we obey
though we know they dont matter.

—*Caprice* (1987, 2010)

People who do crossword puzzles will sometimes encounter a clue
like "Slaughter in the ballpark." If they are experienced solvers, they'll
know they're being prompted to fill four empty squares with the letters
E-N-O-S. That completes the name Enos Slaughter, which belonged
to an American Southerner who had a long career in Major League
Baseball in the mid-twentieth century.

As a lifelong word lover, Bowering likes nothing better than to
settle into a comfy chair with the clever clues of the Sunday *New
York Times* crossword and a pen with which to print the answers.
But his connection with an Enos clue is a lot tighter than the average
puzzler's. When he was a sports-crazy boy, he wrote a fan letter to
Enos Slaughter – and was thrilled when the St. Louis Cardinals' right
fielder sent back a handwritten letter and autographed photo.

George, who has a frighteningly large collection of ballcaps, has
taken delight in baseball since childhood. In Oliver, a mere twenty-four

kilometres north of the U.S. border and blessed with gorgeous summer weather, baseball was the most visible, most accessible sport for a middle-class family in the forties. Both of his parents played – they were catchers – and Ewart Bowering coached and sometimes umped.

A day doesn't go by without George thinking horsehide thoughts, whether it's how his fantasy baseball team is doing, or of major- or minor-league games he's seen, or how he performed as a softball player in parks across Vancouver in the seventies, eighties, and nineties, or of the well-timed *bons mots* with which he amused his teammates. He knows the rules of the game inside out. His recall of team rosters and players' stats, past and present, is encyclopedic. For decades, CBC producers asked for his thoughts on baseball. In September 1998 he had to tear himself away from the cheeky account of Canada's prime ministers he was writing because he'd agreed to opine – live, during a TV newscast – about Mark McGwire's attempt at a sixty-second home run. It may be a stretch to call him Canada's Roger Angell, but if you made that a crossword clue and provided eight squares for the answer, solvers might well give you "Bowering."

Explaining exactly why he loves baseball can be tricky; for George, it's simply part of the rhythm of life, tied in with the seasons. Opening day is "not only the proof of the end of winter ... but a defiance of the end of things," as he once wrote. A person survives life's vicissitudes knowing that "next spring the swing of a 35-ounce bat is going to flash with sunlight." During his many softball-playing years, he often felt as if a higher power were acting through him when he played well. "It's so nice to feel yourself being used" to pull off a particular feat, he said when he, his second wife Jean Baird, and I talked at their place in December 2012. When he plays, he senses something like a divine force in action, something that makes him think, "Oh, it's using me to make a double play, whatever 'it' is." (He has the same sensation when his writing is going well.) His *Baseball: A Poem in the Magic Number 9*, twice published as a pennant-shaped chapbook with a green felt cover, resounds with the jubilant declaration, "In the beginning was the word, & the word was 'Play Ball!'"

Early in 1970, George, fellow writer Brad Robinson, and a sculptor named Glen Toppings helped bring Vancouver's hippie-era Kosmic League into being. Spring was glorious that year, and so the three started playing impromptu games of catch outside Toppings's studio, near Granville Island. Eager to extend the idyll into whole games of softball, they called up the artists and poets they knew and recruited some players. Soon there were two teams of longhairs who preferred tie-dyed T-shirts to uniforms and loose-jointed fun to stiff competition: the Granville Grange Zephyrs, and Flex Morgan and the Mock Heroics. The artists among them used their grant-writing skills to wangle a Local Initiatives Program (LIP) grant for sports equipment and playing time in Vancouver's ballparks. By the end of the first season there were about sixteen teams in the league, including the East End Punks, the Afghani Oil Kings, the Flying Dildos, and the Teen Angels, a team of DJs and radio personalities whose star player was Terry David Mulligan. Brian Fawcett, who played for the Punks, has enumerated "a team of rock 'n' roll musicians, a team of political radicals, a team of motorcycle hoodlums, two teams made up of writers, painters, and serious musicians, a team of women, a gay team, a team of dope fiends," and one of undercover cops.

The original rules were: No spikes, no uniforms, nine innings, and nothing but fun allowed. But Gill Collins, who played for the women's team – Nine Easy Pieces – and then for the Zephyrs, says, "Even though it was not supposed to be competitive, it was serious ball." Bowering bestowed nicknames on players: "Leaky" for Fawcett, "Excruciating" for Gordon Payne, "Expressway" for Dwight Gardiner, and so on. He himself was called Whip, in ironic recognition of the quality of his throwing arm, though Collins remembers him being a sidearm thrower: "Throwing the ball to first base, he would sort of whip it."

The Granville Grange Zephyrs, full of beans in 1971. At the back: Brad Robinson, Glen Toppings, a non-member named Walter, George Bowering, Lionel Kearns. In the middle: Gary Lee-Nova, Gerry Nairn, Dwight Gardiner, Brian Fisher, Dennis Vance, Lanny Beckman. In the front: Liam and Frank Kearns.

In the Kosmic League, George was the Zephyrs' shortstop. He considered himself an infielder with a weak arm and so worked hard at getting the ball out of his glove quickly. In terms of his base running, as he writes in *A Magpie Life: Growing a Writer*, "I always did run the bases like a sewing machine." (As Fawcett puts it, using a different simile, he "runs like a duck.") Yet he was not without talent. Jim Allan, pitcher on a team called the Ball'd Egos, remembers his "good batting eye" and Marke Andrews, who pitched for the Diamond Dazzlers, seconds that: "[He was] a pretty good hitter."

Playing Kosmic ball meant taking pains not to be competitive. It was the seventies, so, as one baseball-loving writer has put it, "grass could be found in the dugout as well as on the field." Each team had "a trademark comestible or beverage," often brought out at a particular juncture. The Zeds (as the Zephyrs called themselves, in analogy to the

Oakland Athletics being the A's) sucked Popsicles in the fifth inning. The Punks eccentrically brought out little stone crocks of imported English cider. On New Year's Day 1972, Kosmic League teams played an all-star game, with a "day-glo painted softball," so it could be seen in the snow, and a bonfire and vat of mulled wine going, for warmth. These all-star games would become a tradition.

Antics and tomfoolery abounded in Kosmic League games. Beth Jankola, who watched part of the league's first – and last – championship tournament, wrote, addressing Bowering, in the *Georgia Straight*: "I saw you do incredible things, in the heat of excitement, I saw you rush over and kiss Brad when he had made a marvellous catch, I saw you goose Dazzy [Dennis] Vance just before he had to face an uptight pitching moment, and I also saw you zip your fly up and down a number of times when you were especially pleased with some Zephyr great play." George has said, though, that the amount of theatre depended on who was playing. "If we were playing a goof-off team with no real shot at the pennant, we would go heavy on the antics." So, try as they might, they didn't quite banish competition. Skill breeds ambition, Fawcett has written, and ambition leads to striving and vying.

George's mouth was his standout feature in the ballpark, and it's what he's remembered for. "He was an active vocal participant in the ball game," states Gill Collins, who won't use the word "heckler" because "we all did it." Maybe we can borrow a term from hockey and say he "chirped." Marke Andrews, then at the *Vancouver Sun*, says, "George was the constant mouthpiece, with that big booming voice." Jim Allan, then with Duthie Books, affirms that "he took joy in kibitzing ... If his bat or his glove didn't do the talking, then he could certainly do the talking." Allan remembers him taunting pitchers by calling them Dogbreath and once memorably denouncing a male player: He called him a peckerhead for running right into a small woman who was playing first base. "It stuck amongst the whole league, and even [the man's] teammates started calling him that."

The Kosmic League dissolved in the mid-seventies, having expanded too fast and strayed from its peace-love-and-revolution roots. But while it was going, Bowering salted his diary with details of how he played. In spring 1975, when he was thirty-nine, he wrote, "Played third base for Afghani Oil Kings against Bum Biters today ... I missed a foul ball, but did some neat running & a pickoff. At bat I walkt twice, then flied to center & singled to left." A few weeks later, he couldn't resist recording that he'd "hit a solo homer over left field, popt to second, hit a 2-run homer over left, and then hit a grand slam homer over left, my greatest day in softball."

In the mid-eighties, newsman Marke Andrews organized a softball league for Vancouver wordsmiths, this one smaller and less outré. The Twilight League, so called because of its large contingent of middle-aged players, was "a super-friendly league, a very literary league," says Andrews, who pitched for a team called the Bat People. Jim Allan, by then working for the Granville Book Company, ran the Paperbacks, a team that George – who'd gone a decade without playing regularly – was delighted to join. He played third, first, and sometimes second base. As time passed and infirmities accumulated, the Paperbacks started thinking of themselves as the Bad Backs. The league's other original teams were the Friendly Club, with art-world figures like Grant Arnold, Reid Shier, and Stan Douglas (who's famous now) as members, and the Write Sox, a team loaded with freelance writers. (The Backs thought of them as the Soreheads.) By the early 2000s there were seven teams – including the Secret Nine and a music-industry team, Zulu – and about seventy players.

George, who'd considered red-bearded Glen Toppings insanely old for playing Kosmic ball in his forties, was entering his fifties. His reflexes were slowing but he was hopeful he could compensate. "In recent games I have been proving that you dont have to be fast on the basepaths, if you are smart," he wrote in his diary in May 1988. By then, though, he'd sustained at least one spectacular injury. In late

August 1987, while playing second base, he got hit in the right eye by a powerful low line drive. His glasses broke, blood streamed down his face and, as an unbylined *Sun* story (surely written by Andrews or his colleague John Mackie, one of the league's first members) put it, he spent "the rest of the afternoon being treated for a shattered cheekbone." Describing a baseball accident that temporarily blinded him, George told *Vancouver* magazine that the game mattered more to him than eyesight. Earlier, he'd written in a letter to his mother, "Got hit in the mouth twice and [on the] back once. It is worth it. One hobbles with pride." The pounding his body took when he was one of the superannuated boys of summer horrified Angela, and it angered her to see him take pride in his injuries.

Still, even late in his career on city sandlots, his playing could occasionally be stellar. Jim Allan remembers a moment when "there was a runner on first base and a really hard grounder to him. He took it and backhanded it, underhand, to second base. It was so elegant, like he'd been doing it eight hours a day, every day, his whole life." Allan also savoured the physical comedy Bowering brought to the park. He'd imitate Pete Rose's hunched batting stance one moment and Kevin Youkilis's madly high elbows the next. (The genius of his mimicry was lost on those who didn't watch Major League ball.) And George and Jim shared the pleasure of having their daughters, Thea and Natasha, with them on the diamond from time to time. Jim loved it when he was on the mound, got a strikeout, and heard Natasha call out, using scorers' jargon, "Nice K, Dad!" And George was proud when Thea showed her flair for comedy by heckling him, a sixtyish guy in shorts, with the immortal line, "Are those your legs, or are you riding a chicken?"

His own witticisms ring out most loudly when he's a specta-tor. In the 1980s and '90s, when the Vancouver Canadians were a Triple-A team, he'd sit in Nat Bailey Stadium's "famous Section 9" with friends like Fawcett, Paul "Popcorn" Naylor, and Michael "Fast

Eddie" Barnholden. He has the kind of voice that really carries. Marke Andrews, who's been at the Nat, sitting some distance from him, says, "He'd time it just so there's a lull, and then he'd come out with something, and *I* would hear him, three sections away."

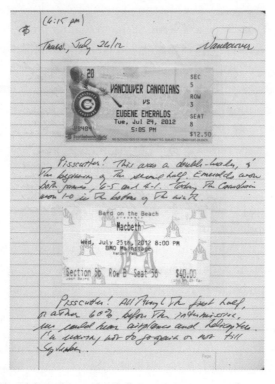

Although he no longer plays ball, Bowering continues to be an opinionated, vocal spectator.

One of the things he's been known to yell at players he considers overpaid is "Do something, millionaire!" But some of his chatter might strike non-sports fans as juvenile. He used to taunt Brad Lesley, a player nicknamed The Animal, by chanting, "We want The Vegetable!" He's been known to tease Latino ballplayers by calling them "Wally," and non-Latinos by calling them "Pepe," taking delight in doing the opposite of what folks might expect. Fawcett says time has softened the sting in his old friend's catcalls: "He's a little sweeter now." It's easy to tell if he's at the park, though. When he's in full rhetorical flight, his contributions are so frequent and distinctive that they led the Canadians to name him their Official Loudmouth Fan.

Nat Bailey Stadium has honoured him by displaying *Word Bird*, Jennifer Ettinger's two-metre-high sculpture of an eagle, wearing Bowering's glasses and ring, with his poem *Baseball* printed on it. In its last stanza, he aphoristically insists that baseball is not a diversion of the intelligence. Rather, "a man breathes differently after rounding the bag."

CHAPTER 13

THE TRICKSTER, THE FUNSTER

In E.J. Pratt's "Towards the Last Spike," what did the railroad builders have in their blood?

- a. Granite
- b. Whiskey
- c. Porridge
- d. Ham & eggs

Answer: c. Pratt doesn't say whether they injected it or took it orally.

—"A TransCanada Poetry Quiz with No Questions about Snow," *Another Mouth* (1979)

George Bowering was not the first Canadian writer to use pseudonyms. In the early twentieth century, Archibald Belaney perpetrated a literary hoax by living and writing as Grey Owl, claiming he was Métis. The Quebec writer John Glassco, who was deliciously eccentric, used the pseudonyms Miles Underwood and George Coleman for his erotica. Raymond Souster, a Toronto poet and publisher who worked at the Canadian Imperial Bank of Commerce, used his middle name, Holmes, in pennames for his novels. Earle Birney, the B.C.

poet who set up the first creative writing department at a Canadian university (UBC), employed such pseudonyms as Earle Binning, B.C. Birney, Earle Robertson, and Henry Scott Beattie. George Woodcock, the staggeringly prolific Vancouverite who was editor of the journal *Canadian Literature* from 1959 to 1977, sometimes appeared in print as Anthony Appenzell.

Bowering, often called a trickster, had several literary aliases that fooled people, at least for a while. When he was a grad student at the University of British Columbia, he slapped a Teutonic penname onto mischievous letters he sent to the *Ubyssey*. He has always been left-wing, but his letters as Helmut Franz were reactionary. He hoped to agitate students and spur them to respond indignantly. That's clear in his first Helmut Franz letter, of March 1962, which began, "I am sure I am speaking for a majority of students when I say that your recognition of the Players Club play, *The Afrikaaner*, was indefensible. If the government and the people of South Africa can be so slandered without any check by responsible people on this campus, then this country is heading toward a gloomy future." His best buddy, Will Thornton-Trump, says, "He was testing the waters to see how much right-wingism there might be at UBC." Not much, it turned out. Many students whose feathers he'd ruffled wrote in.

As a young professor in Montreal in 1968, he came up with a Jewish penname, Eytan Edwin (or E.E.) Greengrass. He'd filched the last name from Jim Greengrass, a National League ballplayer in the fifties. He'd borrowed the distinctive first name from a college student who'd stayed with him and Angela for half a year or so due to problems at home. George didn't have the initials in the name e.e. cummings in mind but, rather, the medical term "EEG," which he'd seen on boxes in the former laboratory at UBC where he and his friends put *TISH* together.

George used "E.E. Greengrass" in the journals *Open Letter* and *Canadian Literature*, which published him so often that he needed a secondary handle to keep the primary one from becoming *de trop*. Greengrass's writing also went to journals in smaller cities, like *Floorboards* in Fredericton and *Salt* in Moose Jaw. And Greengrass sent work that differed from his inventor's then-current approach – for example, lyric poems after George had said he was done with lyrics – to big-name literary magazines like *Descant* (Toronto), *Grain* (Saskatoon), and the *Antigonish* [Nova Scotia] *Review*. The literary career of E.E. Greengrass continued until the year 2000.

In 1971, when the Kosmic League formed in Vancouver and George started playing softball as one of its Granville Grange Zephyrs, the *Georgia Straight* printed his lively reports on the games. Since he couldn't resist mentioning his own performance – once telling of G. Bowering's "four hits, including a titanic triple, and many runs batted in" – he badly needed an alias. Thinking of Eric Whitehead, a sportswriter at the *Province*, he fashioned one: "Erich Blackhead." This imaginary jock occasionally showed a literary side in the *Straight*, reviewing books by Bowering's pet writers, such as Robert Creeley.

Subsequent pennames riffed on the E.E. Greengrass formula: a first name beginning with E and a last name signifying an expanse of lawn. Translating Greengrass into Italian, he got *prato verde* – literally, "green lawn." Edward Pratoverde came into being around 1968. Bowering scored a coup in 1977 when he answered a call for submissions to an anthology of poems by Italian Canadians and, as Edward Pratoverde, mailed half a dozen poems to the editor, Pier Giorgio Di Cicco (later Toronto's poet laureate). In the cover letter, Pratoverde disingenuously said he'd decided to "drop that dumb pen name, and go with my real name, Ed Prato." Di Cicco's elegantly named *Roman Candles* anthology came out the following year and contained two of Prato's poems, "Immigrant" and "Maple." The contributor bio George provided said Prato had been born in Trieste, tossing a hint to readers who might recognize the trickster's favourite city. (Eventually, the truth emerged. Philip Marchand mentioned the deception in his *Toronto Star* column on April 5, 1990; George doesn't know if, or when, Di Cicco found out.) A few years later, Ed Prato reviewed books by Margaret Atwood, Patrick Lane, and Michael Ondaatje in Canadian literary journals. And in the early 1980s, Bowering-as-Prato sent in solutions to several of the CanWit puzzles in *Books in Canada*. George's 1985 book of political poems, *Seventy-One Poems for People*, ends with thirteen by Prato.

Ellen Field, a penname he had fun with in the nineties, was a fan of the poet bpNichol (who had died in 1988, a crushing loss); she was also a feminist who adored word play. The twenty-six poems in her "A, You're Adorable" suite engage with each letter of the alphabet in turn. Ontario's rob mclennan published it as an above/ground press chapbook in 1998. In 2004, when he'd become aware of who Ellen Field was, he brought out a second, larger edition. These poems also appear in Bowering's 2006 book, *Vermeer's Light*.

This trickster has palmed himself off as Helmut Franz, Erich Blackhead,
E.E. Greengrass, Edward Pratoverde, and Ellen Field.

George's foolery has taken other forms, too. People visiting his website, georgebowering.com, will find a non-existent book under "Writings, Fiction, Novels." *Fiddler's Night* isn't one of his hundred-plus titles. The tipoffs are the name of the publisher – Dos Equis – and the fact that there's no "Buy now" link to click on.

Over the years, plenty of readers have found his jokes and games tedious. In 1987, Fraser Sutherland bridled at the "all-pervasive jokey knowingness" and "in-group chumminess" of his *Delayed Mercy and Other Poems*. And Alan Twigg, interviewing him that same year, told him, "I don't hate any of your stories. It's just that sometimes it's irritating to feel this clever guy is so confident about whatever is coming into his head that he won't go back and make it any easier for someone to get a hold of." Yet his cleverness and playfulness don't put everyone off. Perhaps the most flattering use of the word "trickster," in describing him, came from Peter and Meredith Quartermain. In a reference-book profile, they call him a trickster who "uses his considerable wit and restless energy to deflate the pompous, to unsettle the satisfied, to unsettle those whose view of the world rests on such ordered categories as fact and fiction, prose and poetry, real and imaginary ... His writing deliberately looks careless, empty, undisciplined ... It is not."

Readers looking for sustained belly laughs should pick up "The Ryerson Split" in *The Rain Barrel and Other Stories*, one of Bowering's eight short-fiction collections. The story, only lightly fictionalized, lays out the circumstances that led to his humiliating premature exit from a long-ago literary party. It was 1966, he was thirty, and artsy types had been summoned to a Toronto hotel to celebrate the launch of an anthology called *Modern Canadian Stories*. He'd been invited because he had a story in it. Naturally, he was flattered.

As he entered the reception room, he spotted Phyllis Webb and Earle Birney, writers he knew. He also recognized two of the book's older contributors, Morley Callaghan and Hugh Garner. The editors of the anthology, Giose Rimanelli and Roberto Ruberto, were present, too, "being extremely Italian in their suits." Before much had had a chance to happen, George, holding a plate of canapés (courtesy of Ryerson Press), bent down to pick up a dropped napkin. His tight trousers split down the back. Birney, thirty years his senior, offered a spare pair of *his* pants, but the idea didn't appeal: "What would Earle's probably baggy pants with short legs look like?" George felt he had no choice but to back out the nearest door, forfeiting his chance at a media interview. As he retreated toward London, Ontario, where he was then living, a clang from his 1954 Chevrolet told him something had gone horribly wrong with the car. When he got to a garage, he found out he'd thrown a rod. Dryly, he writes, "I did not then nor do I now know what that means."

In "Being Audited," another *Rain Barrel* piece recounting real events, George writes comically about his and Angela's go-round with Revenue Canada when they tried to write off expenses associated with his writing career in the early eighties. An accountant named Garry used to do their taxes; they saved receipts for him. Around that time, the tax department seemed to be taking an extra-hard look at people who gave their occupation as "writer" when they filed. The story includes a few details about the marriage: Angela (simply called "my wife") was the astute money manager, he the spouse who sat at an IBM Selectric generating future income with his mind and fingers.

In the story, the narrator chats with his muse, she noticing improvements to the couple's house and complaining, "I've been wearing this same diaphanous gown since I helped Percy Shelley write *Prometheus Unbound*." He also relates how he and Angela had had urea formaldehyde foam insulation pumped into their house and, a few years later, when it was found to be a health hazard, removed – a costly real-life fiasco. The biggest laugh comes midway through, in an indented passage: "Astute, college-educated readers will have arrived at the opinion by now that the use of the house is symbolic, either of the house of fiction, in Jamesian terms, or as the psyche's image of self in the Freudian sense. That is no lasting comfort to the writer, who has to live somewhere."

"Staircase Descended," also in *The Rain Barrel*, is more of a made-up tale but there's a kernel of emotional truth in it. An unnamed middle-aged man narrates, describing in elaborate detail how much trouble he has getting out of bed in the morning, due to a back problem. In agony, he crawls to the toilet and kneels to pee because he can't yet stand up. Then the narrator addresses the reader. Having stretched his description of temporary morning paralysis over twelve paragraphs, he doubts the reader has stayed with him. "If you have, please sign your initials right here," he asks, at which point there's a little space.

His body finally co-operating, the narrator shuffles downstairs, clad in a tatty bathrobe. His wife and a neighbour are at the kitchen table, chatting over coffee. The neighbour is prettier, the wife smarter, we're told. They don't see him. It's not that they don't *seem* to see him; they really don't see him. To verify this, he lifts the hem of his robe and does a little dance, cutting a scarecrow-like figure with bony legs and swinging genitals. When this elicits no reaction, he dresses and goes up the street to a luncheonette he frequents. He asks an old gent at a table to look him in the eye and confirm that he exists. The fellow obliges. Even so, the narrator has begun to wonder. At the story's end, he asks, "Did I just imagine being downstairs and dancing? Am I not now sitting on a reddish banquette at Daphne's, thinking of my hard bed as down that street, up those stairs? Is there anyone reading or hearing this?" And so a drawn-out comic story ends on a plaintive existential note.

In 1992, Thea, then twenty, wrote her own story in response. "Staircase Descended Again" appeared in one of her college's student publications. Reprising the action in her dad's story, she took umbrage at a man judging his wife less pretty than a neighbour. She also undermined the sympathy a reader might feel for her dad's befuddled narrator by describing the two women at the kitchen table as "his lover and his wife." Bowering's reaction was one of unalloyed pleasure at his story having inspired her to write one.

Standing on Richards, a collection of George's stories published in 2004, opens with the title story, which is set in downtown Vancouver on a street that was a sex workers' stroll for years. The narrator, a tweedy aesthete named Aubrey, has taken early retirement from teaching literature at "the university on the hill" (the students' lack of interest finally got to him) and has decided to sell his mind on Richards Street. He'll set himself up on a corner with a stack of books and, for a price, provide the intellectually hungry with learned conversation. Since he's not about to pose in spike heels like the well-educated sex worker nearby, he strives for a masculine equivalent, "fiddling with my old brier and looking over the top of my glasses." A guy cruising by is curious. He opens his car's passenger door, Aubrey tumbles in, and they negotiate a price of fifty dollars for an hour of cultured talk. Aubrey launches into a disquisition on a long-past European war, and the john calls him a "mind whore," proceeding to speak quite well on the difference between mind and brain. It's an appealing, funny story, though the ending is flippant: The john asks for a kiss and Aubrey, thinking, "What the hell?," gives him one.

"The Lawnmower," one of Bowering's earliest stories, is darkly foreboding and comic at the same time. Leonard Stride gets up one Saturday morning, reads the newspaper, and starts watching sports on TV. As the day passes he's assailed by ads for a powerful lawnmower. The entreaties intensify: A handwritten threat is slipped under his door; a rock with a note tied to it comes through the window; he picks up the phone to hear a man with a European accent say, "You got just ten minutes to buy a Super-Mower, you bastard. And then we're going to beat the living piss out of you." When two thugs show up at his door to carry out the threat, he caves. He hadn't been that averse to getting a new lawnmower, anyway.

TEETH
POEMS 2006-2011

GEORGE BOWERING

A twenty-first-century collection that, says its author, is "certainly supposed to be amusing."

Occasionally, Bowering is funny in poems. "Van, Can," from 1999, pokes fun at British Columbians for having soft lives. With a nod to T.S. Eliot, it begins,

> Sometimes in mid-April we fill our hot-tubs
> with Perrier water, we are so pacific, west
> coasting through spring, casting not a thought
> to our poor cousins in Toronto, slogging
>
> through dirty snow ...

"Van, Can" is what he's been known to call "magazine verse." To him it's "not a throwaway poem but kind of an outside-the-canon thing." As he's grown older, he's felt freer to lark about in verse, tweaking Emily Dickinson's nose and aping Edward Lear. His "'Workshop' Assignment Poem," from a recent collection, begins:

> *Because I could not stop for lunch*
> *my stomach went insane.*
> *It gave my liver one good punch.*
> *It squeezed my kidneys in a bunch.*
> *I have a hunch that I should munch*
> *my breakfast once again.*

Nonsense runs riot in its third stanza:

> *There was a lightbulb up my nose*
> *the night my brain went south,*
> *I should have laundered all my clothes*
> *and then dry-cleaned my mouth.*

In his late-life poetry, though, this friskiness sometimes collides with his sense of time running out. His short, bouncy poem "Epitaphs" begins:

> *Here lies George Bowering.*
> *He could have done better.*

CHAPTER 14

THE SUCCESS

As I watch you walk,
                        your white dress
falling around your thighs in the starlight,
I love you for everybody you have been.

—"Elegy Three," *Kerrisdale Elegies* (1984)

Kerrisdale Elegies, full of passages of surpassing loveliness, is George Bowering's most radiant long poem. He composed it by taking a major work of European literature published between the world wars – the *Duino Elegies*, by Rainer Maria Rilke – and, using his imagination and the personal history he calls his biotext, transmuting it for a different time and place. "An awful lot of my writing is about previous writing, in one way or another," he says; in 2011's *How I Wrote Certain of My Books*, he writes that he has successfully "collaborat[ed] with dead poets," including Milton, Shelley, and Yeats. Published in 1984, *Kerrisdale Elegies* has been aptly described as a "mind-meld between Rilke and Bowering."

Rilke was on Bowering's radar because there was a vogue for the Czech-born, ethnically German lover of Paris in North American poetry circles in the sixties, seventies, and eighties. The *Duino Elegies* also inform the Torontonian Dennis Lee's soul-searching work, *Civil Elegies*. In Vancouver, Karl Siegler translated Rilke, while Robin Blaser taught his work. Jack Spicer had talked to Vancouver's young poets about Rilke at the home of Warren and Ellen Tallman in June 1965.

Spicer believed the universe sometimes sends a poet an opening line, and Rilke had famously had that experience composing the *Duino Elegies* – he "almost felt that he had no part in [his elegies'] creation," as C.M. Bowra wrote in *The Heritage of Symbolism*. On a stormy evening in 1912, as Rilke paced the cliff outside Duino Castle, near Trieste, the wind seemed to carry the first words of the book to him. "Who, if I cried, would hear me among the angelic orders?" is how the J.B. Leishman / Stephen Spender translation renders them. Another, by Martyn Crucefix, reads, "Who, if I cried out, would hear me among the ranks of the angels?"

Kerrisdale Elegies begins colloquially: "If I did complain, who among my friends would hear?" As the poet Stephen Collis says, "It's a cardinal sin in poetry: You never paraphrase [another writer]. And he did an entire book of it, and it's his most beautiful book." For Bowering to drop an upscale Vancouver suburb, known for its clipped lawns and parked Volvos, into a poem sequence shot through with cosmic melancholy creates a jarring effect. "Everybody's got this built-in feeling about Kerrisdale – I mean, that's a joke, right?" he has said. The words "Kerrisdale" and "elegies" don't quite go together.

The *Duino Elegies* are ten philosophical meditations on the spiritual crises of modern life. They speak of "a world after God, after catastrophe, and after any sense of coherent wholeness has been lost." There are correspondences between their wording and that in Bowering's book, but *Kerrisdale Elegies* is neither rip-off nor knock-off. As the Toronto poet Victor Coleman says, "I'd defy anybody who likes to read any kind of literature to read *Kerrisdale* and not be impressed by how solid a book of poetry it is."

Originally, George thought of doing an approximate translation of *Duino* – approximate since he doesn't know German. Writing in longhand, he tried this in March 1982 while on a reading tour in the Southwestern U.S. Then, on a plane to Albuquerque, he decided to scratch out whatever he'd written that he didn't like. "When I got to New Mexico, I had scratched out the whole page, every word ... So I dropped the idea of a guesswork translation and started translating with the help of a number of English translations, and kept my mind clean by reading French poetry as I went along."

Kerrisdale Elegies are meditations on "the strangeness of coming into the world," its loveliness, "and the sadness of leaving it," according to the first edition's back cover. In places, Bowering deftly strengthens the structure Rilke built. Where Rilke writes in his Fourth Elegy about death being part of life, even in childhood, Bowering succinctly (and chillingly) says that a child "carries his shroud with him on the first day of school." He also puts biotext in his Elegy Four, recounting how, when he sat in a pew at his father's funeral (in March 1974), holding his mother's and sister's hands, he thought he heard his dad saying, "It's all right." For Rilke, angels – not Christian angels but starry presences that move between life and death – are present in such moments.

In Rilke's Fifth Elegy, travelling acrobats perform on a carpet they have spread out, spectators encircling it like flowers dropping pollen. (The acrobats Rilke was picturing were the ones in *La famille de saltimbanques*, the famous 1905 Picasso painting.) Elegy Five in the *Kerrisdale* book finds the poet at a baseball game. The athletes run, bend, leap, and "fall to the patchy green carpet" while "[t]he crowd opens, rises like a row of poppies, and subsides, scattering peanut shells like petals." This is in keeping with the Rilke text: Bowering managed to substitute ballplayers for acrobats without losing the elegy's world-weary tone.

Reading the two books side by side reveals not only the correspondences and divergences but also the imitator's consummate skill.

Some brilliant passages are Bowering's own but convey Rilke's awe. In his Elegy Two, he writes,

> God, should he choose,
>
>   can press us into
> sausage patties,
>   he can flatten a car,
> furl up a street,
>   tuck us into our own shoes.

The Toronto novelist Marian Engel – no baseball fan (and, until then, not a huge Bowering fan, either) – marvelled at how George succeeded in capturing the European writer's magical tone. In a review, she wrote that he had "poured all his considerable power into one vessel" and that "he must be read." The book came out on January 3, 1984; by February 26, George was writing in his diary, "I am getting lots of favourable feedback on *Kerrisdale Elegies*, I mean like praise, from people I usually don't hear from, even …"

The original *Kerrisdale* had a stern-looking close-up photo of him on the front. On the back, a blurb from Robert Kroetsch said that Bowering "speaks to the presence of Rilke." One reviewer thought it would have been fairer to readers if the connection between the two sets of elegies had been made clearer. So, on the 2008 reissue from Talonbooks, the front-cover art is split, with ancient, brooding Duino Castle on top and a calm Kerrisdale street scene below. The back-cover copy says the book is "George Bowering's brilliant response to Rilke's call," his elegies "a living, vibrant transformation of the work."

There is almost universal agreement that *Kerrisdale Elegies* is George Bowering's finest writing. It's such a triumph that whatever he published next was bound to suffer in comparison. He would acknowledge this, reflecting that *Kerrisdale*'s success had "put my more recent poetry into a shade."

Praise for Bowering's *Kerrisdale Elegies* came from all over. Annalisa Goldoni's Italian translation appeared in 1996.

In his *Delayed Mercy and Other Poems*, published at the beginning of 1987, there are forty-nine "late-night poems" he wrote after waking himself up at 2 a.m. He wanted to see how his sleepy mind would perform. Another thing he did was start each poem with a line he'd read in someone else's work that day. The borrowed lines came from Canadian poets like Christopher Dewdney and from others such as Herman Melville, Samuel Beckett, and Amiri Baraka. Bowering calls such schemes "baffles," finding it freeing to work within self-applied rules. The idea comes from Oulipo (short for *Ouvroir de littérature potentielle*, literally "Workshop of potential literature"), a literary movement launched in France in 1960. Raymond Queneau, a writer fascinated by science, and François Le Lionnais, a scientist fascinated by writing, were the instigators. They wanted to "investigate the possibilities of applying mathematical structures to literary creations." Georges Perec, who joined in 1967, said, "I set myself rules in order to be totally free." Perec wrote his Oulipian novel, *La disparition* ("The disappearance"), without using the letter *E* – a feat Bowering greatly admires. Coach House, which published *Delayed Mercy*, didn't explain how the late-night poems had come to be – the thinking was that if readers couldn't understand the book, they should just work harder at figuring it out.

In September 1988, Angela came to the park where George was playing softball and told him that their friend bpNichol, the wildly original Toronto poet, had died. Nichol had complained of back and leg pain for years, but somehow a tumour growing around his spine had escaped detection, and he'd died during surgery. "Of all the people in the writing world," George thought, "this is the last person we would want to go." The losses in his world were piling up: Red Lane had died in 1964; Ewart Bowering ten years later. George crumpled with each hit. Sorrow seeped into his soul and, as Margaret Atwood has observed, he became "mellower, sadder, more available in his writing." It's little wonder that death pervades his serious poetry. He has said, if only to himself, "My short poems are few, and a good thing, because they are all about death."

McClelland & Stewart had served up *Touch*, a selection of his early poems, in 1971. *The Catch*, which it published in 1976, contained new poems and some from earlier books. Two subsequent selected-poems volumes attest to his well-rounded success as a poet. *Selected Poems: Particular Accidents* (1980) draws from twenty-nine books of his poetry spanning the years 1961 to 1978. In the introduction, "George Bowering's Plain Song," editor Robin Blaser praises the naturalness of his style and the seriousness of his intent. He also quotes a now-famous thing George had said the year before: When asked which poetic tradition he was dedicated to, he'd answered that he "wouldn't want to shame the language. That sounds very pretentious but it's true." Pauline Butling thinks Blaser may have been the first scholar to take George's work that seriously. She says he gives "a really thoughtful, careful, really serious reading of George" in "Plain Song." The first time she read it, she thought, "Wow!"

George Bowering Selected: Poems, 1961–1992, from McClelland & Stewart in 1993, is a generous showcase. Roy Miki, its editor, included two serial poems inspired by John Keats. In "Irritable Reaching," George pays tribute to Canadian writers and artists. The individual poems are acrostics, so you read the lines' first letters to see which person is being praised. And "Do Sink" is a set of fourteen sonnets beginning and ending with the first and last words of Keats's "When I Have Fears That I May Cease to Be." (The first words are those of the title; the last are "Till love and pain to nothingness do sink.") Relatively recently, Bowering explained that he let Keats "and his concerns and his era, his poem composed in 1817," influence his diction and rhyming. Still, Bowering's biotext is what leaps out. "Do Sink" is a melancholy poem that shows him driving solo through empty countryside in search of his maternal grandmother's grave. He writes,

> *I'm driving this black sedan*
> *too swiftly over rutted prairie roads*
> *and think that I may never live to trace*
> *my DNA another generation*
> *down the route of fate …*

At the end of the book, Miki says in an essay that, rather than hone and polish one style of writing, his friend and colleague Bowering has expanded the boundaries of his poetic vision. He moved from single lyric poems to the extended form, and in his long poems "the limits are set in advance – rigorous limits that cannot be willed away by the poetic self – so that the writing is enacted in and against those limits …"

What some people call "limits" George calls "baffles," and these Oulipian constraints shaped his big, bold serial poem, *My Darling Nellie Grey*. Published in 2010, when he was in his seventies, and named after a song his father used to sing, it began with his New

Year's resolution to write a poem every day of 2006. He also decided he'd set fresh rules for his writing process each month. The thirty-poem section he wrote in April is composed of American-themed sonnets. In "Some Answers," written in June, each day's poem starts with an italicized quotation – a question a poet once posed, like "Did he who made the lamb make thee?" (Blake) and "Shall I part my hair behind?" (Eliot). He gives answers, some of them flippant. The thirty-one-section poem he wrote in August responds to works of art, the individual poems opening with such lines as "According to Caravaggio," "According to Krieghoff," and "According to Chagall."

Sharon Thesen, who considers *Nellie Grey* "one of the most astounding works of Canadian poetry ever published," says Bowering performs his self-set tasks in a "very friendly, witty manner ... with a bit of nudge-nudge, wink-wink off every page."

In 1986, Bowering and his Alberta writer friend Robert Kroetsch, centre, gave readings in Australia. In Geelong, near Melbourne, their host was a fellow writer, Brian Edwards, left.

CHAPTER 15

THE FRIEND

I met him in the Fifties, when all the famous people
had his initials – Mickey Mantle, Marilyn Monroe, Mary
Martin, Mickey Mouse.

We mailed each other letters every week, complaining
about the latest communication devices.

At university he was famous for his barbaric yawp,
and so was Walt Whitman, who had his initials upside down.

—"Magic Mitt," *The World, I Guess* (2015)

Will Thornton-Trump has been Bowering's closest friend since they
met as kids in the mid-forties in Oliver. "That system is hermetic,
sealed from the inside," declares the Toronto writer Brian Fawcett,
another close friend, though not for as many years. "Everyone's an
outsider" to the Bowering–Thornton-Trump alliance, says Fawcett,
adding, "That relationship is so old, it's got its own code."

Soon after George and Will met, they started a club with just the
two of them as members. George, being older, awarded himself the
deciding vote. Will says, "I used to try to propose other members
because I would have liked to be able to outvote him, but he would
put it to a vote and it would be voted down. 'Majority rules' and he's

older, that was his argument." That this inequity still mildly rankles show how the distant past lives on for them, imbued with a mythic quality. In the club, Will addressed George as "Cap'n." His friend would "pretend he was teaching me all about life, and I'd say, 'Is that right, Cap'n?' and sort of go along with it. I tell him sometimes that I'm the world's greatest straight man. I'll do it even at the cost of my own ego because it'll be funny."

Will Thornton-Trump is Bowering's best friend and straight man.

At school, George's classmates considered Will an uncool sort of side-kick, since he was younger, but George didn't care. Their friendship endured. Because of George's Air Force stint, Will graduated from UBC earlier and went off to study in Japan. In the early sixties, George trumpeted his buddy's exotic adventures in the *Oliver Chronicle*. The headline on those columns was "Bill Trump in Japan."

In the eighties, when retinitis pigmentosa had wrecked Will's eyesight, causing him to take early retirement from teaching high-school French, they started going out for lunch regularly. George dubbed the sessions Great Breakfast All Day. I joined them once, at Vancouver's Argo Cafe, a spot that boasts of serving "downtown food at an East Van price." When a server brought their lunches, she gave Will a spoon for his beef goulash, knowing he has a blind man's horror of dribbling sauce down his shirtfront. "Look!" George cried. "My friend's eating his dinner with a spoon. Aw! I did that, too – when I was one and a half!" It sounds childish and mean, but Thornton-Trump knows his friend too well to take offence; once, when Will had sent out a group email saying he'd broken his foot by accidentally stepping in a hole, everyone replied sympathetically but George, who shot back, "Hey, Clumsy!"

During Great Breakfast All Day, or GBAD, Will presents a list of droll observations he's compiled since he and George last met. Will uses a recording device to save and retrieve them. The day I was there, he mentioned a graphic on a TV newscast that had said a piece of legislation needed "royal ascent," instead of "assent." (His sighted wife had spotted that.) And he posed this puzzler: "Why is your sternum at the front of your body" when "sternum" suggests rear placement? At GBAD, still going strong after thirty years, it's traditional for George to say, "Willy, you got off easy," when his old pal finishes presenting his list.

As kids, Bowering and Thornton-Trump cracked up when they saw that Will's dad's name on an advertising sign – W.E. Trump – could be read as "wet rump," and they continue to revel in wordplay in their old age. What's unusual, though, is the ritual nature of their meetings and the expectation that guests will be somewhat familiar with the drill, as if attending a Passover Seder or Japanese tea ceremony for the first time.

📖

Bowering's friendship with Brian Fawcett began memorably in 1968. Fawcett, who was in his twenties, went to a reading that George, nine years older and living in Montreal, gave in Vancouver. He brought a brick with him. "I just sat there, all through the reading," he recalls,

"throwing it up and catching it." Fawcett, who would become a provocative, versatile writer, knew that what he was doing was "fairly
ridiculous adolescent theatre," but he meant it as a joke, and Bowering
got it. "I mean, George was a south Okanagan kid and I was from
northern B.C.," Fawcett says – they were supposed to be tougher
than the big-city poets. With that act, their long friendship was born.

Lionel Kearns is a friend from earlier in the sixties. Kearns was
an aspiring poet who worked hard at his writing and impressed his
professors at UBC, especially Earle Birney. He, George, and Will met
in Spanish class. In February 1961, Kearns and his first wife were living
in married students' housing on campus while George was dating Joan
Huberman. She was twenty and had also been seeing a man in his
thirties who worked at the CBC. One rainy night, George got jealous,
imagining them having sex. He made a desperate move. "I got a late-
night call from Joan," Kearns recalled years later. "She said, 'George is
going to jump off the bridge! You've got to do something.' It was one
of those terrible Vancouver nights, gloomy and wet enough to make
anybody want to jump off a bridge. I jumped into my little Morris
Minor and headed for the nearest bridge to see if I could find him. It
was raining hard. About a third of the way across the Burrard Street
Bridge, there was this lonely, hunched-over figure. I jumped out of
the car and grabbed him, opened the passenger door, and threw him
in. He said nothing. Back at our house, we stripped off his wet clothes
and poured warm soup into him. He was still not talking. We put him
to bed. Next morning, he was himself."

George and Lionel would each dedicate an early book of poems to
the other, and there's a poem about the two of them in George's *Rocky
Mountain Foot*. "The White Station Wagon Strophes" tells of a road
trip they took through the Rockies, at one point cooking enchiladas
"in a can on the manifold."

In 1970, George helped one of his friends in a major way, not pull-
ing him off a bridge but throwing him a financial lifeline: He helped

John Newlove get a job as an editor with McClelland & Stewart in Toronto. Saskatchewan-born Newlove was a fine poet, admired by his peers, but after his books had been appearing for a decade to reviews he considered lukewarm, he'd reached the conclusion that "[t]here is no interest whatsoever in my poetry. Period." He was tired of living from hand to mouth, too. As Bowering would recollect years later, "People were worried about him, partly from reading what he was saying in the poems, partly [from knowing he] was [living] on one potato a day."

In those distant days, the letters they wrote each other had an antic tone – "Dear Glowering," "Dear Newfuck" – but George, literary star on the rise, was suddenly able to help his struggling friend. From Montreal, where he then lived, he said in a letter, "I was talking to [M&S publisher] Jack McClelland in his fancy hotel room the other day, and giving him lots of advice, abt whom he shd publish and so forth. He said who wd I suggest as an editor. I told him you, and built you up for half an hour from every angle, stressing yr knowledge of history and anthropology etc. as well as poetry. He sd it sounded like a good idea, but dont know how sincere he was. Might be a good idea to drop him a letter of enquiry." Things worked out exactly as Bowering and Newlove had hoped – by the end of the year, Newlove was sending his missives on McClelland & Stewart Limited letterhead.

Like Kearns, Fred Wah is a friend Bowering got to know at UBC. Wah would one day write *Diamond Grill*, a memoir about his childhood, much of it spent in his father's eponymous Chinese Canadian café. Wah admits that the book, with its talk of butter pats and coffee urns, its inspiring recipes for Chinese dishes, and its probing of a Eurasian boy's feelings of "hybridity," has sold much better than his poetry.

In the eighties, Wah was the editor of *Swift Current*, Canada's first electronic literary magazine. Its technology gave contributors with modems access to an early version of email. From 1985 to 1988, Fred and George sent each other electronic messages full of warmth, wit, literary talk, teasing, and haikus. One would end his letter with a haiku and the other, receiving it, would finish *his* letter with a haiku in the same vein. While they were imitating the Surrealists in this way, Fred was writing a book called *Music at the Heart of Thinking* and George was working on *Errata*. Ten of *Errata*'s essays had appeared in the magazine *Brick*, and Wah praised them for being easy to read yet at the same time delivering "philosophical twists." He suggested, though, that George try being "a teeny bit more playful/dangerous with the language." Bowering took the opposite tack, teasing Wah for being wilfully obscure in *Music*. "Why," he asked, "do you have to write so much unlike the dear culture's patterns? I mean I like it when I get it; but it is so hard to get it." A few months later, when Fred's publisher asked George to write a cover blurb, George joked, "I think I will say: 'A totally unreadable book! A masterpiece!'"

David McFadden is another of his dear friends. They got in touch when Bowering was twenty-four and McFadden was twenty. An Ontarian, David worked at the *Hamilton Spectator*, first as a proofreader and later as a reporter, before leaving to pursue his creative writing exclusively in 1976. His books of poetry include *Intense Pleasure*, *The Saladmaker*, and *Be Calm, Honey*, each of its poems a sonnet. In 2013 he was the Canadian winner of the Griffin Poetry Prize. In an October 2013 *Globe and Mail* article he publicly acknowledged being slowed down by a form of Alzheimer's disease; he died in June 2018, aged seventy-seven.

Back in 1966–67, when the Bowerings lived in London, Ontario, George introduced David to Greg Curnoe, who would later make 194 drawings to illustrate McFadden's experimental novel, *The Great Canadian Sonnet*. Bowering got a kick out of McFadden's "terrible, awful sense of humour." Once he got a car – a Plymouth Horizon – and "waited extra time so he could get a blue one: Blue Horizon."

Bowering introduced his London, Ontario, painter friend Greg Curnoe, left, to his Hamilton, Ontario, poet friend David McFadden, right.

Writing to each other, they talked about literature, baseball (David having become a fan relatively late in life), and just about everything else. In an October 1986 *Swift Current* message, McFadden declared, "Oh George, it's so wonderful to be totally off the hook romantically, and over the hill sexually. What a blast! I can just lie around reading Proust in peace, finally." But a couple of months later he said one reason he hadn't been in touch was that he'd been getting "a little bit involved with this young woman from Nelson, B.C. (In fact she has her finger in my navel right now as I type.)"

He wasn't the only person having a dangerous liaison. In the mid-eighties, George was in love with Constance Rooke, a writer, scholar, and beloved teacher who was then the editor of the *Malahat Review*. She and her husband, Leon Rooke, were a power couple of Canadian literature. (They rather resembled the Bowerings, both men being tall, jocund, and assertive, both women articulate blondes with strong senses of style.) The Rookes were living in Victoria but would soon move to Guelph, Ontario, where they would start the Eden Mills Writers' Festival in 1989. When Connie was with George, she spoke of a future in which they would leave their partners and live together, she supporting him so he could write full time. George needed to talk about this with someone and confided in Brian Edwards, a writer/professor in Melbourne, Australia, whom he'd met at a conference and liked immediately. Brian met both Angela and Connie and could see why his new friend was torn. He sent notes of understanding and sympathy, but he was far away and they were using snail mail. News of Leon's rage over the affair, after he and Angela found out about it in December 1986, flashed through the literary world, especially after he muscled the marital mattress down a flight of stairs and flung it onto the front lawn. The Rookes stayed together until Constance's death in 2008. Leon told Sandra Martin, who wrote her obituary in the *Globe and Mail*, that their marriage had become stronger after the painful episode.

Mike Matthews, right, whom Bowering met at university in the late 1950s, was a friend for five decades.

The late Mike Matthews, an educator, actor, and writer, was a dear friend who received and replied to Bowering's lively letters a couple of times a month for more than forty years. Mike and his wife, Carol Matthews, were also good friends with the Rookes. In the mid-eighties Carol encouraged Mike to go see George and draw him out about his love life, which clearly had him tied in knots. The two men went out for a beer but, in the end, talked only about sports. George's position tended to be that "feelings are for feeling," not for talking about.

George's letters to Mike, with salutations like "Dear Magic Mitt" and "Dear Math Use," must have been fun to open. In 1987, when George was in Toledo, Spain, with Angela and Thea, he sent a postcard exclaiming, "Olive oil! Olive oil! El Greco! Olive oil! I could go on. I have just found out the Prado closes at 2, and it's 11, and [the] two women havent started their toilet, and its closed tomorrow. I guess we will spend the day having olive oil." On the rare occasions when George discussed his writing with Mike, he was honest. While working on his novel *Caprice* in 1984, he admitted, "I havent got a clue as to what is going to happen next, much less in the next 11 chapters."

📖

Bowering also had a long-running correspondence with the slightly older writer Hugh Hood, whom he'd met in Montreal in the late sixties. Hood was a friend Bowering thought of as "a square, an admirable square." He taught Université de Montréal students the poetry of William Wordsworth and England's other Romantics. The two of them shared a love of baseball and hockey, and both borrowed ballplayers' last names when christening fictional characters. Another thing they had in common was discipline: They plugged away at literary invention despite full teaching schedules and busy personal lives. When Hood died in 2000, Bowering marvelled that the huge project he'd embarked on decades ago, "to write a 12-volume novel series on the century [*The New Age*], and have the 12th volume published in 2000, came true."

George's correspondence with Al Purdy, whom he has famously called "the world's most Canadian poet," was epic, too. It went on for nearly forty years, and though they lived far apart, they managed to see each other and be photographed together "more often than Wayne and Shuster." Because of the eighteen-year difference in their ages, George sometimes used the salutation "Dear Uncle Al." Purdy always replied promptly, while Bowering, with less time on his hands, sometimes took a while to respond. Once, Al complained, "You take so long replying to a letter I'm never sure whether you're dead or mad at me for some reason or living with a new woman who gives you no time apart from fucking. Strike out one of those." They flattered each other in their letters but were frank when discussing poetry and poets. They had a constructive disagreement about William Carlos Williams, Bowering considering all of his work superb but Purdy finding him "so underemphatic he comes out on the other side of emphasis like a reverse gum boil."

George Stanley – who was a stalwart in Bowering's Dads and Tads group – is another member of the inner circle. In 2018, New Star Books published *Some End*, their dos-à-dos poetry flip book combining Bowering's "Some End" and Stanley's "West Broadway." Back when Stanley was teaching college students in Terrace, B.C., from 1976 to 1991, they wrote to each other, Bowering occasionally addressing envelopes whimsically: "George 'Feet' Stanley," "George Stanley, gent." In a 1980 letter, Bowering declared, "Here we are, you who grew up in the USA, teaching Canadian writing, and I who grew up in Canada, teaching American writing. Arent we crazy?" Stanley believes that the comrade with whom he shares an agrarian first name ("tiller of the soil" in Greek) has a great talent for friendship.

It's a talent that inspires others to respond in kind. In the early eighties, the Bowerings' neighbour Gill Collins saw that George and Angela were stressed and weren't getting along. She offered to come and clean their house once a week. Angela called her later in the day to see if she was serious. They agreed on payment of ten dollars an hour, the salary Gill had been making at a church-based counselling service called Divorce Lifeline. "They kind of needed a mother," says Collins. Because Angela was a heavy smoker and George also smoked at the time, "the windows were yellow." Plus, they had five cats, a couple of which sprayed. For fourteen months, Collins washed the windows, floors, and toilets. Her kind efforts not only made the family's surroundings more pleasant, they brought emotional benefits: Angela, who'd been seeing a psychiatrist for years, was able to stop once Gill had whipped through half a dozen times with mops, rags, and cleansers. It's a rare friend who sees what's needed and supplies the elbow grease herself.

CHAPTER 16

THE NOVELIST

In the post-modern novel you do not identify with the characters. If you are to identify with anyone it is likely to be the
author, who may lay his cards on the table & ask for your
opinion or even help in finishing the book ... you are offered
a look at the writer writing, not left in the dark waiting for
the stage lights to be lit ...

—"The Three-Sided Room: Notes on the Limitations of
Modern Realism," *The Mask in Place: Essays on Fiction in
North America* (1982)

Though primarily known as a poet, Bowering has been writing fiction
since 1959. *Mirror on the Floor*, his first published novel, appeared
in 1967. Set in Vancouver, it's a realistically told story redolent of its
time – you can almost smell the patchouli oil.

The central figure is Andrea Henderson, a nineteen-year-old who
has recently fled the home of the parents she hates. Andrea, who is
renting a many-windowed turret room in an old wooden house in
the West End, is alarmingly mercurial. Her more conventional boyfriend – Bob Small, a university student majoring in French – worries
that one day she'll do herself in.

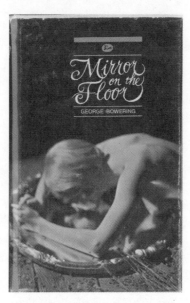

The original cover of Bowering's first published novel – set in Vancouver, which was rare in 1967.

Bowering's friends and fans will know he based Bob on his best friend from childhood. They'll also know that George Delsing is a stand-in for the author, his perennial avatar. Things happen in *Mirror on the Floor* – dramatic things, some even tragic. But many readers are satisfied by the supple writing alone, as when the omniscient narrator shows us Andrea at a window, watching "the cars moving along the street, dusky September light … the driveway empty, parents away in the evening dusk, driving to Granville Street … sunset destroyed by massive bank of purple clouds … everyone beating the arriving dark." In the *Province*, columnist Lorne Parton called it a "flaunting, evocative, nostalgic, sometimes annoying and irritating, always readable story."

In his later fiction Bowering became more of an anti-realist. On the whole, he'd rather not write books in which readers lose themselves; he likes to remind them of his authorial presence, practically waving at them from between the lines. In 1977's *A Short Sad Book*, a send-up of Canadian literature and Canadian identity, Chapter Thirty begins, "George Bowering sat at his desk writing history." Later in the book he all but shakes the hapless reader, saying, "[D]ont imagine any more that you can put on your invisibility suit & watch what [the characters] are doing ... what they are saying to each other ... Literature is not a one-way mirror."

In taking this approach, Bowering knowingly forfeits a wide readership. He once wrote that "as soon as an author begins to fool seriously with the trappings of the conventional novel, he is relegated to either neglect or notoriety, both places outside the mainstream." As Bowering recounts in *Pinboy*, his agent (Denise Bukowski) has begged him to produce more commercial work, telling him, in so many words, to stop thinking up odd little projects and "get back on the A-list, dope."

A Short Sad Book is written in the manner of Gertrude Stein. (The title inverts one of her titles: *A Long Gay Book*.) Although the story should be easy to grasp, given its simple language and large type, it's full of obscure jokes – it features Sir John A. Macdonald as a character, for example, and describes him having sex with Evangeline, from the poem by Henry Wadsworth Longfellow. Speaking about the novel's many obscure references, Rolf Maurer, whose New Star Books published the 2017 edition, says alert readers will "turn to Google on their wrist watch, just like in the old days they might have gone to the library to figure out who this Gogarty was that Joyce is on about. Not that we're comparing *A Short Sad Book* to *Ulysses*. They're just using the same literary device."

Several of Bowering's ideas for subsequent novels came from history. He's written three that take place in the Canadian west. *Burning Water*, from 1980, is a taut double story glinting with half-buried bits of mischief. In the dominant narrative it's 1792 and George Vancouver, a commander in Great Britain's Royal Navy, is sailing the HMS *Discovery* into Nootka Sound, on Vancouver Island's outer coast. Two

Indigenous men ("the first Indian" and "the second Indian"), watching, can't believe their eyes. They wonder if the ninety-nine-foot ship and the *Chatham*, an accompanying tender under the command of Lieutenant William Robert Broughton, could be giant wooden birds with folded wings. Vancouver and his crew of more than a hundred take up temporary residence on the waters of the New World. They will stay for four years and do such a meticulous survey of the coast, north to latitude 60, that their charts will serve mariners for generations.

The secondary narrative is set not in the 1790s but in the 1970s. It concerns the author, a modern-day George who makes his home in a city named after the historical George. A family man, he happens to be on his own in Trieste, Italy, writing the book we hold in our hands. In the dominant storyline, Vancouver feeds his crew sauerkraut to prevent scurvy; in the secondary one, George the writer goes into a trattoria and sympathetically orders *salsicce con krauti* (sausage with sauerkraut).

In a short prologue, Bowering tells how he will handle the two tales. He decided to use the third person throughout because "I cannot spend these pages saying *I* to a second person. Therefore, let us say *he*, and stand together looking at [both Georges]. We are making a story, after all ..." Sometimes the reader is momentarily confused about which George, which "he," is under discussion. (The scholar Jessica Langston has suggested that, by entangling a modern story with a historical one, Bowering was striving to "highlight the shakiness of the subject and the self" – that is, trying to show that all written history is unreliable.) Anachronisms, a feature of postmodernism, abound. When George Vancouver asks Coast Salish Chief Tyee Cheslakees about the weather in Johnstone Strait, a channel along the northeast coast of Vancouver Island, he's told that "in the winter it rains all the time, but we always say that at least you don't have to shovel it."

Bowering had read George Vancouver's account of the voyage and also one by Archibald Menzies, the Scottish naturalist who collected plant samples on the voyage. Menzies's plant cuttings, growing in cold frames, devour more and more precious deck space. Vancouver fumes about the activities of the botanist, that "porridge-faced little Scot." When the ship's doctor is indisposed, Menzies steps up to look after the captain and crew. Vancouver, weakened by hyperthyroidism and gout, resents the fact that the crew member he likes least knows all about his physical condition. Where might their accelerating animosity lead?

Bowering paints a sympathetic portrait of Vancouver, who, according to an outside source, "led a surprisingly short and unhappy life" from 1757 to 1798. His most daring act of historical revisionism was to posit a homosexual affair between Vancouver (in his thirties, with little sexual experience) and the elegant, older Don Juan Francisco de la Bodega y Quadra. The Peruvian-born Spanish naval officer met with Vancouver in Nootka Sound over whether lands in the area were Spanish or British. They failed to resolve the issue, but in *Burning Water* their discussions take place over posh dinners on Quadra's ship, the *Activa*, lubricated by anachronistic sips of "California grape" and Blue Mountain coffee. Bowering had found, in his research, that Vancouver "actually did speak very fondly" of Quadra; he exaggerated this. In Chapter 16, Quadra asks Vancouver, "Now wouldn't you rather be doing this than making war?" Quadra's lips touch his, and then the older man bends "like an indulgent mother to strip his clothes from him."

This embroidery made some readers howl. W. Kaye Lamb, a former national archivist and an authority on the voyage in question, fulminated in the *Vancouver Sun* that Bowering assumes a homosexual relationship between Vancouver and Quadra "without a shred of supporting evidence."

As for his portrayal of Indigenous Peoples, calling one character "the first Indian" and another "the second Indian" wouldn't fly today. And there's another problem. Chapter 26 describes a session of lusty lovemaking between Sir Joseph Banks and an unnamed Indigenous woman. (Banks, the botanist – or, as Bowering writes, the "green-thumbed busybody" – on an earlier expedition led by Captain James Cook, wasn't in Nootka Sound in 1792, so the three-page chapter is a sort of flashback.) To Banks, the Indigenous woman smells like a dolphin. He "didn't love it, but he didn't hate it, either." He rather admires the warm colour of her bare skin, compared with his own pasty hide. The passage ends when both are sexually satisfied, at which point the supine botanist fleetingly forms "a picture in his mind's eye of Mrs. Banks."

Despite the frankness and humour, it's easy to see how an Indigenous woman reading the chapter might take offence at a fictional sister "slopp[ing] up and down" on Banks's erect penis. Marcia Crosby, a Tsimshian-Haida writer and art historian, encountered *Burning Water* in a Canadian literature class. While she knew it was a historiographic metafiction, she still felt queasy. For the "uninformed reader who does not understand the theoretical intention behind Bowering's work," she has written, "there is the comforting recognition of the drunken, dirty, promiscuous, yet 'natural' Indian." Bowering acknowledges that the chapter is "not like the things around it; it stands out." He considers it a comment on imperialism and colonialism, but it doesn't always land that way – it strikes many readers as gratuitous.

For those turning the pages to see where Vancouver's and Menzies's mutual antagonism will lead, Bowering provides a climactic finale. The botanist, goaded beyond endurance by the explorer, fetches his gun and shoots Vancouver in the chest. The book's last sentence has a lovely archaic quality: "A gust of wind punched into the mainsail, and every man took a little shuffling step to stay erect, save their captain who seemed to be lifted by some strength unwitnessed, over the rail and into the unsolicitous sea." In real life, Vancouver didn't die violently at sea – but this is a work of fiction.

"Burning water" is an Aztec metaphor for "imagination." A sentence on the prologue's first page says, "Without a storyteller, George Vancouver is just another dead sailor." Bowering had wanted to call the book *The Dead Sailors*, but General Publishing told him readers wouldn't go for a novel with "dead" in the title (Norman Mailer's popular and critically acclaimed *The Naked and the Dead* notwithstanding).

Bowering was excited as *Burning Water* landed in bookstores. Reviews were impassioned and all over the map. One critic with a particularly negative stance said its postmodern touches made him feel that "somewhere in the wings of this book there is a clever little boy snickering." John Moss, an Ontario professor of Canadian literature, disliked it intensely at first but later changed his mind. In a textbook he wrote, he called it "a blast, force without form, like a directed explosive used to make a rockcut for a new highway." Six years later, in the text's second edition, he wrote that "its achievements [are] more apparent in retrospect. That is the way it often is with revolutions."

Certainly, George's fiction-writing skills had improved. *Burning Water* is smoother and more gratifying to read than *A Short Sad Book* and better researched and more complex than *Mirror on the Floor*. Timothy Findley, Constance Beresford-Howe, and Sheila Watson were the judges for the 1980 Governor General's Award for Fiction in English. They had three books on their shortlist, the others being debut novels: Susan Musgrave's *The Charcoal Burners* and Leon Rooke's *Fat Woman*. The winner was *Burning Water*, and the citation, signed by Findley, called it "exciting, informative and gripping ... a brilliant piece of writing." George hadn't rewritten history, as some were complaining. Instead, he'd made a fiction based on history, "an accounting of what it means to go in search of a place that only exists in the mind."

Sheila Watson with Bowering in the 1980s. He calls her novel, *The Double Hook*, "the watershed of contemporary Canadian fiction."

It's rare for a writer to win a GG for poetry and another for fiction (though Michael Ondaatje has won two for poetry and three for fiction). But while *Burning Water* made a splash, what Bowering was hearing through the grapevine made him feel he'd alienated people. In his diary, he wrote, "I'm living with the fact that most of the Can. literary world does not like me, resents me, etc."

New Star Books reissued *Burning Water* in 2007. In his splendid introduction, Stan Persky says there's a name for Bowering's trademark playfulness: *tapinosis*, a rhetorical device with which serious things are said in offhand, slangy language. New Star publisher Rolf Maurer dimly remembers that when *Burning Water* and the next two books in the trilogy came out, "a lot of people kind of sneered at them because they were overly po-mo [postmodern]. They didn't like those aspects of them. But those are the aspects that I think stand up." The New Star *Burning Water* went into a second printing in 2013.

Caprice is the trilogy's second book. Cynthia Good, who had started a Canadian publishing program at Penguin Books Canada in 1983, read the manuscript two years later and was anxious to publish it. She wrote to George, offering him a $5,000 advance and explaining what the royalties would be. He was so pleased the novel had found a home that he quickly replied, "Regarding the terms of your offer – okay." He added, "You are wonderful, just what I needed, this news."

Having taught a graduate course on western novels and movies, Bowering wanted to take the classic western – like those by Louis L'Amour – and "turn over some of the furniture." In his book the lone rider on a revenge quest is not a grim, tough man but a woman. Her sweetheart, Roy Smith, is one of the Old West's few male school-teachers; he works at a residential school for Indigenous children (now notorious for their legacy of cultural alienation and abuse). At the story's end, Roy, tied to his job, stays behind in Kamloops while Caprice rides off into the sunrise. "Couldn't resist that one," Bowering chuckles.

Caprice is a striking character, cinematic in her distinctiveness. George, generally not big on describing characters' looks, made her "a five-foot-eleven-inch red-headed freckle-faced French Canadian woman." She rides a glossy black stallion and expertly handles a bull-whip. She's out to avenge the death of her brother and is tracking Frank Spencer, the American who killed him. Oh, and she reads Goethe and writes poetry, too.

The story – a postmodern tale laced with parody and irony – takes place in 1889, when, as the narrator puts it, "the west had started to shrink." The Thompson Valley, with its cottonwoods, ponderosa pines, sagebrush, and cactus, and place names like Bonaparte, Savona, and Deadman River, provides the perfect backdrop. As in *Burning Water*, there are two Indigenous men commenting on the action; Bowering delights in such recurrences. This time they're Tsilhqot'in, not coastal, people.

Clearly having fun, he gave the secondary characters, many of them immigrants, marvellous handles – there's Soo Woo, proprietor of Fairview's Canadian Café, and Luigi Martino, nicknamed Everyday

Luigi, for example. The prose is pitch-perfect for the genre he's shaking up. A late chapter opens: "She had undone the belly-cinch and reached to jerk the thirty-pound saddle from the damp blanket on [her horse] Cabayo's back, when she saw a rifle pointed at her. She dropped to the hay-strewn floor and rolled even as she heard the report of the Winchester. There was a second shot."

Doing his research, Bowering had read Mary Balf's *Kamloops: A History of the District Up to 1914* and was tickled to learn that people there started playing baseball in 1885. "Now those readers & critics are going to say, oh come on, you put baseball in everything," he wrote in his diary. "But get this: the town & the CPR team had a game New Year's Day, 1889, and the game was held up for a solar eclipse!"

Caprice is the first book Bowering wrote on a computer. Tormented over troubles in his marriage with Angela, he approached the job with discipline, turning out four pages a day. Penguin published the novel in April 1987, its front-cover painting showing a cowgirl with russet braids. A chorus of approval came from most of the critics, and headline writers outdid themselves. The *Maclean's* review, by John Bemrose, was titled "Angel with a Lariat"; the one by Ken McGoogan, in *Books in Canada*, was called "As for Me and My Horse." Maggie Helwig said in the *Toronto Star* that while the writing has "some patchy moments, especially early in the book, Bowering's prose is for the most part a delight, vivid, strong and musical." The *Vancouver Sun*'s reviewer found the prose reminiscent of Kurt Vonnegut's.

Frank Davey, *TISH* editor turned academic, taught *Caprice*, which he considers "probably as close as a man can come to writing a feminist novel." He believes Caprice to be loosely based on the Quebec writer Nicole Brossard, since allusions to her poetry are "salted away covertly" in the book. As well, a number of women George knew said he must have modelled Caprice on them. Some were tall and horsey; one had a small C-shaped scar on her face, as Caprice does. "None of them were!" Bowering exclaims. "She was the only thing in the book that was entirely made up." When the Vancouver bookseller/ publisher William Hoffer produced a small excerpt as a hand-sewn limited edition, he had a tall woman named Caprice – who liked to go horseback riding in Ashcroft, B.C. – do the stitching. Bowering had named the character before he met her. When he learned her name, he shivered.

In Toronto, Cynthia Good had been promoted from editorial director to editor-in-chief and vice-president of Penguin Canada. She thought George was "ahead of his time in having a woman protagon- ist" and had "reflected a woman in those situations extremely well." But *Caprice* didn't sell as well as she'd hoped. "I had a feeling that westerns were going to become very popular again, which actually didn't happen at that moment." One thing that did happen, though, was that Denise Bukowski offered to represent him. Sprinkling extra question marks into a September 1987 letter, she asked him, "Why in blazes did you let Penguin retain film rights to your novel????" Seeing that she could do him some good, he signed on as a client.

Following the publication of *Caprice*, Bowering was wildly busy. Reviews of his *Delayed Mercy and Other Poems* were coming in. He was turning out essays, short stories, poems, and articles; he was also looking for a publisher for *Harry's Fragments*, a high-concept novel he'd written in 1985. (Coach House would publish it in 1990 with the subtitle *A Novel of International Puzzlement*. Readers who know the ancient Greek philosopher Heraclitus – famous for saying, "You cannot step into the same river twice" – and his *Fragments* are more likely to get it.)

In November 1992, his Ontario friend Greg Curnoe died unexpect- edly. A few days before his fifty-sixth birthday he'd gone out cycling with friends and been hit by a truck – a cruel end for a popular artist who loved to paint bicycles and their wheels. Bowering wrote a book in tribute, *The Moustache: Memories of Greg Curnoe*. It's a collection of a hundred short reminiscences, each beginning with the words "I remember." One thing George remembered was Peter Gzowski interviewing him and Greg together on the CBC Radio show *Morningside.* "For years people had been saying that Greg looks like Gzowski and that I sound like Gzowski."

The opening sentences of *Shoot!,* the third novel in Bowering's historical trilogy, are arrestingly simple: "There were three brothers walking around the dry country, doing their best to change things. The sun was beating on their heads, but they had a job to do. The sky was wide and blue, just as it is today. Red willows grew beside the river."

First published in 1994 by Key Porter Books, *Shoot!* is based on real people and events, with George cleaving more closely to facts than he had in *Burning Water.* The time and place are similar to those in *Caprice*: We're in British Columbia's high, lonesome Interior in the second half of the nineteenth century. The brothers are Allan, Charlie, and Archie McLean – "the wild McLean boys" George had heard about growing up in the south Okanagan Valley in the forties. The McLeans were mixed-race youths, then called half-breeds or "breeds." Their Scottish father, Donald McLean, chief fur trader at the Hudson's Bay Company post in Kamloops, had died in the Tsilhqot'in Uprising of 1864. Their mother, Sophie Grant, had Secwépemc and Scottish blood.

In Bowering's telling, Donald McLean is contemptuous of Indigenous Peoples despite having married Indigenous women and fathered eleven mixed-race children. The boys are growing up without education, opportunities, and status. The story's narrator tells us, "The Indians and the white men had different reasons not to like [mixed-race offspring] all that much ... Each side saw them as a degeneration, though. Tag ends."

The boys' teenage sister, Annie, works as a servant in the home of a rich settler. In 1879, the settler gets her pregnant and her infuriated brothers seek revenge. With Alex Hare, a Métis friend, they act out the rage they feel toward entitled white men, stealing a stallion from a rancher against whom Charlie has a grievance and breaking into houses with larcenous intent.

Readers of *Shoot!* learn that Special Constable Johnny Ussher thinks the wayward McLeans can be talked into better behaviour but doesn't get a chance to prove his theory: During their rampage in the Nicola Valley they kill him, and another man, in cold blood. (While no reason is given in the novel, we guess that the young men of the McLean gang are so angry about what happened to Annie that they lash out at the first men who happen into their line of fire.) The McLeans end up in a cabin beside the Spahomin Reserve on the west side of Douglas Lake, and a posse of more than a hundred white citizens representing the law lays siege to it. As the standoff drags on, the cornered youths grow cold, thirsty, and weak, and they surrender. They are jailed and tried twice, the reported details enlivening the front pages of Victoria's *British Colonist* newspaper for days. In court, Judge Henry Crease tells them, "You have caused great terror throughout the country, and by a campaign of robbery and assault and murder you have disgraced British Columbia ... you know that you need not expect mercy here."

In *Shoot!*'s strong penultimate chapter, a photographer comes to the prison to take what are now the only extant photos of the McLeans. Bowering writes, "Archibald Minjus waited for the rain to stop. He waited for almost a week, and then on Tuesday morning the sun came out, bright as a new axe. Brighter." In January 1881, the four are hanged. Archie McLean, the youngest brother, is only fifteen.

Bowering's disdain for colonialism is evident throughout *Shoot!* and he has the skills to make us care about the McLeans. To show their predicament as lads with a place in neither culture, he marshalled an impressive amount of Indigenous language, lore, and recovered history. Doing research in the summer of 1992, he went to the Secwépemc Adams Lake Reserve with Dwight Gardiner, his linguist friend and former student. They spoke with Aimee August, Adeline Willard, Bill

Arnouse, and other Elders, who told Bowering about Digging Roots Month, Things Getting Ripe Month, and Deer Travel Month. "This is a great bonus," he wrote in his diary. "They're funny & smart."

It's impossible for the average reader to know which parts of the story are invented. Did Donald McLean, the cruel patriarch, really hate Indigenous Peoples so much that he murdered an Indigenous child? When the McLean gang was holed up in the cabin, did the purloined stallion really wander off to an ice-covered lake, step onto the ice, and drown? When the boys were jailed in New Westminster before their hangings, did the warden's young wife really read aloud and sing to them? The scholar Sherrill Grace notes in the afterword to the novel's 2008 reissue that it contains so many stories it must be read as "a story about telling stories." Some are "factually true," she says, "while all are fictionally true."

Bowering had wanted to write the novel "without any yuks" – but he also wanted to ensure that it wasn't a conventional historical account. Sherrill Grace felt that, by using several narrative voices, he succeeds. In a review, the journalist and novelist Don Gillmor called *Shoot!* "a poet's novel," writing that it is constructed in a "cyclical rather than linear fashion, the events circling back repeatedly."

Shoot! was Bowering's second book with Bukowski as his agent. Seeking to follow Canadian publication with American, Bukowski showed it to senior editors at the best houses, including Jonathan Galassi at Farrar, Straus and Giroux. Richard Beswick, of Little, Brown and Company, replied that he saw its appeal but was put off by the treatment: "too many flash-forwards with the twentieth-century narrator making rather smug observations." But by March 1995, Bukowski had good news for Bowering: Hope Dellon, a senior editor at St. Martin's Press, considered *Shoot!* "a brilliant work." Dellon wasn't sure how well it would do but, as it turned out, the print run of fifteen hundred copies sold out and a second was ordered. In February 1996, Bowering had the pleasure of seeing the novel receive a brief but positive notice, nicely illustrated, in the *New York Times Book Review*. The item pronounced *Shoot!* "intricately plotted, meticulously researched and shaded with nuance," and made a point of mentioning the author's "unflinching examination of bigotry and intolerance."

Partly thanks to Bukowski, Bowering was on a roll. In January 1994 she sent him a two-word postcard responding to some good news he'd received from Penguin Canada: "Yippie!!!! Denise." And in September of that year he sent her a fax that began, "Dear D. Book-wowski."

CHAPTER 17

THE CRITIC

... the animator of poetry is language. Not politics, not
nationalism, not theme, not personality, not humanism,
not real life, not the message, not self-expression, not con-
fession, not the nobility of work, not the spirit of a region,
not the Canadian Tradition – but language.

—"Unexpected Objects," *Craft Slices* (1985)

In the early eighties, when his marriage to Angela was in an uproar,
Bowering wrote an essay that stands out in his critical oeuvre as a
straightforward work of scholarship. "Home Away: A Thematic Study
of Some British Columbia Novels" argues that, startlingly often, the
literature of Canada's westernmost province is about the attempt
to find a home. Recalling the Bible-citing description of Canadians
as "hewers of wood and drawers of water," he writes that the main
livelihood in British Columbia was "the harvesting and processing
of house-building materials" – in other words, logging and milling
timber. "But the houses that the families of the harvesters and pro-
cessors live in most often seem temporary and unstable ... British
Columbia novels often offer tents, brush shelters, shacks and boats
for their characters to pass short times in." Where Margaret Atwood

had contended that Canadian literature is about survival in a land of brutal winters and Northrop Frye had written of a "garrison mentality" in response to threats from nature, Bowering saw something different in fiction from the milder West, where workers tended to be "the kind who move around for their work – loggers, miners, fishermen, cowboys, fruit pickers."

To show how a homing instinct ran through novels written or set in B.C., George picked eleven and discussed each at satisfying length. One is Malcolm Lowry's 1970 *October Ferry to Gabriola* ("the apotheosis of B.C. fiction"); another is Jane Rule's 1977 *The Young in One Another's Arms* ("trees against bulldozers and concrete, home versus real estate developers"); yet another is Hubert Evans's 1954 *Mist on the River*, in which, Bowering notes, the word "home" appears on almost every page.

Bowering had these riches at his fingertips because he'd fought for local curriculum in his first decade of teaching at Simon Fraser. He remembers suggesting, during a committee meeting in the seventies, that the English department offer a B.C. Studies course. "Laughing and guffawing" ensued because the idea seemed like such a stretch: Canadian literature, okay, I guess; B.C. Studies, give us a break. George decided that, when teaching Canadian lit, he'd draw up a reading list of B.C. books and pretend it was a coincidence.

The journal *BC Studies* published "Home Away" in the summer of 1984. The essay proved its durability when, nearly three decades later, editor Graeme Wynn and associate editor Richard Mackie were deciding which essays from the journal's long backlist to include in a greatest-hits anthology. They snatched up "Home Away," seeing its search-for-home theme as one that could guide them to assemble a cohesive book. Their *Home Truths: Highlights from BC History* both nods to its title and uses the essay as its opener.

In the seventies, *Canadian Literature*, a journal produced at UBC, published several Bowering essays that shed light on individual

Canadian writers with a care and devotion bordering on tenderness. A prime example is "That Fool of a Fear," George's close reading of Margaret Laurence's 1966 novel *A Jest of God*. The essay's title comes from the book: Rachel Cameron, the novel's protagonist, an unmarried rural schoolteacher with incipient schizophrenia, is afraid of becoming a fool. "Yet," she says to herself at a crucial juncture, "I could almost smile with some grotesque lightheadedness at that fool of a fear, that poor fear of fools, now that I really am one." While sketching out the story and highlighting Laurence's skills as an author, George applauds *A Jest of God*'s first-person narration. "The subject of the book is Rachel's mind," he writes, so it's right that readers get to see it, with all of its "unsureness and confusions." He writes with affection, wanting others to like the book as much as he does. (A few years later, when he and Laurence were corresponding, she thanked him for the article, saying he'd "pointed out things about the use of language that I'd given up hope of anyone ever seeing.")

Another of his essays in *Canadian Literature*, "Purdy: Man and Poet," surveys Al Purdy's artistic development. (In the documentary film *Al Purdy Was Here*, there's a clip in which Pamela Wallin, then a TV journalist, tells Purdy, "You were a high school dropout, a demoted soldier, a bankrupt businessman, an inconsiderate son, a problem husband." He replies, "Look, if you start feeling guilty about yourself, it isn't going to help things, is it?") Al improved his writing over time, George writes, shedding the pretentious classical allusions of his early work and instead using what he'd seen in the Cariboo, the North, and other little-known regions of Canada. His poetry came alive, reflecting his bumptious personality.

That essay became Chapter I of *Al Purdy*, a 1970 monograph in publisher Copp Clark's Studies in Canadian Literature series. These books of a hundred or so pages were aimed at a general and scholarly readership, with five thousand copies in the initial print run, retailing for $1.85 each. Bowering's *Al Purdy* is an even-handed, lively piece of work – and it impressed Jean Baird, George's future second wife, when she read it near the end of her studies in high school. It was the first book of Bowering's that she had read, and she remembers thinking it was unlike all other criticism she'd come across.

In *Al Purdy*, a book-length essay from 1970, Bowering called Purdy, right, "the world's most Canadian poet."

By the end of the seventies, he was producing essays about the craft of writing, with several defending his favourite kind of prose – the avant-garde, anti-realist variety. He has long considered realism dishonest because writers don't acknowledge their presence in the text, conspiring, instead, to respect what's known in the theatre as the fourth wall. Bowering's introduction to *Fiction of Contemporary Canada*, a short-story anthology he edited for Coach House Press in 1980, makes this point in a vivid, likeable way: "If James Joyce starts you off with Ulysses, you know that you are going to enter the chamber of Penelope at the close." Readers of conventional fiction observe the structure but mustn't meddle with it, whereas a postmodern writer "invites his readers, & sometimes his characters, to take a hold somewhere & help him move the damned thing into position."

George formulated so many thoughts about writers and literature that he was able to publish five books of essays in the eighties. *A Way*

With Words and *The Mask in Place* came out in 1982, *Craft Slices* in 1985, and *Errata* and *Imaginary Hand* in 1988. He was a professor, but he didn't go in for academic publishing. Instead, he sent batches of his essays to small literary presses such as Oberon in Ottawa, Turnstone in Winnipeg, and NeWest in Edmonton. His industry and intellectual rigour were on view but not in the conventional places.

A Way With Words contains essays about Canadian poets. Bowering had been dismissive of the Ontario postwar poets Jay Macpherson, Douglas Le Pan, and James Reaney, and their inspirer, Northrop Frye, because of their reliance on classical myth and imagery. But in the essay "Why James Reaney Is a Better Poet," he praised Reaney for speaking with his own voice in lines he'd written about drinking from Ontario's Avon River. Reaney seemed to be changing from a "Fryed" poet to a "raw" one.

The Mask in Place is a collection of essays about fiction. Here he writes not only about Mordecai Richler and Audrey Thomas but also about Nathaniel Hawthorne and Jack Kerouac. Bowering was also alive to women's writing in North America. In "Sheila Watson, Trickster," he calls her strange but influential 1959 novel, *The Double Hook*, "the watershed of contemporary Canadian fiction."

In 1985, Oberon Press must have expected his cleverly titled *Craft Slices* to find educated readers, for the back-cover copy says, "[T]hese mini-briefs on CanLit will remind you of Pope's *Dunciad*." The eighty-eight short essays, alphabetically arranged, broadcast his love for Canadian writers. In the middle, there's a run of essays about Gwendolyn MacEwen, Eli Mandel, Daphne Marlatt, and David McFadden. *Craft Slices* succinctly presents some of George's most deeply held beliefs. In the ultra-short "Stained Glass," he again makes a pitch for postmodern writing, saying he doesn't value fiction that acts like a window on the world. "If it is a window, let it be a stained-glass window," he writes. "It has to be interesting itself." In "Stories," he insists that an artist tunes into the world, rather than making up a world. "No artist can really create," he states. "He gathers and arranges materials found at hand." Some of the essays are tough on other poets. Patrick Lane and Joe Rosenblatt come in for a drubbing because of language Bowering deems excessively brutal or adjective-laden. (This led the anthologist Russell Brown to write that he's at his most cantankerous in *Craft Slices*.)

Bowering poses with a cardboard cut-out of bpNichol, one of whose books is called *Craft Dinner*. Loving the title, George adapted it for *Craft Slices*, which he dedicated to Nichol.

As a critic, Bowering came to value brevity; each of *Errata*'s ninety-nine meditations is just a paragraph long. While *Errata* looks as if it could be read in one sitting, it is surprisingly dense and takes some time to digest. Cryptically, he contends in its thirty-fourth essay that while autobiography "replaces the writer," biotext is an extension of him or her. How so? He doesn't say enough for readers to grasp the distinction. When he states, in the thirty-sixth essay, that the best poetry is written – and read – in fear, he again doesn't fully explain. Yet *Errata* has fervent fans. David McFadden told him, "I much prefer the Bowering in *Errata* for some strange reason" to the Bowering in *Kerrisdale Elegies*. And Ryan Knighton was drawn to the postcard essays because he could handle them when he was losing his sight and no longer "chasing down novels with voracious appetite."

Some of the essays, prefaces, and afterwords George has written stick in readers' minds because only he could have formulated them. The preface to *Another Mouth*, a particularly unruly book of his poems, is a dialogue between him and the Canadian Tradition ("C.T."). Responding to flak he'd taken for having been influenced by American poets early in his career – in a way, creating his opponent in order to neutralize the anger and defensiveness he'd felt when under attack – he has "G.B." telling "C.T." that his influences are international, something for which he won't apologize.

Bowering edited *My Body Was Eaten by Dogs*, a book of David McFadden's selected poems, in 1981. The introduction he wrote for it is affectionate, like his earlier essay on Laurence, and marvellously detailed. He saw McFadden as a romantic who, like him, had American influences. "His is Whitman's ear," Bowering wrote, adding that his friend often seemed to "stop the poem before an expected punch line – Robert Frost with a witty pair of scissors."

"The End of the Line," a short essay at the end of *Imaginary Hand*, discusses poetic line breaks in a particularly jaunty way, suggesting that it's as if a poet is walking a dog when he or she starts a new line: "My little dog runs ahead of me & comes back to my feet, then off she goes again … She can turn, & turn, & yet go on, & turn again." Citing a magazine poem (without giving its author or title), he points to some line breaks he considers clumsy. But he doesn't offer guidelines for generating better ones, since knowing where to end a line of poetry is a highly personal affair.

In an essay on Michael Ondaatje, right, Bowering says that while he and fellow Vancouver poets could be said to have descended from Robert Duncan, Ondaatje descended from W.B. Yeats and Wallace Stevens.

George was the subject of two critical works at that time. *A Record of Writing*, Roy Miki's annotated, illustrated bibliography of his work, appeared in 1989. It's an exhaustive catalogue of everything he'd published, and everything published about him, enlivened with photos and quotations. Miki, an SFU colleague of Bowering's, told me, "I knew George and I thought, while we're still active and alive and doing stuff, to put on record what he'd gone through in this particular phase of his life. He was pretty young when I finished that bibliography; we knew there was going to be a lot more writing to come. But it's the formative years."

In 1992, Talonbooks published *George Bowering: Bright Circles of Colour*, by Eva-Marie Kröller. She analyzes his work, pointing out how his friendships with the visual artists Greg Curnoe, Jack Chambers, Roy Kiyooka, and Guido Molinari influenced him. A reviewer called the book highly readable and said it puts him in historical and cultural perspective.

In the nineties, Bowering wrote a ten-thousand-word essay about himself, "Alphabiography." Conversational in tone, it seems to flit all over the place until you realize it's alphabetically arranged, at which point the title becomes clear. In the G section (G is for "George"), he says, "I have always liked the work of George Oppen, George Stanley, George Economou and Georgia Savage. People who have read more than I have tell me that Lord Byron is pretty good." In the W section (W is for "Writing"), he recounts preparing to go to Trieste, where he would write *Burning Water*: "I went to Chinatown and bought a number of thick hardcover notebooks made in the People's Republic and called 'Sailing Ship.' Robin Blaser had showed me one at his house. They were perfect, because ten pages held a thousand words ..." Under "Y" (for "Youth"), he talks about the swift passage of time, saying, "I have always refused to sleep in the daytime, because I hate to have hours of my life happen when I dont know about it. But everyone has to sleep sometime ..." Tailing off, that last sentence is a fluid segue to the abbreviated final section, "Zzzzzz."

Bowering has done some of his best phrasemaking in articles and essays. In "Confessions of a Failed American," which appeared in *Maclean's* in November 1972, he lists ten beloved Canadian things, including the scent of the Okanagan Valley in apple blossom time and the Moose Head Ale label. Using diction worthy of Gertrude Stein, he brings the piece to a close with two sentences that people often quote: "The best thing about Canada is that it is not this. It is this and that."

CHAPTER 18

THE AMATEUR HISTORIAN

When I finally got to see [the Plains of Abraham] in 1968, after a leisurely climb, I was disappointed to see that the Plains ... take up less space than the boys' playground at my old elementary school in Oliver, B.C.

—*Stone Country: An Unauthorized History of Canada* (2003)

Mourning Dove, an Indigenous woman of Sinixt, Colville, Syilx, and Irish ancestry, was born in the United States' Pacific Northwest around 1885. An itinerant farm labourer who lived for a time in Alberta and south-central B.C., she managed to buy a typewriter and, lugging the heavy machine from pickers' camp to pickers' camp, write several books in English, her second language. Her best-known novel, *Cogewea, The Half-Blood*, came out in 1927.

Sophia (or Sophie) Grant was a woman of Indigenous and Scottish descent. The three sons she had with Hudson's Bay Company trader Donald McLean went on a crime spree in B.C.'s Interior in 1879. Bowering told the McLean Gang's story in his historical novel, *Shoot!*

George's flair for reaching back in time and spinning lively stories from half-forgotten events led to his producing three quirky popular histories: *Bowering's B.C.: A Swashbuckling History* (1996), *Egotists and*

217

Autocrats: The Prime Ministers of Canada (1999), and *Stone Country: An Unauthorized History of Canada* (2003). He dedicated the first one to Mourning Dove and Sophia McLean.

Mourning Dove (*née* Christine Quintasket), "the first Native American woman ever to write a novel," according to Bowering.

Penguin Books Canada had published *Caprice* in 1987, and Cynthia Good, publisher at Penguin, thought he'd be able to make the shift from historical fiction to history. "I have a proposition for you," she wrote to him in the summer of 1993. "We are finding that we're doing quite well with regional histories, particularly if they are written in a lively and entertaining manner. Would you consider the possibility of writing a short history of British Columbia? We'd like it to be anecdotal (as well as informative and accurate) and even humorous. In short, we'd like it just the way you write."

For inspiration she sent him a copy of *Don't Know Much About History: Everything You Need to Know About American History but Never Learned* by Kenneth C. Davis, a best-selling book with an irreverent approach. George could be every bit as lively and funny, she was sure. Eventually, she thought, Penguin might produce a whole set of regional histories. (It commissioned Lesley Choyce – another ener-getic, versatile wordsmith – to write a Nova Scotia history around the same time.)

For the B.C. book, Good negotiated the terms of the contract with Denise Bukowski. Part of the deal was that Bowering's advance would be $21,000, payable in equal thirds on signature, delivery of the manuscript, and publication. Good, a Toronto Blue Jays fan who'd bonded with George through baseball talk, sent him a cute note: "My dear, you have been a bullshitter your whole life. History is nothing but bullshit. I have total confidence in you."

His task was a tall order, partly because B.C. is vast – bigger than the United Kingdom and Ireland, bigger than California. He loved the Okanagan Valley, he'd taught for short periods at the David Thompson University Centre in Nelson, and he of course knew Vancouver and Vancouver Island. But he had a lot to cover, both historically and geographically, and not much more than a year in which to work the facts up into a breezy yarn. When he'd written a narrative up to the year 1858, he sent Good a sample, saying, "It might be not as droll as you'd like. I seem to keep getting caught up in accuracy. But I can get the funny in later, maybe?"

In the fall of 1995, just as he was leaving for Europe (where he would teach a course on his favourite B.C. novels at a Danish uni-versity), he sent Good his 171,000-word first draft. After she'd read sixty pages, she faxed him a reassuring reply: "I have only one thing to say – it's brilliant. If I may go on, it's idiosyncratic, it's touching, it's personal, it's wild, it's real, it's new, it's going to revolutionize the way we think about history. In other words, it's exactly what I wanted." But he would continue to be diffident as he soldiered through the research and writing. Early in 1996, Mary Adachi, a copy editor at Penguin, suggested a number of cuts and revisions. He made them, but by the end of March, when he'd had no further feedback, he wondered if

Penguin was annoyed with him for not doing enough or was even considering dropping the project.

Not at all. The book came out in fall 1996 with the grand title *Bowering's B.C.* While Good thought George had the name recognition to carry it, he quailed a bit at the presumption, writing in his diary that it had "a title I dont like, but couldnt seem to get changed." He also questioned the subtitle, *A Swashbuckling History*, asking her, "Do you think the readership will think it's all right?" (Lesley Choyce's *Nova Scotia Shaped by the Sea: From the Beginning of Time* hit bookstores in the same season.)

Bowering's approach in the book bearing his name is folksy in the best possible way. "I didn't write it for history professors but for people like my mother and daughter," he told the *Simon Fraser News*. He had tried not to write a "Great Man"–style history, since enough had already been written about politicians. "Instead," he said, "I wanted to give voice to athletes, painters, lifeguards, and writers." He also made a point of giving Indigenous Peoples much more prominence than was customary. He writes that they have been on Canada's West Coast for five hundred generations, "whereas there have been only 90 generations since Jesus's time." *Bowering's B.C.* begins and ends with First Nations – a corrective to the Eurocentrism that normally dominates the genre.

The book contains some lovely insights. George writes that while Christianity is about transcendence (the belief in an afterlife better than this life), Indigenous beliefs highlight transformation or mutability – shape-shifting. In Northwest Coast Indigenous art, the image of an orca with what looks like an eye on its back is sometimes seen. It's as if the creature is "becoming something else," he writes. "The Indian carvings, for all their massiveness, are verbs in wood." He confidently states that "the Indians adjusted to the strangeness of the Europeans faster than the Europeans adjusted to them." His discussion of the Potlatch – a northwest coast ceremony involving feasting, dancing, displays of wealth, and gift-giving – is illuminating. He tells about the Anglican missionary William Duncan, who lived among the Tsimshian at Metlakatla, near Prince Rupert, in the 1850s. Duncan's administration, not adjusting very well to the Tsimshian, forbade five of their traditional practices: They were "to give up Indian devilry, to cease calling in conjurers when sick, to cease gambling, to cease giving away property for display, to cease painting faces." The Canadian government outlawed the Potlatch in 1884, but Bowering points out that Matthew Begbie, B.C.'s chief justice from 1870 to 1894, disagreed with the anti-Potlatch law and went after it, "writing decisions against it, evading it, mocking it."

Bowering's tone throughout the book is chatty. In his chapter on the fur trade, he talks about how sea otter fur was sought after for its luxuriance and durability in the late eighteenth century. Yet he can't help but bring up the friskiness and sheer charm of otters in the wild. "Who," he wonders, "could kill an animal that looks so happy?"

Early on, he describes the Okanagan – or uk^{w}naqín, to use the region's Indigenous name – as a place where rattlesnakes doze in the sun or "slither past some low-lying cactus and speargrass, looking for the shade of some crumbling shale. Small owls burrow in the dust, and once in a while a scorpion can be seen walking on his shadow across a lump of basalt … If a breeze comes up, it blows through crisp sagebrush and greasewood, scenting the air with a kind of spice." As is his way, *Bowering's B.C.* is often a personal history, too – bestowing the title of "loveliest valley in the western world" on the Okanagan, for example.

Cynthia Good didn't mind him writing himself into the story. It's a pretence, she believes, to think that writers offering accounts of the recent past are talking about something outside themselves. "So why not be up-front with it and say, 'I am here,' 'I'm writing this,' 'I'm thinking this,' 'This is what happened to me,' 'This is what I thought'?"

There's much in the book that could be new even to knowledgeable readers. A Portuguese sailor named Gaspar Corte-Real found the fabled Northwest Passage around 1500, Bowering writes, after which the sea route through the Canadian Arctic between the Pacific and Atlantic Oceans would be "found over and over again in the next few years, and sought ... for the next four centuries." Another noteworthy nugget is that Lytton, the village at the confluence of the Thompson and Fraser Rivers, is named for Edward Bulwer-Lytton, a British colonial secretary who took a special interest in the Crown Colony of British Columbia (and wrote the novel that famously begins, "It was a dark and stormy night ..."). Yet another little-known fact: Rudyard Kipling, author of *The Jungle Book* and *Just So Stories*, "bought a couple of lots in Vancouver in 1899 and sold them at a tidy profit thirty years later, just before the Wall Street crash."

Bowering also braids literature into his account. He highlights writers like Penticton's Jeannette Armstrong, who happens to be Mourning Dove's great-niece. In describing how the Great Depression affected British Columbians, he recommends Dorothy Livesay's short story, "A Cup of Coffee," as a fine depiction of one woman's struggles. He knows the Canadian canon, as Rolf Maurer points out.

Of course, he's not a professional historian; he has a bachelor's degree in history. So he was brave in taking on the project. Jean Barman, the leading expert on the province, thought he did surprisingly well. In a review, she declared that he "swashbuckles his way through three centuries of human history with an aplomb and self-confidence that many writers must wish they possessed." She did feel, though, that he hadn't tried to tell a story much different to the standard one; he'd basically kept "the orthodoxies ... intact." She also thought he could have made women more central. Overall, however, reviews were enthusiastic. Most arbiters thought he'd put together a fast-paced, fresh, informative account, and the word "page-turner" was bandied about. Early in 1997, Good faxed him a clipping from *Quill*

& *Quire*: A feature called "The Season's Stars" listed *Bowering's B.C.* in the Regional Faves category alongside Janet and Greta Podleski's first *Looneyspoons* cookbook. "We are so thrilled with the performance of *Bowering's B.C.*," Good wrote.

If George wasn't his usual chipper self during this gratifying breakthrough, those who knew him knew why. Angela was in distress. She had been coping with multiple sclerosis since at least the early nineties, but now she was in agony, racked with bladder and lower back pain. She suspected a new pathology and dreaded finding out what it was. In November 1996, shortly after the release of *Bowering's B.C.*, she was diagnosed with a rare gynecologic cancer. Radiation treatment and surgery were ordered. She and George were frequently in tears. Their marriage was far from ideal: They'd been antagonists more than helpmeets, and each had often felt lonely and unloved. But they knew each other so well that they could only cling to each other. When she was wheeled to the operating room, he saw anew her "dear familiar face." Her operation took thirteen hours, with four surgeons taking part. She made it but emerged in rough shape.

📖

By the end of January 1997, Good and Bukowski were urging George to write a second non-fiction book. With the twenty-first century looming, publishers were hustling to get meaty look-back volumes – political, historical, cultural – onto their lists. *Maclean's* supplied a useful angle of attack in April when it came out with an article ranking the twenty prime ministers Canada had had since 1867 – a catchy, if reductive, exercise. The magazine had asked the historians Jack Granatstein and Norman Hillmer to get together with some colleagues and rank the leaders according to their achievements. Landing on top was William Lyon Mackenzie King, the longest-serving prime minister and the one at the helm in World War II. Sir John A. Macdonald – the founding PM, appreciated for his railroad-building but damned (today) for his residential schools – ended up in the second spot. The historians ranked Sir Wilfrid Laurier third and, surprisingly, Louis St. Laurent fourth. Pierre Elliott Trudeau wound up in fifth place, while the lone woman, Kim Campbell (who, with only 132 days in office, didn't get much time to prove herself), finished last.

In April, Good sent Bukowski a fax saying a book on Canada's prime ministers would be a perfect project for George, "and I would of course like to exploit the terrific reviews and profile he achieved with *Bowering's B.C.*" Penguin would pay an advance of $40,000 and hoped to publish before January 2000. The women worked on him, and he eventually agreed, probably because a project would distract him from his despair over Angela. He joked that he didn't think the new book should be called *Bowering's PMS*, saying, "I may be undergoing a lot of stress, but not that kind."

For this task, even the world's most agile writer would need to do a fierce amount of background reading. It wasn't going to be easy to have a multiplicity of past political dust-ups at his fingertips. And yet he finished the first draft fourteen months after signing the contract. His diary doesn't shed light on how he went about crafting what would become *Egotists and Autocrats*. It only shows him keeping count of a growing number of finished pages and reluctantly leaving his desk when an unrelated commitment cropped up.

Angela's health deteriorated as he wrote sections, and then chapters, devising clever titles for them. Some are arguably too clever, like the one on the 1929 Wall Street Crash, which he called "Thud!" – a reference to people who'd been financially ruined jumping from skyscrapers' windows. As he laboured at the keyboard, Angela underwent a series of painful and humiliating treatments that changed her body ever more radically. Seeing such a smart, forceful person yield to the ravages of disease was frightening for those around her. Jamie and Carol Reid, close friends for decades, visited her in hospital when she knew she didn't have much time left. "She was very spirited," Carol recalls. "She was fired and wired till she died." Although Angela wasn't one to exercise or spend time outdoors, Carol heard that she'd ridden a bicycle – "down a hill, freewheeling" – to celebrate life while she still had it. "She had a lot of courage: MS *and* cancer?"

The title *Egotists and Autocrats* comes from the statement, made by one of Laurier's biographers, that the Canadian political system forces prime ministers to be both. Bowering opens the book with the suggestion that although Sir John A. Macdonald was the first PM, one of three people born earlier might be considered the first true leader. There was Sir Robert Walpole (1676–1745), "the first prime minister of British North America, and therefore of the parts that would become Canada," he writes. Another was Armand Jean du Plessis, commonly known as Cardinal Richelieu (1585–1642), who was chief minister of King Louis XIII and president of the Company of New France. A third was Allan Napier MacNab (1798–1862), who served in the War of 1812 as a teenager and became premier of Upper and Lower Canada in the mid-nineteenth century.

Macdonald, nation-builder extraordinaire, had the nickname Old Tomorrow. George gave the title "Young Tomorrow" to his chapter on Laurier, whom he succinctly calls "a ninth-generation French-Canadian with a love of British Liberalism." Laurier, he writes, was an eloquent orator who, for the fifteen years he led the nation, was "the brightest prime minister in the British Empire." He informs us that when Laurier died, in February 1919, his last words to his wife, Zoé, were "*C'est fini.*" Writing about R.B. Bennett, Conservative PM for the first half of the thirties, Bowering tells of a "hard-working, teetotalling Methodist" in Calgary, "a wild-west town, full of hard drinkers and men with missing fingers" – again, a nutshell of confident concision. Bennett, he writes, was the first millionaire to lead a national party in Canada, and one who thought a government should be run like a business.

Using a journalist's modus operandi, he starts each PM profile with the jazziest facts he could muster. "Prairie Lightning" is his chapter on John Diefenbaker, Conservative prime minister from 1957 to 1963. It opens with an anecdote about Dief giving a stump speech from the top of a rural town's manure pile, declaring, "This is the first time I have ever spoken from the platform of the Liberal Party." The chapter on Pierre Trudeau, dashing Liberal prime minister from 1968 to 1979 and 1980 to 1984, is called "Guns and Roses," shorthand for his invocation of the War Measures Act and his oft-worn rosebud boutonnière. Bowering writes, "You should try to remember what kind of year 1968 was," and then proceeds to summarize the cultural tumult in a paragraph. Later, introducing Brian Mulroney, PM from 1984 to 1993, he writes that Mulroney came from a Liberal family but fell into Conservative ways. Early in his political career, he was "not yet a right-winger, just an opportunist. In fact, he admired Pierre Trudeau, and wished that he could be like him."

In a weird burst of synchronicity, *Egotists and Autocrats* hit bookstores in fall 1999 along with two other guides to the country's prime ministers, Will Ferguson's *Bastards & Boneheads: Canada's Glorious Leaders, Past and Present* and *Prime Ministers: Ranking Canada's Leaders*, in which Granatstein and Hillmer expand their 1997 *Maclean's* piece. Cynthia Good had been in the publishing racket long enough to know that the zeitgeist can sometimes prompt three publishers to issue remarkably similar books at the same moment. They competed for Christmas shoppers' dollars. Wistfully, she recalls that George's irreverent doorstop was "not a failure, but it just was not the kind of bestseller we had hoped for."

Reviewers had no choice but to weigh in on all three books at once because, as an *Ottawa Citizen* columnist remarked, evaluating prime ministers had become "somewhat of a cottage industry at century's end." One critic wrote that the historians' prose didn't hold a candle to that of "hot-doggers like Ferguson and Bowering." Rex Murphy, who assessed the three books in the *Globe and Mail*, favoured George's, pronouncing him a stylist who could "make a mission statement readable." In the *Georgia Straight*, Verne McDonald teased po-mo George, saying he seemed to be forever trying to perfect "the technique of economical author intrusion." In a newspaper in Atlantic Canada he was taken to task for calling Americans "USAmericans" – something he'd been doing for years. The reviewer wrote, "Once would be cute, twice sufficient, but running across it every other page is annoying."

Angela May Bowering, his wife for nearly thirty-seven years, died on September 8, 1999. She had spent her last afternoon with "Finnish genealogists," family members with whom she'd been researching her origins. She was fifty-nine, and *Egotists and Autocrats* had recently arrived in bookstores. The author, blinded by grief, for once had no interest in seeing the reviews.

In his poem, "Death," he writes that the loss of a lover means never again being able to put an arm around a "dear waist" or touch "a lovely hip." In his eight "Imaginary Poems for AMB," written after her death, he tells her spirit that the twenty-first century was the one:

> *we all wanted you to*
>
> *see, those eyes wide*
> *& still green after all*
> *these tears.*

📖

In January 2000, Penguin Canada sent George a contract for a third popular history. This time, Good hoped he would tackle the story of Canada. Since he'd done the prime ministers, it was a natural next step. "I knew he could do it," she remembers, "but I also understand why someone doesn't want to overreach … So we had … to make him

feel comfortable and [reassure him that] he would be able to do it."
The contract sat unsigned on his desk for a couple of weeks. With
his wife gone after protracted suffering, he couldn't stop replaying
her final hours in his mind. "I will never get over this," he thought.

Writing the country's history would theoretically give him something else to think about, and he eventually signed the contract. But
he couldn't motivate himself, couldn't get into his usual productive
groove – he could barely rouse himself to fulfill his final teaching
commitments. He had applied Penguin's advance to his mortgage
and felt guilty every time he put off doing the work. In the spring,
he used his diary to spell out his state of mind: "In the past few days
I have had a lot of sad missing of dear Angela. I think I haven't hit
bottom yet. I'm very unhappy."

Stone Country: An Unauthorized History of Canada came out in
May 2003, when he was Parliamentary Poet Laureate. In the first
chapter he explains why he chose the title. Before European explorers
and settlers arrived in Canada, Indigenous Peoples lived in a "broad
stone country, and along the spine of that country they left stones
that they had banged together in order to make sharp points." Ending
the chapter in his own special way, he quotes from Al Purdy's poem,
"Lament for the Dorsets." In its last lines, an Inuit hunter is carving
an ivory swan that will survive long after he and his people are gone.
"After 600 years / the ivory thought / is still warm."

In a chapter on the fifties, "Nuclear and Unclear," he tells of the
Louis St. Laurent government setting up the Canada Council for
the Arts, a body that would become "the most important factor in
the country's fight to stay out of Hollywood's sock drawer." Who
else would put it that way? Ryan Knighton thinks fondly of how his
grandmother enjoyed George's histories. They're "just told so bass-ackwards," he says. "She liked that."

Like *Bowering's B.C.* and *Egotists and Autocrats*, *Stone Country*
exhibits a mastery of facts paired with jaunty narration, authorial

intrusion, literary references, and punchy chapter titles like "Get Riel" and "Mackenzie Kink." By that time Bowering had the formula for animating the past down pat. All three of his histories contain a small private joke: a reference to Eugene "Bomber" Lacy, supposedly a madcap Greyhound bus driver from Princeton, B.C. There was no such person; a high school classmate of George's made up the character.

What sets *Stone Country* apart from its two predecessors is its nifty leitmotiv. In Chapter 13, Bowering mentions Tom Longboat, Onondaga from the Six Nations of the Grand River Reserve in Ontario, who became a Canadian sports hero when he won the Boston Marathon in 1907. Sportswriters called him "the racing redskin" and two hundred thousand people turned out to greet him when he returned from Boston. George keeps track of Longboat after his burst of fame, mentioning him five more times. Longboat served in World War I and joined the Home Guard during World War II. In the thirties, he supported himself unglamorously by collecting garbage, including horse manure. Bowering notes that a sportswriter who had it in for Longboat "really enjoyed the image of the ex-world champion with a shovel." After World War II, the marathoner moved back to his home reserve, "where he had been a child named Cogwagee." Asked about the genesis of this superb storytelling element, George, who pored over sports magazines as a boy, said he'd known about Longboat practically forever. Most people, if they know the name, just know about the marathon running.

The reviews of *Stone Country* were decent, or better. A teacher in Ontario called it "an unorthodox work of genius." In the *Globe and Mail*, Don Gillmor, whose *Canada: A People's History* had recently appeared, praised it for blending the standard architecture of a Canadian history with "the tone and language of a Kurt Vonnegut novel" (the second time, at least, that Bowering had been compared to the novelist). A third reviewer in Ontario found it short on solid analysis and a little too cute. And, in B.C., George Fetherling questioned

Bowering about the "gobs of praise" he lavishes on PM John Diefenbaker, mentioning a couple of things Dief did that he surely wouldn't endorse. The fact was, Bowering liked Dief's style and was willing to overlook his failings.

After a few years had gone by, the historian Patricia Roy considered his three popular histories in a journal article. She deemed *Bowering's B.C.* the strongest, since his own province is the part of the country he knows best. In the subsequent books she saw him overemphasizing some minor issues and paying scant attention to others, misjudging their relative importance. With *Stone Country: An Unauthorized History of Canada*, she felt that neither the title nor the subtitle worked. She enjoyed reading it more than *Egotists and Autocrats* but thought its post-Confederation chapters cannibalized passages from Bowering's earlier prime ministers book. Having a trained historian make an assessment is valuable, and Roy, treading carefully, found some weaknesses. The extenuating factors were the toughness of Bowering's triple task, the brutally tight deadlines, and his spouse succumbing to terminal illness as he worked. In hindsight, he probably should have said no to Cynthia Good a little more often.

CHAPTER 19

THE POET LAUREATE

When I was the Parliamentary Poet Laureate of Canada I was asked by the Governor General whether I would write a poem for her to take to the president of Spain, and I didn't. A few Members of Parliament asked me for poems for some occasions too, and I didn't. But when Little League Canada asked me for a poem to print in the program for their annual tournament, I said sure.

—*The Diamond Alphabet: Baseball in Shorts* (2011)

Canadian legislators voted in December 2001 to establish a poet laureate, following the lead of Great Britain, which has had one since 1668, and the United States, which appointed its first in 1937. Jerahmiel "Jerry" Grafstein, a Liberal senator with passionate convictions, made the idea a reality by way of a Private Member's Bill – a rare triumph of personality and persuasion. He believed Canada's major cultural institutions ought to show they cherish poets and writers; he also thought a laureate would bring poetry to the people, help bolster the written word against the onslaughts of the digital age, and possibly even elevate the quality of debate in the House of Commons and the

Senate. As a *Globe and Mail* editorialist would later put it, "Three out of four ain't bad."

After the bill passed, 175 to 60, on December 11, newspaper articles about Grafstein's dream come true said Canada's published poets could write letters of application for the post. In Vancouver, George Bowering thought, "Ah, well, why not?" Throughout his career as a professor he'd written letters recommending students, colleagues, and fellow writers for programs, scholarships, promotions, and awards, so he was adept at making a case. He wrote quite a long letter "tellin' them exactly why I was a good choice."

The first Parliamentary Poet Laureate would serve a two-year term, receiving a nominal stipend of $12,000 a year and an annual travel budget of $10,000. Although the laureate's web page today says the role involves writing poetry for use in Parliament on important occasions, Richard Paré, then the Parliamentary Librarian – the person to whom the laureate reports – didn't want the poet in the national spotlight to feel obliged to write on demand, since "creativity cannot be quantified."

Evidently, thirty-five poets were considered solid candidates and, by the summer of 2002, that long list had been whittled down to a short list of three. Bowering's diary shows he knew he was among those nominees by August 15, 2002. Grafstein had in mind someone like Robert Pinsky, U.S. Poet Laureate Consultant in Poetry from 1997 to 2000. While Pinsky had the title, he managed to "go into the classroom, to go across America, and to inspire people in poetry," says Grafstein. "The project he did for the millennium was magnificent: He went across the country and got a thousand people, from every walk of life, to read their favourite poem."

Predicting who would be named Canada's first Parliamentary Poet Laureate was something the B.C. writer John Moore had attempted. He wrote in the *Ottawa Citizen* that Margaret Atwood, bill bissett, Leonard Cohen, Lorna Crozier, Gary Geddes, Don McKay, John

Newlove, John Pass, Harold Rhenish, and Patricia Young were likely candidates. After it was decided that Bowering would wear the laurel wreath (he got the official phone call on October 21), Moore wrote in the *Vancouver Sun* that he was "hardly the mainstream favourite you'd expect Parliament to put its money on."

Why not? Well, there was the issue that had dogged him early in his writing life – the feeling that because American (and English) poets have been his major influences, he isn't embedded in Canada's literary tradition. Then there was the fact that he doesn't always aim to be reader-friendly. And, mostly, there was his outsize personality. The outspokenness that had led the CBC to call on him for radio and TV commentaries again and again might be a liability on state occasions. He wouldn't be a shrinking violet – he'd yuk it up in public.

And yet he triumphed. The Speakers of the House of Commons and the Senate, choosing from three names put forward by the Parliamentary Librarian, the chair of the Canada Council for the Arts, and the heads of three other cultural institutions must not have wanted "a smarmy President's Choice laureate who tries to please everyone," as Ottawa poet Susan McMaster wrote George in a 2003 email. Bowering, who would later tell the *Toronto Star*'s books columnist that he "never felt any compulsion to keep my mouth shut about anything," was the bard they went for. He considered himself lucky to be the inaugural laureate because he'd be defining the job as he went along. "It's like starting a poem," he told a magazine writer. "If you know what's going on [at the outset], you shouldn't be writing the damn poem."

At the time, he was a widower with a new partner. Jean Baird, who has a Ph.D. in English (her dissertation was an annotated bibliography of Edna O'Brien) and is a former creative director of Canada Book Week, has top-notch organizational skills. Besides rescuing the legendary A-frame house that Al Purdy built on Roblin Lake, in Ontario's Prince Edward County – it was set to be demolished and she oversaw, instead, its renovation into a writers' retreat – she has investigated the effect of prize-giving on literature by reading and evaluating 255 novels that won or were finalists for the Booker Prize. Because she comes from southern Ontario and is a whirlwind of efficiency, George sometimes calls her "the Lake Erie fury." She has auburn hair and takes pleasure in dressing well, with an emphasis on shoes and jewellery. Her signature earrings are tiny gold dragonflies.

Bowering has called Jean Baird, left, a "blessed order in the happenstance of my late years." *Material republished with the express permission of* Vancouver Sun, *a division of Postmedia Network Inc.*

Baird knows, appreciates, and promotes Bowering's work. Before they got together, she started a vogue for it among teenage writers in Port Colborne, Ontario, where she lived. The young people were contributors to *In 2 Print*, a full-colour national magazine she published. When George's first young-adult novel, *Parents from Space*, appeared in 1994 with what she considered weak cover art, she suggested the teens hold a contest to elicit better pictures for a future cover. The magazine received piles of submissions, a winning picture was chosen, and the students invited George to come east to present the prize. He did so on October 26, 1996, which the city had designated George Bowering Day thanks to Jean's advocacy.

During George's term as Poet Laureate, he moved in with Jean in Port Colborne. He was closer there to Ottawa and Toronto, where he'd be making appearances, and to the University of Western Ontario, where he'd be writer-in-residence starting in fall 2003. Bowering and Baird were heading east on November 11, 2002, when the news of his appointment broke. Reporters couldn't reach him easily because he was in transit. Somehow, the orderly disclosure Parliament had been striving for went sideways and November 14 ended up being the big media day in Toronto. Journalists across the land wanted a piece of him.

At year's end, he wrote a poem to order for the *Vancouver Sun* in answer to an editor's request. "A Poem for the New Year" appeared on December 28. Its short lines incorporate the seasonal phrases *lang syne* and *auld acquaintance*, yet it warns of impending environmental disaster. It's about the ruined world that parents are handing to their children. A little girl is sleeping under a tree and, he writes,

> *Whatever you do, do not*
> *slam the year open with a bang,*
> *waken the child*
> *sleeping under that tree*
> *into terror, that tree*
> *dying in our back yard,*
> *birds lining up to mourn. You*
> *wanted a cheer for new*
> *lang syne? Have you looked at the under*
> *cutting of the North Shore mountains,*
> *have you heard the four wheel drives*
> *passing your sweet coupe*
> *on the rain slick of Burrard?*
> *Let that babe sleep, let*
> *chainsaw rest in watershed ...*

Mere weeks into his new role, he found out how much trouble a celebrity can get into when chatting with a reporter. The *Globe and Mail*'s Alexandra Gill phoned to ask a few questions for an arts feature. She wondered if the fact that a cluster of Vancouver poets had recently won major prizes owed anything to the city's vibrant spoken word and performance poetry scenes. He replied with surprising vehemence: "Horseshit!" He went on to say that treating poetry as performance is "crude and extremely revolting" and likened performance poets to "dogs who walk on their hind feet." What he meant by this Johnsonian simile, but didn't make clear enough, was that poetry slams seem to him to be all about "suck[ing] up clapping from your audience." He's leery of those who don't do as he does: approach the language humbly and try to write without shaming it.

T. Paul Ste. Marie, a stylish young Vancouverite who produced and hosted a weekly open mic night called Thundering Word Heard, circulated the article to all of his contacts. In an accompanying note, he wrote, "Don't get me wrong – any press is good press." On the other hand, he was appalled to see the new laureate maligning the many young poets drawn to spoken word and slam. "His discouragement is damaging, in my eyes," he wrote, asking for responses.

The media love a controversy, and this one exploded. Performance poets across North America started crying foul and a photo of Bowering's face with crosshairs superimposed on it turned up online. A person using the name Tuxedo raved incoherently about the perceived insult, going so far as to set up a mock website in George's name, "full of infantile vulgarities and spelling errors," recounted Mark Cochrane in the *Vancouver Sun*.

George and Jean spent most of January 2003 enmeshed in the war of words, trying to mend the rift. Newspapers published letters to the editor pointing out that poetry has a venerable oral tradition – as if Bowering might not have known. Emails flew all over the place. Jamie Reid sent Ste. Marie a note saying, "Try not to hurt him too badly,

T-Paul. We have only one poet laureate just now and the government won't pay for another one if this one gets broken."

It looked as if a February 7 reading by George (with Roy Miki, who'd recently won a Governor General's Award for Poetry) in Vancouver might be the site of a nasty confrontation. Two of George's muscular former students offered to provide security. Luckily, the event proceeded without disruption, but the laureate was wary. He remembers the crowd being "really, really big. Somebody anonymously gave me a cake. I thought, 'Yay!' and then I thought, 'Uh-oh. I'm not eating this cake.'" A few weeks later, he wearily told the editor of an online literary magazine that the contretemps was "a bore, and has had more ink than it deserves."

One of Bowering's plans as laureate was to start a Poem of the Week feature on the web page. The poems were Canadian, of course, and he chose them himself. He wanted to get poets' names and faces onto postage stamps, too, but that couldn't be done within two years. He thought it would be terrific if Canadian poems could appear on Canadian wine bottle labels (Oliver, B.C., was calling itself the wine capital of Canada, fruit orchards having given way to vineyards), but that required endless meetings with vintners and, again, would take more than two years to organize. One thing he could do was visit schools and get young people excited about poetry, as Pinsky had done in the States.

National limelight made George busy. Literary festival and conference organizers wanted him in their lineups and he accepted many of those invitations, especially when they took him to places he'd never been, like Timmins, Ontario. (George gravitates to smaller places in much the same way as he champions smaller presses.) In March 2003, he delighted Campbell River, B.C., by appearing at its Words on the Water Festival. He even wrote a poem for it. In July, Oliver feted him with a special dinner at Tinhorn Creek Vineyards to which dignitaries and everyday people came. He was presented with a barrel of private-label commemorative wine, the equivalent of three hundred bottles. The following summer he returned to present a high school student with a creative writing bursary and received more wine. A town councillor told the *Oliver Chronicle*, "He will be able to entertain Canadians and international visitors with some wonderful wines and will be an excellent ambassador for our wineries."

The year 2003 was one in which poets laureate, their numbers growing, gave concerted thought to their role and responsibilities. Earlier, New Jersey's laureate, Amiri Baraka, had caused an uproar by reading his long poem, "Somebody Blew Up America," at a festival. Four of its lines struck many listeners as anti-Semitic and some began trying to strip him of his title. In the wake of that flap and others, the first U.S. conference for state poets laureate was planned for late April. Marie Harris, New Hampshire's laureate and one of the organizers, said, "It's interesting that so many states have a poet laureate, yet most have not defined the position." Writers accepting the appointments generally "cook up their own plan." Billy Collins, U.S. poet laureate at the time, commented that the laureateship was part of his country's "fascination with things British, like the Burberry trench coat." Yet he conceded that "poetry is easier to understand if you have a head of poetry, just like a country needs a leader."

In Canada's Parliamentary debates leading up to the creation of the position, Grafstein had quoted the Bible, saying, "In the beginning was the Word." He'd called Parliament a "word factory" and said, "Poetry encapsulates popular history and popular memory in a way that history alone cannot ... Is not World War I ... best remembered by the poem 'In Flanders Fields'?" Some members of Parliament, including Marlene Jennings, a Quebec Liberal, and Wendy Lill, a playwright who was the NDP's culture critic, embraced the idea, but others thought it wrongheaded. Madeleine Dalphond-Guiral, a Bloc Québécois member, had said (in French), "What next? When will we be getting our official parliamentary dancer and musician?" MPs and senators alike worried about showcasing poets who write in French as much as those using English. It was decided to alternate between anglophone and francophone laureates.

As for whether an official poet would have to write for state occasions, Noël Kinsella, who would become Speaker of the Senate, quoted Britain's laureate, Andrew Motion, who'd said he wanted to honour the traditional responsibilities but not write poems that were "sycophantic or sentimental." Bowering's approach was to write poems to order only when the assignment fit into his constellation of pleasures and preferences. Here's how "Opening Day," the poem he wrote for Little League Canada, finishes:

> *read about base,*
> *read about ball,*
> *read about baseball.*
>
> *I mean don't delay it.*
> *Get down and play it.*

"Lost in the Library" is a similarly effervescent poem from his term, and a filmmaker named Elvis Prusic made a video of him reciting it, delightfully accompanied by live jazz.

One evening in early September 2003, after Bowering and Baird had had a pleasant Mexican dinner with friends in Ontario, their hosts' dog got into a fight with a neighbour's dog and George lent a hand in trying to separate them. He didn't get bitten, but he fell and broke his right hip. He needed surgery, recovery time in hospital, and occupational therapy. A wheelchair, a walker, and a cane would be necessary as he regained mobility. Several of his scheduled appearances had to be postponed or cancelled. He found it ironic that when he went before a *standing* committee of Parliament to answer questions about the laureateship, he was *seated* in a wheelchair. The experience was

The scoreboard attested to his laurels when Bowering threw the first pitch in a Milwaukee Brewers ball game in June 2003.

frustrating for other reasons, too. Naively, he hadn't been expecting there would be political grandstanding during the session. He was asked such things as, "How many poems have you written so far?" The questioner was looking to do a cost-benefit analysis, as if he were a factory worker rather than an ambassador for poetry.

In the *Winnipeg Sun* on April 24, 2005, an article by Kathleen Harris, "Public Poet's Slim Volume Criticized," expanded on the belief of some parliamentarians that he didn't give Canadians value for money. It said he wrote two poems, eighty-seven lines in total, during his two-year tenure. Pat Martin, New Democrat MP for Winnipeg Centre, weighing this against the laureate's stipend and travel budget, called his output "expensive."

Halfway through his term, Bowering told an interviewer that when it came to accomplishing anything significant as poet laureate, circumstances tied his hands. For one thing, "Parliament gave me no budget for big projects," with the result that he had to spend "enormous amounts of time going to offices in Ottawa and Toronto, begging for money." What's more, "nothing in Ottawa or Toronto gets done in less time than the Iron Age." (Grafstein sympathizes. During his twenty-six years in the Senate he fought for other cultural causes, such as the establishment of a national portrait gallery. He's told his wife he wants his tombstone to summarize his life in two words: "He tried.")

In a report to Parliament on the whole heady experience, dated September 30, 2004, Bowering called the position "the best job I ever had." He said he particularly appreciated having a travel budget, which had made possible a "constant round of readings, lectures, consultations, interviews, press and broadcasting sessions, visits." He suggested future appointments be announced more smoothly and that new laureates be introduced to Parliamentary Library staff. In his diary, though, he tells a funny story. Preparing to return to Vancouver after the sale of the emotion-soaked Kerrisdale house, he was arranging for electrical service to the one he and Baird had bought in West Point Grey. A young man with BC Hydro asked if he was employed. George told him, "I am the Parliamentary Poet Laureate." The Hydro staffer replied, "We'll mark you down as retired."

THE OLD GINK

He hung out of an Expeditor at 1,000 feet
taking pictures ...

He doesn't know
how to do any of these things
he did as a youngster.

But then he had no idea whatever
how to be an old man.

—"How To," *Teeth: Poems, 2006–2011* (2013)

George Bowering and Jean Baird got married on July 20, 2006, at Vancouver's Sylvia Hotel. It was an afternoon wedding. Advising the guests on how to dress, the deckle-edged invitation said, "It will be the middle of summer. This is Vancouver. Just look nice."

Having come through seven eventful decades, George felt lucky to have a dynamic younger woman with his best interests at heart as his partner. He describes her in a poem as a "blessed order in the happenstance of my late years." Jean would become his "first reader, manager, publicist, agent, and sweetheart." She even enjoys baseball, accompanying him to places like Ohio to watch the Toledo Mud Hens play ball. Once they'd become a couple, his diary entries got blander: The impending-train-wreck tension he'd often felt in his first marriage was no more.

At the beginning of October, when he and Jean had been married for less than three months, their lives were rocked by tragedy. Returning to Vancouver after a visit to San Francisco, they learned that Jean's twenty-three-year-old daughter, Bronwyn Dixon, had died in a car crash. In 2006, George had been writing a poem a day for the 2010 book that would be titled *My Darling Nellie Grey*. He was basing each October poem on a funny, misleading, or ambiguous headline in that day's newspaper. If there were ever an excuse to shelve the poetic task he'd set himself, "the insane days before and after Bronwyn's funeral in small-town Ontario would have provided it," he writes in the book's introduction. Yet he stuck with it, feeling the discipline would steady him during a "time of raw crazy grief."

The couple soon began channelling their anguish into a project. Jean had turned to books in her bereavement, reading Joan Didion's *The Year of Magical Thinking* and Katherine Ashenburg's *The Mourner's Dance: What We Do When People Die*. She saw a need for an anthology of Canadian essays on the many forms mourning can take. She and George commissioned such pieces as "Good Grief," in which William Whitehead writes about surviving the death of Timothy Findley, his partner of forty years, and Jill Frayne's "Her Great Art," about the loss of her mother, June Callwood. There are twenty essays in all. Random House Canada published *The Heart Does Break: Canadian Writers on Grief and Mourning*, edited by George Bowering and Jean Baird, in 2010. *Reader's Digest Canada* reprinted two of the essays and a brief excerpt from George's introduction, "May I Bring You Some Tea?"

In his seventies, he had to accept that he was an old gink – "gink" being a semi-derogatory slang term for a man and a tiny but noteworthy part of his lexicon. (Once, he was telling me how a certain popular Canadian author, reading from his work at literary festivals, would trot out the same passage at every podium. The fellow's name didn't spring to mind but he threw out a couple of descriptors: He set his fiction in Nova Scotia and had a son who's also a writer. Alistair MacLeod? Yes, he affirmed, "that's the gink.")

Receiving an honorary degree from the University of Western Ontario in 2003, Bowering wore his Three Stooges tie, as is his wont on such occasions.

Though he's an old gink himself, George has managed to stay frisky. Having a young wife has helped, and so did having an extremely long-lived mother. He couldn't be *that* old if Pearl, nineteen years older, was still alive and cheerful, could he? He'd phone her on Sunday evenings, reaching her in her assisted-living home in Oliver and fondly calling her Cookie. Every time he had a new book out, he'd send her a copy – except for *Pinboy* (2012), which depicts a female teacher seducing his teenage self. Asked, soon after its publication, if *Pinboy* was causing a stir in his hometown, he replied, "I was kinda hoping that nobody there would ever find out about it, especially my mother."

At a time of life when it's normal to slow down or stop, George has been publishing with a rat-a-tat-tat rhythm, one or more books a year. His twenty-first-century output includes *Left Hook: A Sideways Look at Canadian Writing*, a book of essays; *Baseball Love*, a memoir that celebrates his baseball road trips with Jean; *The Box*, a collection of stories of sixties Vancouver; and *10 Women*, ten stories with women's names for titles. His friend Stan Persky has said that while he (Persky) and Brian Fawcett have each written a decent number of books, "George is beyond prolific – [his drive is] a kind of graphomania in a league with John Updike or Joyce Carol Oates." George's 2018 novel, *No One*, shows him unwilling to leave anything he has created on the cutting-room floor. In fact, he considers it his best fiction. *No One* follows the sexual exploits of a post-*Pinboy*, married George Delsing. To some of ECW Press's employees, the extramarital couplings are described in a way that objectifies women, and those who were offended were excused from working on it. In an open letter to them, titled "The Objects of My Affection" and posted on his website, Bowering said he would rather see the novel "attacked by the critics than semi-censored before its birth." Jack David, co-publisher at ECW, sees the novel not as pornography but as evidence that George "writes in as many different ways as it's possible to write." *No One* rings clever changes on Homer's *Odyssey* and James Joyce's *Ulysses* (there's an inversion of Molly Bloom's soliloquy at the end), but it fictionalizes some of Bowering's real-life liaisons only lightly and paints a dismaying picture of sexual competition between unhappily married spouses.

Even as he grumbles about his hearing aids and frets about his likely imminent demise, George continues to drum up workable ideas. When he was a juror for the 2008 Griffin Poetry Prize – something "Mike Ondaatje" had talked him into – he read so much bad poetry that he contemplated making a chapbook "entirely of things such as title page, dedications, quotations, thanks, notes, etc., leaving either no room for the poetry or room for one little poem."

His standout achievement this century has been *My Darling Nellie Grey*. It's a long poem of more than four hundred pages and, for once, he explains in the introduction the writing strategies he used. The book was shortlisted for B.C.'s Dorothy Livesay Poetry Prize, which he would have loved to win. (He knew Livesay, an ardently political poet who lived from 1909 to 1996, and once wrote an essay about her called "Say Live.")

Nellie Grey led to him acquiring a young, influential fan. Daniel Zomparelli, founder of *Poetry Is Dead* magazine, loved the book and analyzed its twelve sections, one by one, in a series of blog posts he called Summer of Bowering. It was thorough coverage, almost always wildly positive. As the series wound up, Zomparelli wrote, "After spending the summer with his book, I can't help but think that he's a good friend that I can call up anytime. Fortunately for Bowering, I don't have his number and I am a lazy stalker." They've since become friends.

Another young friend of George's is Charles Demers, the comedian, novelist, and onetime SFU student. When he and his wife, Cara Ng, were expecting their first child, he and George started writing each other letters about fatherhood. This was a brainwave of Jean's: She could see a book in it. Their "daughters book" would gradually take shape and, after the birth of Demers's and Ng's daughter, Joséphine, be published as *The Dad Dialogues: A Correspondence on Fatherhood (and the Universe)*.

A further blessing in his late years is the Georgettes, a writing group that formed after he gave a week-long workshop in Victoria in 2005. Nine women and one man participated, and when it ended, they didn't want to let him go. He and the Georgettes still get together to write and talk about poetry.

📖

In 2015, Bowering had a health crisis that brought him to the brink of death. One rainy spring afternoon, he put on a broad-brimmed hat and stepped out to run errands on 10th Avenue. Mickey, his and Jean's forty-five-kilogram Bernese mountain dog, accompanied him, though it's normally Jean who walks her. On his way into the West Point Grey branch library, he swayed and crumpled to the sidewalk. He'd had a cardiac arrest.

Ivy Zhang, a fourteen-year-old student at a nearby private school, happened to be walking to the bus stop near the library. "At first, I thought he tripped and fell," she would later tell a *Vancouver Sun* reporter, "but when I went up to him, he wasn't responding." She immediately called 911 and, because there's a firehall close by, response was quick. He was given CPR and rushed to Vancouver General Hospital, where he was treated in the cardiac care unit for twelve days.

George and Jean also give Mickey credit for having sharp senses: The dog had insisted on going out with him. A week after the terrifying close call, Baird told concerned friends her husband was on strong pain meds and was physically weak but that "cognition is huge, though the speech is slow. Looking very good." He recovered more quickly and better than is expected of seventy-nine-year-olds. Baird told *BC BookWorld* that health care workers assessing the progress of his recovery asked him if he could jump, and he jumped. "They said they'd never had another before who was able to jump."

In *Sitting in Jalisco*, a long poem he wrote while in Mexico in January 2016, Bowering writes,

> *What a terrible green the umbrellas are, the sea*
> *another green, my chance of seeing it was*
> *eight percent, and we are so glad we didn't know.*

The poem echoes Wallace Stevens's "Sea Surface Full of Clouds" which begins, "In that November off Tehuantepec," and features umbrellas, ocean, and "paradisal green." Unlike Ondaatje and the late John New-love, Bowering hasn't been a devotee of Stevens. But to a reporter who'd asked what legacy he'd like his poetry to leave, he once said, "Writing poetry is a group job. It's a bunch of people, over hundreds of years, doing it as a group ... I feast off other poets all the time."

With Ivy Zhang, who saved his life with a timely 911 call in April 2015. Mickey the Bernese mountain dog made Bowering take her with him that day. *Photograph by Jeff Vinnick, used with permission.*

Bowering's mother's death had to happen sometime, and he'd been dreading the phone call for years. It finally came on November 8, 2016, just as Americans were electing Donald Trump as their president. Pearl had managed to celebrate her hundredth birthday. On December 26, the anniversary of her and Ewart's wedding, the family buried her ashes with his. They played a recording of her favourite song, "Danny Boy," and all hearts were stirred because the valley really was hushed and white with snow. It would soon seem as if her passing touched off a cascade of losses in the family: Within six months, her daughter, Sally Bowering Brown, and second son, Roger, were also gone.

Since his cardiac arrest, George has been saying he's in extra innings, and by now he's figured out how to be an old man. He cheerfully grouses about never wanting to use such newfangled products as body wash (what's wrong with soap?) and about never seeing teenagers reading books these days. He, on the other hand, has read six thousand. The University of British Columbia Library has accepted his massive collection, organized in categories such as Great Modernists, Other Modernists, Beats, Black Mountain, Anti-Novelists, and Language Poets. Though he's been buying books all his life, he knows he can't take them with him.

Notes

CHAPTER 1: MR. PROLIFIC

she spoke of a TV camera crew: Rebecca Wigod, "Canada's First Poet
Laureate Turns the Page," *Vancouver Sun*, May 14, 2005, D17.

"measured for your coffin": James Atlas, *The Shadow in the Garden:
A Biographer's Tale* (New York: Pantheon Books, 2017), 296.

where Pittsburgh was: George Bowering, "Five Cents' Worth of Sports,"
Five Cent Review 1, 2, August 1969.

"couldn't face the idea": George Bowering, interviewed by the author,
Vancouver, December 9, 2011.

"typewriters at the open windows": George Bowering, "The Great
Grandchildren of Bill Bissett's Mice," in Bowering, *Urban Snow*
(Vancouver: Talonbooks, 1992).

"He's a painter": Bowering tells this story in his book, *The Moustache:
Memories of Greg Curnoe* (Toronto: Coach House Press, 1993), 111.

"beautiful lyric poems": Thea Bowering, interviewed by the author,
Edmonton, February 18, 2013.

"refreshing approach": Erín Moure, email to the author, September 8, 2013.

join a group to study: Fred Wah told me, "A couple of years ago in
the Kootenay School of Writing, I formed a little reading group
around ... Erín Moure's *O Cidadán* [2002], which is a very difficult
kind of book. There were only half a dozen people interested, and
one of them was George."

Imago ... *achieved*: Karis Shearer, "*Imago* & the Canadian Long Poem:
The Cultural Work of George Bowering," *Open Letter*, Fourteenth
Series, 4, Fall 2010, 18.

Wayde Compton: Interviewed by the author, Vancouver, October 4, 2012.

genesis of title Errata: Bowering interview, November 9, 2012.

"It was sent to me": Marc Côté on the telephone from Toronto, November 12, 2012.

T.F. Rigelhof review: "Pinboy Wizard," *Globe and Mail*, October 13, 2012, R20.

"High School Anthologies": In Bowering, *Another Mouth* (Toronto: McClelland & Stewart, 1979).

Nick Mount's Arrival: Toronto: House of Anansi Press, 2017.

Encyclopedia of Literature in Canada: W.H. New, ed. (Toronto: University of Toronto Press, 2002).

"nobody knows": George Bowering and Jean Baird interview, Vancouver, July 26, 2011.

"avant-gardism": John Bemrose, "Technical Risks and a Great Catholicity of Taste from a Spirited Poet," *Globe and Mail*, October 2, 1982, E15.

CHAPTER 2: THE BOY

Writing the Okanagan: Excerpts from Bowering's literary writing concerned with the region (Vancouver: Talonbooks, 2015).

"Nature's Gentlemen": Sherril Foster, *According to the Giant: A History of Summerland and the Okanagan Valley in British Columbia* (Summerland, B.C.: Okanagan Annie Productions, 1998), 39.

a viable career: Rosemary Neering, *A Traveller's Guide to Historic British Columbia*, revised edition (North Vancouver: Whitecap Books, 2002), 110.

The desert bloomed: "They found a desert & made it bloom" is a recurring line in "Desert Elm," a poem Bowering wrote in 1973 in homage to his father and the poet H.D.

"He liked the way": Pearl Bowering, interviewed by the author, Oliver, B.C., August 4, 2013.

"mask ... chest protector": George Bowering, *The Diamond Alphabet: Baseball in Shorts* (Toronto: BookThug, 2011), 70.

"schoolgirl athlete": George Bowering, *A Magpie Life: Growing a Writer* (Toronto: Key Porter Books, 2001), 14.

baby looked bruised: Daniel Wood writes in "George Bowering's Home Run," *Elm Street*, November 2003, 54, that newborn George had "two blackened eyes and a head dented from the doctor's forceps." And Bowering writes in *A Magpie Life*: "My enormous head [at birth] was black and all mushy, they say ..."

sailor suit: For proof, see the photo on the cover of Bowering's *Autobiology* (*Georgia Straight* Writing Supplement, Vancouver Series #7, 1972).

started ... lives ... Depression: In interviews on February 27 and October 15, 2015, Bowering referred to himself as a "Puritan," seeming to mean an upstanding person or goody-goody.

raspberry canes ... arch: These details come from *Autobiology*.

nearly ... a ghost town: Daniel Francis, ed., *Encyclopedia of British Columbia* (Madeira Park, B.C.: Harbour Publishing, 2000), 305.

propaganda images: George Bowering, *Stone Country: An Unauthorized History of Canada* (Toronto: Penguin Canada, 2003), 258.

"eggs in there": George Bowering, "Eggs in There," in Bowering, *My Darling Nellie Grey* (Vancouver: Talonbooks, 2010) – the source of much of the colourful detail in this chapter.

didn't talk ... "four going on five": Bowering, *A Magpie Life*, as above, 44.

puzzling out articles: "I started reading the Vancouver *Province* when I was four, I guess," he writes in "Eggs in There."

"such peril": George Bowering, "The Brush Fire," in *Autobiology*, 16. He was five at the time, he writes in his 2006 memoir, *Baseball Love*.

"The Egg": First published in Bowering's *The Gangs of Kosmos* (Toronto: House of Anansi Press, 1969).

second coming: "When I was about five I thought there was a chance that I was Jesus come back," Bowering told the American poet Rachel Loden in an interview published in 2007 in the online poetry magazine *Jacket*.

sense of being different: George Bowering, email to Gerri Sinclair, December 17, 1985, Library and Archives Canada (LAC), George Bowering fonds (1999–2003), second accession, Series A, Box 34.

repeating jokes: Dr. John Boone, interviewed by the author, Vancouver, July 30, 2014.

"family was not rich": George Bowering, *Pinboy: A Memoir* (Toronto: Cormorant Books, 2012), 114.

freeze tag: Or, as Bowering writes in *Pinboy*, "It was Carol Wilkins who gave me my first broken nose in a failed game of statues."

"you ... knew of everybody": Will Thornton-Trump, interviewed by the author, Vancouver, March 25, 2014.

William ... Lyttle: His new surname came about after his mother suddenly died, his father left the family, and an uncle adopted him.

"Wanna ... play guns?": Will Thornton-Trump interview, November 15, 2011.

Kickapoo Joy Juice: George Bowering, *Delsing* (unpublished autobiographical novel), 1961, LAC, George Bowering fonds (1985–2004), Series B, Boxes 38 and 39a; also in Contemporary Literature Collection, W.A.C. Bennett Library, Simon Fraser University (SFU), Burnaby, B.C.

Blue Mountain: George Bowering, *Writing the Okanagan*, 18.

Cryhat Valley: In 1986, Will Thornton-Trump wrote an essay about the episode with this title. It was published in *Essays on Canadian Writing* 38, Summer 1989 (a special George Bowering issue), 81–85.

"summertime smell": George Bowering, *Swift Current* (proto-email) message to Fred Wah, June 27, 1986, Special Collections, Simon Fraser University Library.

urging Will: "George has a habit of getting other people in trouble and staying out of trouble himself," Bowering's brother Roger said in a telephone interview on August 23, 2013. "He would pick a fight with someone on Will's behalf and go behind a door and shout encouragement."

writing down the titles: Pamela Paul, editor of the *New York Times Book Review*, has done this, too, though not for as many years.

"share a brain": George Bowering, "It Happened," *Autobiology*, 51.

"closer to the sun": Will Thornton-Trump interview, March 25, 2014.

motorcycles and rifles: George Bowering, conversation with the author, Vancouver, September 28, 2017. And see George Bowering and Ryan Knighton, *Cars* (Toronto: Coach House Books, 2002), 87.

"running a rock slide": Bowering phrases it that way in *Writing the Okanagan*, 209.

adult at a … keyboard: Bowering interview, February 27, 2015.

"postwar kids": In *Delsing*, an unpublished autobiographical novel from 1961, Bowering writes of a family much like his, with "two Depression kids and two postwar kids."

"he was enjoying it!": Roger Bowering interview, August 23, 2013.

"plaster bandage": George Bowering, "Roger Falling," *Autobiology*, 56.

the greatest year: Bowering, "Feller and the Sunsplash," in *A Magpie Life*, 96, and also in Bowering, *The Diamond Alphabet*, 18.

"marvellous sports year": Bowering, *Baseball Love* (Vancouver: Talonbooks, 2006), 19.

source of delight: George Bowering and Ryan Knighton, *Cars*, as above, 33.

"horseplay, my friend?": George Bowering, email to Gerri Sinclair, December 15, 1985, LAC, as above.

"regimental tie": Bowering interview, October 31, 2014.

"cheek by jowl": David Amor on the phone from his home in Illinois on October 8, 2017.

"no eyebrows, to speak of": George Bowering's diary, February 18, 1977. Wendy Amor Arnold, mother of three, had died of cancer ten days earlier, aged only forty.

"different shapes … of boy": George Bowering, *Delsing*, as above.

back pain: George Bowering, "Alphabiography," in *A Magpie Life*, 40.

sunstroke: George Bowering, "The Pool," in *Autobiology*, 77–78. See also "Scrubbing the Pool" (part of "Four Jobs"), in *West Window: The Selected Poetry of George Bowering* (Toronto: General Publishing, 1982), 142.

pinsetter: Hence the title of his fictionalized memoir, *Pinboy*.

taking the job away: Hence the title "Deking Dad," an essay in *A Magpie Life*, 47–52.

rule book memorized: George Bowering, *Baseball: A Poem in the Magic Number 9* (Toronto: Coach House, 1967).

per column-inch: Bowering, "Deking Dad," as above, 50.

Bob Broeg's letter: Reproduced on pages 344 and 345 of Bowering's *Writing the Okanagan*.

madly in love: Victoria College alumnus George Bowering speaking with Daniel Zomparelli in "In His Own Words," *UVic Torch*, Autumn 2011, 33.

red ink: George Bowering with Daniel Zomparelli, "Red Ink: Memoirs of Victoria College," on YouTube ("George Bowering[:] Memories of Victoria College & excerpts from *My Darling Nellie Grey*," 10:29, https://youtu.be/XhqeovvLMok).

"fizzle[d] out": Roy Miki, *A Record of Writing: An Annotated and Illustrated Bibliography of George Bowering* (Vancouver: Talonbooks, 1989), xvi.

"fivestar period of remorse": Bowering, *Delsing*.

shelter in movie houses: Bowering diary, July 10, 1959 (the fifth anniversary of his signing up).

high IQ: Bowering, *Delsing*.

calibrate a camera: Bowering, "Air Camera," in *The World, I Guess: Poems* (Vancouver: New Star Books, 2015), 103.

"acey-deucy": Bowering interview, July 23, 2014.

"look in the ... mudroom": Bowering interview, as above.

carrot sticks: Bowering interview, November 20, 2013.

"drinks and women": George Bowering, "The Next Place," in *Auto-biology*, 76.

lost his virginity: While in Manitoba with his wife, Angela, he wrote in his diary on September 17, 1966: "We lookt a bit at Portage, saw house where I finally lost my cherry."

emulating James Dean: Bowering, *Pinboy*, 148.

"shared his ... Underwood typewriter": Bowering, "The Memory of Red Lane," in his essay collection, *A Way With Words* (Ottawa: Oberon Press, 1982); reprinted in *Writing the Okanagan*, 115.

"The ABCs": Ever since, Bowering has found the alphabet a marvellous way to organize a piece of writing.

He didn't recognize: Bowering interview, December 11, 2012.

"my life decisions": Daniel Zomparelli, "In His Own Words," as above, 33.

"I matured some": Bowering diary, July 10, 1959.

"We want ... knowledge": George Bowering, ed., introduction to *Letters from Geeksville: Red Lane to George Bowering, 1960–1964* (Prince George, B.C.: Caledonia Writing Series, 1976).

CHAPTER 4: THE DIARIST

"high in the chicken wire box": George Bowering, *Baseball: A Poem in the Magic Number 9*, as above.

"bowling scores and ... baseball": Bowering interview, November 20, 2013.

"Edison of postmodernism": Alan Twigg, "Two Angles on the Short Story," *Province* (Vancouver) magazine section, March 4, 1984, 6.

sixty-six: Bowering, *Baseball Love*, 127.

"performed brilliantly": Edna Davis, email to the author, October 24, 2017.

"full shelf of Farrell": Bowering diary, October 20, 1958.

It was bliss: The poet bpNichol (Barrie Phillip Nichol) got a different feeling from library stacks. As Bowering says in his introduction to *An H in the Heart*, a 1994 book of Nichol's poems which he and Michael Ondaatje edited, "When bpNichol worked for his keep in the basement of the library at the University of Toronto, he would feel the weight of all those floors full of books above him. What would be the use of adding another book or two to those millions of heavy volumes, he would think."

value of a poet's vision: Peter Middleton, "The Voices in 'The Desert Music,'" *William Carlos Williams Review* 27, No. 2 (Fall 2007), 169.

"the book dropped": Bowering tells this story in several places, notably in "My Heart in Hiding," in *A Magpie Life*, 56.

man carry an umbrella: Bowering, "Alphabiography," 34.

"sunsquare shadows": Bowering diary, November 6, 1958.

a loner by nature: Pat Slater's "Poetry and Politics Blend in Bowering," in Calgary's *Mount Royal College Reporter*, February 28, 1983, contains this Bowering statement: "I have always been a loner. Friends tell me that I am a lone kind of figure. Perhaps that is an inevitable outcome when you grow up smart in a small town." And on page 82 of *Pinboy*, he writes, "My extra-curricular reading [at age fifteen] went along with my loneness, as it still does."

"gathering material": Bowering, "The Great Grandchildren of Bill Bissett's Mice," as above.

"wonderful time of one's life": Bowering diary, June 12, 1959.

"ridiculous-looking figure": Jamie Reid, interviewed by the author, North Vancouver, June 6, 2013.

"plastic RCAF raincoat": Donald Cameron (now Silver Donald Cameron), *Conversations with Canadian Novelists, Part Two* (Toronto: Macmillan, 1973), 3. According to Bowering, it wasn't made of plastic.

"Baseball and the Canadian Imagination": *Canadian Literature* 108, Spring 1986. Reprinted in Bowering's 1988 essay collection, *Imaginary Hand* (Edmonton: NeWest Press).

"flashed himself around": Fred Wah, interviewed by the author, Kelowna, B.C., August 1, 2013.

"good-looking ... woman": Bowering interview, April 28, 2014.

"written in strict iambs": Lionel Kearns, interviewed by the author, Vancouver, November 15, 2012.

"little tiny world": Bowering interview, April 28, 2014.

walked her back: Maria Hindmarch, interviewed by the author, Vancouver, April 20, 2012.

"uncolumnist of the decade": Bowering diary, February 2, 1959.

"loudness and brashness": Bowering diary, April 1, 1959.

sweet-natured: Jake Zilber was "gentle and quiet and unassuming and modest," with "these big huge brown eyes that you almost fell into," Bowering told me on December 11, 2012.

"mushroom earwig": In Bowering's *Another Mouth* (1979) and in his *Selected Poems: Particular Accidents* (1980).

"baths once a week": Bowering interview, April 28, 2014.

curdled glop: Will Thornton-Trump, "The Card Table," April 1995, unpublished.

"inward beauty": Bowering diary, September 25, 1958.

Bronislaw Huberman: Known as "the Jewish Schindler" for founding the Palestine Symphony Orchestra and filling it with European Jewish musicians exiled by Adolf Hitler.

"tiny little thing": Bowering interview, April 28, 2014.

"avant-garde, far-out": Bowering interview, November 9, 2012.

he bought ... a print: Bowering reminisces about this in a May 2, 1969, diary entry.

music based on it: Barbara Pentland's "Three Piano Duets after Pictures by Paul Klee," 1958–59.

The Good Woman of Setzuan: Today the Brecht play's title is generally rendered as *The Good Person of Szechwan*.

"*blitzed a book store*": Bowering diary, November 8, 1958.

"*sweater and bare bottom*": Bowering diary, November 12, 1960.

"*the neatest year*": Bowering, "Alphabiography," 32.

$200 a month: Bowering, "Alphabiography," 32.

sixty-five-cent dinners: Bowering diary, April 24, 1962.

lifting … sandwich halves: Bowering interview, April 28, 2014.

uncertain about his future: W.H. New, interviewed by the author, Vancouver, March 21, 2012.

their own turf: Lionel Kearns interview, November 15, 2012.

Hut B-6: Frank Davey, *When TISH Happens: The Unlikely Story of Canada's "Most Influential Literary Magazine"* (Toronto: ECW Press, 2011), 129.

Wordsworth and … Coleridge: Eva-Marie Kröller, *George Bowering: Bright Circles of Colour* (Vancouver: Talonbooks, 1992), 20.

"*required reading*": John Newlove, "The Poetry Scene: It's Alive, Man, in B.C. – But the Poets Are Unknown," *Vancouver Sun*, Leisure section, July 26, 1963, 17.

"*snugged so tight*": Robert Hogg, interviewed by the author, Ottawa, August 2, 2017.

"*a very tight group*": Pierre Coupey, interviewed by the author, West Vancouver, October 22, 2015.

"*the* Ubyssey *crowd*": Bowering interview, July 26, 2011.

"*cheerful fellow*": Frank Davey, interviewed by the author, Kelowna, July 31, 2013.

"*pretty dominant*": Daphne Marlatt, interviewed by the author, Vancouver, January 11, 2013.

George Delsing character: "He's not me – I am me. But he is a projection of myself more than anyone else is," Bowering writes in "Delsing and Me," published in a short-fiction anthology, a journal, and, in 1985, in his essay collection *Craft Slices*. For the character, he wanted a surname ending in "-ing," like his own. From the world of Major League Baseball, he chose that of Jim Delsing, an outfielder from 1948 to 1960.

CHAPTER 6: THE *TISH* MAN

"most people … better poetry": Bowering, "Years of Lyrics," preface to *Changing on the Fly: The Best Lyric Poems of George Bowering* (Vancouver: Polestar / Raincoast Books, 2004), 7.

"makes the thing manifest": Jamie Reid interview, June 6, 2013.

his best-known poem: Earle Birney's emotive "David," first published in a book in 1942, had a similar place in its author's career. Despite the many fine poems Birney wrote later, "David" remains the one that most readers know and like best.

mildly irksome: In "Rewriting My Grandfather," an essay in his *Vermeer's Light: Poems, 1996–2006* (Vancouver: Talonbooks, 2006), 187–215, Bowering explains that its stubborn immortality grates on him, as do the minor biographical errors it contains.

more than once: George Bowering, "How I Wrote One of My Poems," in *A Magpie Life*, 62–70. See also "Rewriting My Grandfather," in *Vermeer's Light*. As well, the burlap-wall incident appears in *Piccolo Mondo* (Toronto: Coach House), a 1998 novel he wrote with Angela Bowering, David Bromige, and Michael Matthews. He has continued to mention the 1962 incident. On page 183 of *Pinboy*, the narrator says: "I took to smashing walls with my fist, until I hit a concrete wall with burlap pasted to it."

"you'd better marry me": Angela Luoma, letter to George Bowering, May 29, 1962, LAC, George Bowering fonds (1985–2004), first accession, Series A.

"linoleumated … digs": Bowering, "Rewriting My Grandfather," as above, 193.

"He was really steamed": Will Thornton-Trump interview, November 15, 2011.

eminently teachable: Frank Davey interview, August 2, 2013.

Survival: Toronto: House of Anansi, 1972, 2012. In *Arrival* (as above, 70), Nick Mount calls this "the most ambitious book ever written on Canadian literature, the only one to attempt to define all of it – from start to date, English and French – in a single word."

analyzing a few lines: "In Tallman's courses, you might spend the whole second half of the year on three poems," Bowering told me on July 1, 2013.

close friend of hers: "Ellen and Duncan always had a fabulous time together," Karen Tallman, the Tallmans' daughter, a psychologist, said in an interview in Vancouver on April 17, 2012. "They were wicked, playful, gossipy."

"whimsy ... bebop": Ekbert Faas with Maria Trombacco, *Robert Creeley: A Biography* (Montreal: McGill-Queen's University Press, 2001), 66.

strong enjambment: Stephen Burt, "What Life Says to Us" (a review of four posthumous Creeley collections), *London Review of Books* 30, 4, February 21, 2008.

"no bullshit man": Bowering diary, July 16, 1962.

"a joy": Maria Hindmarch interview, April 20, 2012.

"What an inscape!": Maria Hindmarch, email to the author, April 19, 2012.

Ginsberg sleeping: Karen Tallman interview, April 17, 2012.

"From Lucky Luciano": Pauline Butling, "TISH: The Problem of Margins," in *Writing in Our Time: Radical Poetries in English (1957–2003)*, ed. Butling and Susan Rudy (Waterloo, Ontario: Wilfrid Laurier University Press, 2005), 53.

myth, erudition, and magic: Robert Duncan had "a very complicated, rococo mind," Bowering told me on July 23, 2014.

"my faculties at large": The young Vancouverites whom Duncan influenced loved that phrase – Michael Matthews, particularly. After his death in 2012, his widow, Carol, collected his writings in a book called *My Faculties at Large*.

each kick in five dollars: Pauline Butling, "Robert Duncan in Vancouver: On Reading, Writing, and Non-upmanship," in *W*, No. 10, "A Duncan Delirium" (Vancouver: Kootenay School of Writing, 2005), 10–20, http://www.kswnet.org/texts/KSW_W10.pdf.

"He said almost everything": Michael Davidson, in his foreword to Lisa Jarnot's *Robert Duncan, the Ambassador from Venus: A Biography* (Berkeley and Los Angeles: University of California Press, 2012), writes: "I once invited him to give a lecture on Ezra Pound as modernist at which he proceeded to talk about aerial bombardment during World War II, the DNA code, his Jewish ancestry (he had none), his grandmother's life on the frontier, art glass, what is wrong with pop art, the Waite tarot deck, and various sexual experiences during the late 1940s – all without mentioning Pound. If this was disconcerting for the audience, it was to me a brilliant demonstration of Pound's collage method."

lightly scrambling: Frank Davey said on July 31, 2013, "There was some discussion of how [the name *Shit*] would be misinterpreted or just seen as some kind of irresponsible naming. That was when Duncan suggested a phonetic inversion of 'shit' [to make] 'TISH.'"

TISH: Issues are held in the Contemporary Literature Collection, Special Collections, W.A.C. Bennett Library, Simon Fraser University, Burnaby, B.C.

"rip-off of … Ginsberg": Frank Davey interview, July 31, 2013.

"Where were they?": Bowering interview, October 31, 2014; Marlatt interview, January 11, 2013.

the stillborn collection: To rectify the fact that *Sticks & Stones* barely saw the light of day in 1962, Talonbooks would publish a handsome version – illustrated by Gordon Payne, as originally planned – in 1989.

friends … appalled: Fred Wah and Pauline Butling interview, August 1, 2013.

took the criticism to heart: Scotch-taping the Bromige letter into his diary on February 15, 1963, Bowering sheepishly wrote below it, "This from Bromige, to my embarrassment, sums up the opinion of people whom I respect most, including, belatedly, alas, myself."

"special antipathy": Ekbert Faas with Maria Trombacco, *Robert Creeley*, as above, 287.

last issue he, Davey ... and Wah: David Dawson would become the new editor of *TISH*, replacing Frank Davey.

TISH: No. 1–19: Ed. Frank Davey (Vancouver: Talonbooks, 1975).

"heat and sandals": Carol Reid, interviewed with husband Jamie on June 6, 2013.

"Poetry Summer": In Bowering, *Words, Words, Words: Essays and Memoirs* (Vancouver: New Star Books, 2012), 117–23.

"chalk seemed to leap": Warren Tallman, "Poets in Vancouver," in Warren Tallman fonds, Special Collections, SFU Library. See also Aaron Vidaver's blog: "Warren Tallman: 'Poets in Vancouver' (1963)", August 10, 2009, https://vidaver.word press.com/2009/08/10/warren-tallman-vancouver-1963/.

The Line Has Shattered: (Vancouver: Non-Inferno Media Productions, 2013). The film's subtitle is *A Documentary Film about the 1963 Vancouver Poetry Conference.*

lectures ... readings ... discussions: Warren Tallman asked Fred Wah to record the readings and panel discussions. The tapes, which have been digitized, can be heard online at https://slought.org/resour ces/vancouver_1963.

"anthropology, metaphysics ...": E. Fredric Franklyn, untitled article, in *El corno emplumado / The Plumed Horn* 9, January 1964, 151.

mostly his belt buckle: See Bowering's word portrait of Olson in his 1973 long poem, *Curious* (Toronto: Coach House Press).

"positive stuff": Dan McLeod, interviewed by the author, Vancouver, June 10, 2015.

Ode to the West Wind: In *A Magpie Life*, 60–61, Bowering calls this "maybe the simplest-sounding most complicated poem in the English language."

"*Ginsberg got me interested*": Bowering interview, March 29, 2013.

Bobbie Louise Hawkins: Over lunch some years later, Bowering and friends Stan Persky and George Stanley envisioned a movie in which Joan Baez would play Hawkins, Warren Beatty would be Creeley, Orson Welles would act the part of Olson, Peter Ustinov would appear as Duncan, Vincent Price as Blaser, and Ginsberg would play himself – this according to George's diary, August 11, 1971.

unusual childhood: For a transcript of the session, prepared by Charles Watts, see Robert Duncan, "A Life in Poetry," in *W*, No. 10, 89–116, http://www.kswnet.org/texts/KSW_W10.pdf.

"*fantastic experience*": Robert Hogg interview, August 2, 2017.

CHAPTER 7: THE HUSBAND

"*temperamental*," "*bossy*": Angela Luoma, letter to George Bowering, May 28, 1962, LAC, as above.

"*cut the BS*": Roger Bowering interview, August 23, 2013.

"*true selves*": Thea Bowering interview, February 20, 2013.

"*kind of abrupt*": George Bowering in his and Charles Demers's *The Dad Dialogues: A Correspondence on Fatherhood (and the Universe)* (Vancouver: Arsenal Pulp Press, 2016), 97.

"*club you to death*": Luoma letter to Bowering, May 29, 1962, LAC, as above.

"*be prepared for anything*": Luoma letter to Bowering, June 18, 1962, LAC, as above.

"*see about your chest*": Luoma letter to Bowering, June 23, 1962, LAC, as above.

"*pack of safes*": George Bowering's diary, January 13, 1962.

mental illness: George Bowering interviews, October 31, 2014, and October 22, 2016.

fictional character: Angela Bowering et al., *Piccolo Mondo: A Novel of Youth in 1961 as Seen Somewhat Later*, as above, 38.

"letting people down": Bowering diary, May 14, 1962.

"best ... knower of literature": Bowering diary, July 1, 1962.

"softly loving": Bowering diary, April 1, 1962.

"their emotional energies": Brian Fawcett, interviewed by the author, Vancouver, July 24, 2013.

age of his father: Roy Miki fonds, Special Collections, University of British Columbia (UBC) Library.

fifteen minutes late: Bowering, "Alphabiography," 10.

wouldn't be able to fart: Bowering diary, December 20, 1962.

Faulkner ... list: Bowering interview, July 1, 2013.

"lovely great supper": Bowering diary, December 16, 1962.

"It wreaked havoc": Sharon Thesen, interviewed by the author, Vancouver, June 9, 2013.

"Don't hassle, baby": Angela Bowering et al., *Piccolo Mondo*, 113–14.

a stylist's model: Bowering diary, February 4, 1964.

"anxiety about her looks:": Thea Bowering interview, February 18, 2013.

keeps applying makeup: Margaret Atwood, *Surfacing* (Toronto: McClelland & Stewart, 1994 [1972]), 43–44.

stripping off: Atwood, *Surfacing*, 134–37.

a troubled marriage: Bowering would respond to *Surfacing* years later. His mischievous essay, "Desire and the Unnamed Narrator," appeared in *Descant* in fall 1988 and can now be found in his book *The Rain Barrel* (Vancouver: Talonbooks, 1994).

half of ... Canadians smoked: "Why Prohibition Failed," editorial, *Globe and Mail*, September 23, 2017, F6.

"they both got it": Carol Matthews, interviewed by the author, Victoria, B.C., August 8, 2013.

"No record stores": Bowering, "What I Saw and Heard in the Sixties," in *A Magpie Life*, 117.

"more than ... a housewife": Lynn Spink, interviewed by the author, Toronto, May 29, 2014.

Points on the Grid: Toronto: Contact Press, 1964.

loved him one moment: Bowering diary, February 25, 1963.

"collapsing" nature: Bowering diary, June 13, 1963.

"a girl I like and love": Bowering diary, December 14, 1963.

Mother Goddess: Carol Reid interview, June 6, 2013.

"Big Boom Boom": George Bowering, ed., *Letters from Geeksville*, as above.

their chihuahuas: Earle Birney, the older B.C. poet of "David" fame, had written to Bowering on May 18, 1965, "It's a bloody shame you have had to give up that pleasant flat because the landlady insisted on classifying those two ethereal animalcules of yours as Dogs." Special Collections, UBC Library, George Bowering Box 1.

alarming aerogram: Angela Bowering, letter to George Bowering, June 6, 1966, LAC, as above.

"killing pigs": George Bowering, "Athens," in *Europe Journal 1966*, LAC, George Bowering fonds (1985–2004), first accession, Series B, Box 34.

"Eye-Kicks in Europe": This hasn't been published, but Bowering has drawn on it to create short fiction and poetry.

"It pleased me": Antony Bellette, letter to the author, April 15, 2014.

educated men: "We just assumed that it was the natural order of things to get university jobs around the country," Bowering writes about himself and Roy Kiyooka in "What I Saw and Heard in the Sixties," as above, 123.

educated women: The literary critic Pauline Butling, who was at university in the same era, recalls that women were "not automatically assumed to have a place [in the academe]. When I was in graduate school, all these guys – there was just an open door and pathway leading right to a job … I didn't see that at all … There was maybe one female prof [in UBC's English department] at the time."

stop a single bullet: George Lyttik, "George Bowering: Portrait of a Poet as an Alive Man," *The Albertan*, August 27, 1966.

vibrant hues: Bowering interviews, October 31, 2014, and February 27, 2015.

eighteen dollars: Bowering diary, March 17, 1967.

$11,000: According to Nick Mount in *Arrival: The Story of CanLit*, 72, the Canada Council for the Arts had initiated writer-in-residence programs in 1965 and paid half of Bowering's salary.

"poor wooden apartment": Bowering diary, November 13, 1967.

superb reading series: In "On Not Teaching the Véhicule Poets," in *A Magpie Life*, 154–55, Bowering writes, "The poets were flown to Montreal, met at the airport, lodged at the Ritz-Carlton Hotel, given lots of attention and room service, a dinner, the reading, and a party that was not BYO anything." Recordings of the 1966–74 readings can be found at http://spokenweb.ca/sgw-poetry-readings/.

Ted Berrigan: Bowering diary, December 6, 1970.

"genial … nincompoop": Margaret Atwood, "Bowering Pie … Some Recollections," *Essays on Canadian Writing* 38, Summer 1989, 5.

cartoon of him: Jean Baird, David W. McFadden, and George Stanley, eds., *71(+) for GB: An Anthology for George Bowering on the Occasion of His 70th Birthday* (Toronto: Coach House Press, 2005), 115.

"naughty jokes": Margaret Atwood, quoted by Brian Busby in *A Gentleman of Pleasure: One Life of John Glassco, Poet, Memoirist, Translator, and Pornographer* (Montreal: McGill-Queen's University Press, 2011), 212.

"widow's weeds": Frank Davey, *When TISH Happens*, as above, 270.

"someone intelligent": Davey, *When TISH Happens*, 271.

"Weeping Willow": In Sharon Thesen's *The Good Bacteria: Poems* (Toronto: House of Anansi Press, 2006).

"constant nagging": Antony Bellette, letter to Mr. and Mrs. A. Bellette, of Sandy Bay, Tasmania, Australia, October 1970; given to the author.

Atwood tried to help: Bowering, "Fall 1969. Montreal," in *His Life: A Poem* (Toronto: misFit / ECW Press, 2000). Atwood isn't named in the poem, so only insiders know which "she" is meant.

"taking a snooze": Bowering diary, March 16, 1971.

"busting pomposity": Bowering diary, February 20, 1971.

polluted air: There was so much heavy industry in Montreal then that the outside windowsills of their apartment were "piled an inch high with grimy black dust," George writes in *Baseball Love*, 105.

"just about everybody likes it": Bowering diary, April 17, 1971.

"desertion," "abandonment": Bowering diary, September 25, 1989.

"People ... loved listening": Jim Allan, interviewed by the author, Vancouver, February 27, 2012.

"exhilarating and moving": Smaro Kamboureli, interviewed by the author, Salt Spring Island, B.C., April 7, 2017.

"a wonderful book": Angela Bowering, *Figures Cut in Sacred Ground: Illuminati in "The Double Hook"* (Edmonton: NeWest Press, 1988). The book grew out of her master's thesis on Watson.

The Letters of Dido: Begun in the seventies and revised in the early eighties, the manuscript is at Library and Archives Canada, George Bowering fonds (1985–2004), first accession, Series B, Box 40.

intriguing structure: George Bowering, *How I Wrote Certain of My Books* (Toronto: Mansfield Press, 2011), 111–14.

"delivered straight up": Denise Bukowski, letter to George Bowering, September 26, 1988, LAC, George Bowering fonds (1999–2003), second accession, Box 7.

"tone of disillusionment": Eva-Marie Kröller, *George Bowering: Bright Circles of Colour*, as above, 42.

"slightly cautious shuffle": Ryan Knighton, interviewed by the author, Vancouver, January 10, 2012.

"I could tell": George Bowering interview, December 9, 2011.

"just ... one speed": Wayde Compton interview, Vancouver, October 4, 2012.

"half a stanza": Bruce Lord, quoted in Charlie Demers, "Legendary Bowering Retires," *The Peak* (Simon Fraser University's student newspaper), March 19–25, 2001, 3.

"a writing community": Roger Farr, interviewed by the author, Vancouver, July 21, 2012.

"an odious job": Bowering diary, November 14, 1963, and December 14, 1964.

As I Lay Dying: Bowering diary, February 9, 1966.

how he found time: Kathy Mezei, interviewed by the author, Vancouver, March 27, 2013.

"happen for me magically": Dwight Gardiner, interviewed by the author, Vancouver, December 18, 2013.

"completely knockt out": Bowering diary, October 26, 1968.

"pretty good schedule": Bowering diary, September 16, 1969.

a major flap: Details in Chapter 10: The Lightning Rod.

"speak plainly": Bowering diary, June 22, 1971.

seventy-five people: Hugh Johnston, *Radical Campus: Making Simon Fraser University* (Vancouver: Douglas & McIntyre, 2005), 13.

"your creative work": Sandra Djwa, interviewed by the author, West Vancouver, November 29, 2012.

"instant university": This was Donald Stainsby, writing in *Saturday Night* magazine in March 1964, quoted in Hugh Johnston, *Radical Campus*, 12.

"ugly and ... sublime": Clint Burnham, "Reaching for the Sublime: The Ineffable Vision of Arthur Erickson," *Vancouver Sun*, May 27, 2006, F3. In Thea Bowering's short story, "The Sitter," (in her

collection, *Love at Last Sight* [Edmonton: NeWest Press, 2013]),
a character named Eira knows a certain West Coast university
is said to have grey, brutal architecture. However, "her father
had been an English professor there for thirty years; she had
known it since childhood and found the wet, porous cement and
the hard, fixed lines comforting. In the quadrangle, beneath the
long downward-looking eyes of the offices, Eira killed the hours
waiting for her father by wading up to her knees in the expansive
courtyard pool."

"He put on a good show": Miriam Nichols, interviewed by the author,
Vancouver, August 16, 2012.

"Protestant enclaves": George Bowering, "Vancouver as Postmodern
Poetry," in *Vancouver: Representing the Postmodern City*, ed. Paul
Delany (Vancouver: Arsenal Pulp Press, 1994).

"performative tricks": Chris Turnbull, interviewed by the author,
Ottawa, May 25, 2014.

"a third of the poets": rob mclennan, interviewed by the author, Ottawa,
May 18, 2014.

"life and art blur": Stephen Collis, interviewed by the author,
March 28, 2018.

"so diligent": Pauline Butling interview, August 1, 2013.

"illiterates ... getting a B": Bowering diary, October 17, 1973.

essay with a "W": Carl Peters, interviewed by the author, Vancouver,
February 13, 2015.

"George was excited": Colin Browne, interviewed by the author, Vancouver, March 20, 2017.

"some notion": Reg Johanson, interviewed by the author, Vancouver,
July 21, 2012.

Tads: Issues are held in Special Collections, Simon Fraser University.

like samizdat: Jamie Reid, who edited the fifth issue of *Tads*, dated
August 1999, made the analogy there.

"one bird": Charles Olson, "Projective Verse," *The New American Poetry, 1945–1960*, ed. Donald Allen (Berkeley and Los Angeles: University of California Press, 1999), 390. The original Grove Press edition was published in 1960. Note, though, that Olson was using metaphor, another kind of likening.

"between boards": Bowering diary, April 26, 1964.

"saw what Sidney saw": Bowering diary, October 19, 1964.

It's been said: Nick Mount, *Arrival: The Story of CanLit*, 155.

"here to tell us all": Keith Harrison, writing in the *Tamarack Review*.

"merely brutal": Louis Dudek, "Trouncing the Younger Poets," *Canadian Literature* 34, Autumn 1967, 81. Bowering's crude little poem, "Revenge Against Louis the Dud," in his Montreal book, *The Concrete Island* (Véhicule Press, 1977), settles the score.

"sense of wonder": Hugh McCallum, in the *University of Toronto Quarterly*.

"Goddam": Antony Bellette, letter to George Bowering, August 10, 1967, LAC, George Bowering fonds (1985–2004), first accession, Series A.

affectionate, clever poem: Scott wrote it in blue ink on a piece of white cardboard, which Bowering Scotch-taped into his diary on March 28, 1968. Loving Scott's witty verb, George would write in his 2001 memoir, *A Magpie Life*, about how he and Angela had spent Christmas 1970 in New York City, returning to Montreal on New Year's Eve. They'd been invited to a party across the street from their apartment but "said let's just go to bed instead. We bowered, and Thea Bowering was conceived either at the end of 1970 or at the beginning of 1971."

like the ... pennants: The non-traditional shape has always been a little awkward, since the booklet won't sit squarely on a shelf. Memorably, in the early 2000s, a U.S. border guard handling one asked Bowering, "You call this a book?"

"*A genius ... might be*": Fetherling's review appeared in *Five Cent Review*, a Canadian little magazine, in June 1969.

"*do yrself justice*": Margaret Atwood, letter to George Bowering, January 15, 1969, LAC, as above.

"*poets who would follow*": Bowering, *Writing the Okanagan*, 40.

"*any short poem*": The definition, which Bowering cites in "Years of Lyrics," his preface to his *Changing on the Fly*, comes from the 1957 edition of M.H. Abrams's *A Glossary of Literary Terms*.

CHAPTER 10: THE LIGHTNING ROD

"*refused ... a citizen*": It wasn't that Tallman had refused; he just couldn't face doing the paperwork. His daughter, Karen, says he regarded himself as "a citizen of the West Coast."

"*the faddish American style*": Cited in John Richmond, "Four Montrealers Win Literary Honors." The article probably appeared in the *Montreal Star*; Bowering affixed a clipping of it to his diary on April 26, 1970.

"*dirty little fingernail*": Cited in Richard Lemm, *Milton Acorn: In Love and Anger* (Ottawa: Carleton University Press, 1999), 158.

"*put another [poet] down*": Nicholas Bradley, ed., *We Go Far Back in Time: The Letters of Earle Birney and Al Purdy, 1947–1987* (Madeira Park, B.C.: Harbour Publishing, 2014). Purdy told Birney about this in a letter dated June 14, 1970.

MacEwen had asked ... Weaver: Chris Gudgeon, *Out of This World: The Natural History of Milton Acorn* (Vancouver: Arsenal Pulp Press, 1996), 135.

"*a substantial sum*": Richard Lemm, *Milton Acorn*, as above, 160.

"*Acorn wasn't 'colonized'*": Robert Hogg interview, August 2, 2017.

Explaining the attraction: George Bowering interview, March 16, 2018.

Georgia Straight Writing Supplement: These had evolved from Tishbooks, the book-publishing outgrowth of *TISH*.

"physicists ... Niels Bohr?": Bowering, *How I Wrote Certain of My Books*, as above, 43.

"three-year-old voice": Peter and Meredith Quartermain, "George Bowering," in *Dictionary of Literary Biography: Canadian Writers Since 1960, First Series*, Volume 53 (Farmington Hills, MI: Gale, 1986), 84–92.

"warmed over Gertrude Stein": Bowering, *A Short Sad Book* (Vancouver: New Star Books, 2017), 148. Originally published by Talonbooks in 1977.

"ugly at first": Bowering cites this in "Beauty," in his essay collection *Horizontal Surfaces* (Toronto: BookThug, 2010), 15.

synonym for "careful": Cited in Roy Miki, *A Record of Writing*, as above, 36.

"I hated him": Al Purdy would remember this and call Bowering on it. "Sounded like you didn't like Auden in *Curious*, whereas I think some of his stuff wonderful," he said in a January 1, 1991, letter. Purdy raised the issue again in a June 22, 1992, letter: "Do you still feel the way you seemed to then about Auden? I really don't give a shit what his sexual preferences are, but some of his poems enthrall me." Library and Archives Canada, George Bowering fonds (1999–2003), second accession, Series A, Box 32.

how she dressed: Daphne Marlatt interview, January 11, 2013.

selected poems volume: *West Window: The Selected Poetry of George Bowering*, as above, 1982.

"man on the street": John Oughton, "Lives of the Poets," *Books in Canada* 11, 10, December 1982, 20.

like a family: Robert Fulford, "Canadian Poetry Resembles Forsyte Saga," *Toronto Star*, February 16, 1974.

Sheila Watson: Her thoughts on *Curious* come from her preface to Bowering's *West Window*.

"a small circle": Colin Browne interview, March 20, 2017.

Allophanes: Bowering uses the Greek pronunciation, *a-LOH-feh-neez*.

"The snowball appears": Bowering, *How I Wrote Certain of My Books*, 55.

the title means: Bowering, cited in Miki, *A Record of Writing*, 43.

"virtually incoherent": Jon Peirce, reviewing *West Window* in the Canadian Forum in 1982.

attractive, intelligent: Patrick Holland in *The Canadian Book Review Annual 1976*, ed. Dean Tudor, Nancy Tudor, and Linda Biesenthal (Toronto: Peter Martin Associates), 180.

main question … audience: See "Tradition," in Bowering's *Craft Slices* (Ottawa: Oberon Press, 1985), 131–32.

"the one everyone *liked"*: Bowering diary, January 5, 1975.

"a different Romantic poet" … Rob Dunham: Bowering interview, March 29, 2013.

"such a profound ache": Gary Geddes, "Reading This Bowering Would Be Small Pickings Indeed If It Weren't for a Few Brief Moments," *Globe and Mail*, November 20, 1976, 45.

"how to make verses": Cited in Roy Miki, *A Record of Writing*, 48.

seldom names colours: He is partially colour-blind. On April 28, 2014, he told me he often doesn't know the colours of his own clothes. "Someone said to me, 'How nervy [of you] to wear green pants!' I said, 'They're *green*?' I thought they were, like, grey."

"silly accommodating smile": Bowering diary, March 3, 1974.

fluid, moving: Mary Novik, who has since become known for her historical novels, in a March 4, 1977, *Vancouver Sun* review titled "A Fine Catch."

read "the ones you love": Stephen Collis interview, March 28, 2018.

CHAPTER 11: THE FATHER

"sexiness and detachment": Antony Bellette, letter to "Geo and Ange," January 26, 1967, LAC, George Bowering fonds (1985–2004), first accession, Series A.

"tremendous turn-on town": George Bowering, letter to Margaret Randall and Sergio Mondragón, September 9, 1966, Special Collections, SFU Library, Burnaby, B.C.

"most competent person": Stan Persky, interviewed by the author, Vancouver, August 13, 2012.

"NUTS TO YOU": Maria Hindmarch interview, April 20, 2012.

"all ugly apartments": Bowering letter to John Newlove, June 14, 1971, LAC, as above.

"owner ... was a sexist": Bowering interview, June 29, 2017.

"he tried": Bowering interview, July 1, 2013.

"takes his turn": George Bowering, "Summer 1971. Vancouver," in *His Life: A Poem*, as above, 53.

"loosey-goosey stuff": Jamie Reid interview, June 6, 2013.

imprecise hippie sentiments: Angela Bowering et al., *Piccolo Mondo*, 114–15.

finishing ... Autobiology: George Bowering, *How I Wrote Certain of My Books*, 45.

"I thought 'Althea'": Bowering interview, May 27, 2016.

"more powerful personality": George Stanley, interviewed by the author, Vancouver, July 2, 2013.

impressed her mightily: Beth Jankola, "Don't Ever Call Me 'Chicken' Again, George Bowering," *Georgia Straight*, August 31–September 3, 1971, 20.

"Angela ... is expected to whelp": Bowering letter to Newlove, July 24, 1971, LAC, as above.

Lamaze birth classes: George Bowering and Charles Demers, *The Dad Dialogues*, as above, 47.

excited diary entry: *The Dad Dialogues*, 52.

"I used to envy": Thea Bowering interview, February 18, 2013.

"never says anything": Bowering diary, November 4, 1971.

music by white people: Bowering interview, March 29, 2013.

"the Stupids": "I had to pass up the Stupids in Guelph, burnt out on conferences," Bowering wrote to George Stanley on June 12, 1984, Special Collections, SFU Library.

"involved with sketchy people": Thea Bowering interview, as above.

"this is not normal": Bowering diary, May 10, 1984.

"blah blah blah": Bowering, letter to Margaret Atwood, October 1, 1973, LAC, as above.

"hundred thousand dollar": Newlove letter to Bowering, May 22, 1974, LAC, as above.

At War with the U.S.: Vancouver: Talonbooks, 1974.

"constantly redecorating": Karl Siegler, interviewed by the author, Vancouver, October 16, 2011.

facing west: Hence the title of *West Window: The Selected Poetry of George Bowering*, though Bowering also had in mind Shelley's *Ode to the West Wind*.

George followed at a … distance: Carol Matthews interview, August 8, 2013.

"stories of killers": Thea Bowering, writing about the character Anna in "The Cannibals," a short story in her book, *Love at Last Sight*, as above, 52.

"gets ghastly": George Bowering's diary, March 20, 1976. See also page 76 of Bowering's *His Life: A Poem*. Rosemary Sullivan writes in *The Red Shoes: Margaret Atwood Starting Out* (Toronto: HarperCollins, 1998) that this same movie had depressed and worried Atwood when she was a girl because of its message that women who want to be artists must sacrifice their personal lives.

"playing Mozart": Bowering, letter to George Stanley, March 31, 1983, Special Collections, SFU Library.

guacamole: Bowering diary, June 26, 1984.

"part of being a … writer": Thea Bowering interview, February 20, 2013.

"She sits and reads": George Bowering, letter to Michael Matthews, July 10, 1979, lent to the author by Matthews's widow, Carol.

"in a wink": Bowering diary, April 22, 1991.

sent back a … letter: George Bowering, *The Diamond Alphabet: Base-ball in Shorts* (Toronto: BookThug, 2011), 42.

Both … parents played: Bowering, *The Diamond Alphabet*, 35, 70, and 174.

cheeky account: This was *Egotists and Autocrats: The Prime Ministers of Canada*, which Penguin Canada would publish the following year.

Opening day: Bowering, "Baseball and the Canadian Imagination," in *Imaginary Hand*, as above, 46.

"swing of a … bat": In his *Baseball: A Poem in the Magic Number 9*.

jubilant declaration: Reviewing Bowering's *Touch: Selected Poems, 1960–1970* (in which "Baseball" appears) in the October 1972 issue of *Books in Canada*, the writer/professor Stephen Scobie said he thought the poem "tremendous, even though personally I can't stand baseball."

impromptu games: Brad Robinson, "Kosmic Baseball," *Geist* 19, 76 (Spring 2010), 24.

Granville Grange Zephyrs: Brad Robinson writes in "Kosmic Baseball" that Bowering, who "nicknamed everything," had dubbed the sculpture studio the Granville Grange.

LIP grant: Bowering, *Baseball Love*, as above, 125.

sixteen teams: Brad Robinson, "Kosmic Baseball," 26.

Teen Angels … star player: Max Fawcett, "A League of Their Own," *Vancouver* Magazine, April 18, 2016, http://www.vanmag.com/go/east-van-baseball-league.

"dope fiends": Brian Fawcett, "Losers," in *Taking the Field: The Best of Baseball Fiction*, ed. George Bowering (Red Deer, AB: Red Deer College Press, 1990), 196.

"serious ball": Gill Collins, interviewed by the author, Vancouver, March 20, 2014.

infielder with a weak arm: Bowering, *The Diamond Alphabet*, 43.

"like a sewing machine": Bowering, *A Magpie Life*, 90.

"like a duck": Brian Fawcett interview, July 24, 2013.

"good batting eye": Jim Allan interview, February 27, 2012.

"pretty good hitter": Marke Andrews, interviewed by the author, Vancouver, January 17, 2012.

"grass ... in the dugout": Tom Hawthorn, "Bowering on Deck," *Capilano Review* 3.24, Fall 2014, a special issue called "Bowering's Books," 177.

"a trademark comestible": Bowering, *Baseball Love*, 132.

"day-glo painted softball": Bowering diary, January 2, 1972.

"incredible things": Beth Jankola, "Don't Ever Call Me 'Chicken' Again, George Bowering," as above.

"the amount of theatre": Bowering, *Baseball Love*, 133.

Skill breeds ambition: Brian Fawcett, "Losers," as above, 199.

the Soreheads: Bowering, *Baseball Love*, 176.

seven teams ... seventy players: Guy MacPherson, "Writers with Balls," *Vancouver* Magazine, May 2002, 14.

mattered more ... than eyesight: Guy MacPherson, "Writers with Balls," as above.

"hobbles with pride": George Bowering, letter to Pearl Bowering, June 29, 1986, LAC, George Bowering fonds (1999–2003), second accession, Series A, Box 5.

"riding a chicken": Bowering, *Baseball Love*, 177.

"famous Section 9": See "Nat Bailey Stadium 1987," part of "Yards," a serial poem about ballparks, in Bowering's *Urban Snow*, as above.

"Do something, millionaire": Yvonne Zacharias, "Loudmouth Fan Finds Poetry in Devotion," *Vancouver Sun*, August 21, 2010, H2.

Official Loudmouth Fan: Yvonne Zacharias, as above.

CHAPTER 13: THE TRICKSTER, THE FUNSTER

Grey Owl: James Doyle, "Pseudonyms," in *Encyclopedia of Literature in Canada*, ed. W.H. New, as above, 904–5.

Earle Birney: Elspeth Cameron, *Earle Birney: A Life* (Toronto: Viking/Penguin, 1994), xi.

George Woodcock: Alan Twigg, "George Woodcock Biography," https://bcbookawards.ca/george-woodcock/biography.

"testing the waters": Will Thornton-Trump interview, March 25, 2014.

genesis of the name Eytan: Bowering interview, July 1, 2013.

"a titanic triple": George Bowering as Erich Blackhead, "Zephyrs Gust into First Place," *Georgia Straight* 5, 181, July 6–10, 1971, 18.

Edward Pratoverde: Roy Miki covers all of this in his Bowering bibliography, *A Record of Writing*, 134.

CanWit puzzles: In November 1981, the CanWit feature gave readers mangled titles of Canadian books and asked them to supply the real ones. One CanWit challenge in 1991 was for readers to send in short essays in which they imagined how it would be if Canada and the United States exchanged leaders as part of the free-trade deal then in the news.

"jokey knowingness": Fraser Sutherland, "Literary Tricks and the Larger Concerns," *Globe and Mail*, August 8, 1987, C19.

"I don't hate": Alan Twigg, 1987 George Bowering interview. Search "George Bowering" on www.abcbookworld.com.

"uses his … wit": Peter and Meredith Quartermain, "George Bowering," *Dictionary of Literary Biography: Canadian Writers Since 1960*, as above.

The Rain Barrel: Vancouver: Talonbooks, 1994.

Modern Canadian Stories: Ed. Giose Rimanelli and Roberto Ruberto (Toronto: Ryerson Press, 1966).

"Being Audited": First published in *The Bumper Book*, ed. John Metcalf (Toronto: ECW Press, 1986).

"Staircase Descended": First published in *West Coast Review* 23, 1 (Spring 1988), 33–51. It also appeared in *90: Best Canadian Stories*, ed. David Helwig and Maggie Helwig (Ottawa: Oberon Press, 1990).

"Staircase Descended Again": The story appeared in *The Liar*, Capilano College (North Vancouver), Spring 1992.

Standing on Richards: Toronto: Viking/Penguin, 2004.

"The Lawnmower": First published in the U.S. literary magazine *Wild Dog* in 1964 and then in Bowering's *Protective Footwear: Stories and Fables* (Toronto: McClelland & Stewart, 1978).

"outside-the-canon thing": Bowering interview, June 29, 2017.

"'Workshop' Assignment Poem": In Bowering's 2015 collection, *The World, I Guess*, as above.

"Epitaphs": In Bowering's *Teeth: Poems, 2006–2011* (Toronto: Mansfield Press, 2013).

CHAPTER 14: THE SUCCESS

"about previous writing": Bowering interview, March 18, 2017.

"dead poets": Bowering, *How I Wrote Certain of My Books*, 136.

"mind-meld": Mary di Michele, untitled review of Bowering's *Delayed Mercy and Other Poems*, in *Books in Canada* 16, 74 (June/July 1987), 23.

Rilke ... a vogue: Eva-Marie Kröller, *George Bowering: Bright Circles of Colour*, 77.

The Heritage of Symbolism: London: Macmillan & Co., 1947, 73.

"a cardinal sin": Stephen Collis interview, March 28, 2018.

"built-in feeling": Cited in Roy Miki, *A Record of Writing*, 75.

"a world after God": Karen Leeder and Robert Vilain, eds., *The Cambridge Companion to Rilke* (Cambridge, U.K.: Cambridge University Press, 2010), 3.

"I'd defy anybody": Victor Coleman, interviewed by the author, Toronto, May 28, 2014.

"I dropped the idea": Rachel Loden, "Like a Radio in the Dark: An Email Interview" (interview with George Bowering), *Jacket* Magazine 33, July 2007. http://jacketmagazine.com/33/loden-bowering-iv.shtml.

first edition: Toronto: Coach House Press.

The acrobats ... saltimbanques: C.M. Bowra, *The Heritage of Symbolism*, as above, 79.

"poured his ... power": Marian Engel, "Shapely Lyrics on Death," *Globe and Mail*, April 7, 1984, E21.

would have been fairer: Ronald Hatch, "*Kerrisdale Elegies*: A Feast of Familiar Scenes," *Vancouver Sun*, August 18, 1984, C13.

the 2008 reissue: Karl Siegler, then publisher at Talonbooks, re-edited the work. He told me, "I actually found, in three different places in *Kerrisdale Elegies*, a statement by George in English that I considered to be perfectly in the voice of Rilke ... He ... came up with three Rilke-isms that Rilke never wrote in German."

"my more recent poetry": Bowering diary, December 17, 1991.

a writer ... a scientist: Andrew Gallix used this phrasing in "Oulipo: Freeing Literature by Tightening Its Rules," the *Guardian*, July 12, 2013.

"applying mathematical structures": Bowering, introduction to *My Darling Nellie Grey*, as above, 12.

La disparition: Translated by Gilbert Adair as *A Void* in 1995.

"the thinking was": Frank Davey, email message to the author, August 31, 2012.

died during surgery: Frank Davey, "This Gentleman, bpNichol," in *The Heart Does Break: Canadian Writers on Grief and Mourning*, ed. George Bowering and Jean Baird (Toronto: Random House Canada, 2009), 110.

"the last person": Bowering diary, September 28, 1988.

"mellower, sadder": Margaret Atwood, "Bowering Pie ... Some Recollections," as above, 6.

"My short poems": Bowering diary, February 19, 1988.

Selected Poems: Particular Accidents: Vancouver: Talonbooks, 1980. Talon simultaneously brought out selected-poems volumes by Daphne Marlatt, Fred Wah, Frank Davey, bpNichol, and bill bissett.

"shame the language": George Bowering in an interview conducted by Bill Schermbrucker, Sharon Thesen, David McFadden, and Paul de Barros: "14 Plums," *The Capilano Review* 15. 1 (1979), 100.

"a ... really serious reading": Pauline Butling interview, August 1, 2013.

George Bowering Selected: Toronto: McClelland & Stewart, 1993.

"Irritable Reaching": The title comes from Keats's famous idea of negative capability, which he defined as a state in which people are "capable of being in uncertainties, Mysteries, doubts, without any irritable reaching after fact and reason" (letter to brothers George and Tom Keats, December 21, 1817).

he let Keats: Bowering, *How I Wrote Certain of My Books*, 131.

his maternal grandmother: Her name was Maple Brubacker Brinson, though she isn't named in the poem.

"most astounding": Sharon Thesen interview, June 9, 2013.

CHAPTER 15: THE FRIEND

"its own code": Brian Fawcett interview, July 24, 2013.

"'Majority rules'": Will Thornton-Trump interview, November 15, 2011.

"I got a late-night call": Lionel Kearns interview, November 15, 2012.

"no interest whatsoever": John Newlove, letter to George Bowering, June 16, 1971, LAC, George Bowering fonds (1985–2004), first accession, Series A.

"worried about him": George Bowering in the documentary film, *What to Make of It All? The Life and Poetry of John Newlove*, dir. Robert McTavish (Vancouver: Moving Images Distribution, 2006).

"talking to Jack McClelland": Bowering letter to Newlove, July 26, 1970, LAC, as above.

Diamond Grill: Edmonton: NeWest Press, 1996.

has sold much better: Fred Wah interview, August 1, 2013.

marriage had become stronger: Sandra Martin, *Working the Dead Beat: 50 Lives That Changed Canada* (Toronto: House of Anansi, 2012), 202.

"Feelings are for feeling": Thea Bowering interview, February 20, 2013.

"Olive oil!": George Bowering, postcard to Michael and Carol Matthews, July 26, 1987, lent to the author by Carol Matthews.

"an admirable square": George Bowering interview, July 23, 2014.

"12-volume novel series": Bowering diary, August 4, 2000. On Shelagh Rogers's CBC Radio show, *The Next Chapter*, on September 3, 2016, contributor Jason Proctor recommended *The New Age* to fans of novel series, calling Hood "the Canadian [Karl Ove] Knausgaard."

"most Canadian poet": George Bowering, *Al Purdy* (Toronto: Copp Clark Publishing Company, 1970), 1.

"Wayne and Shuster": George Bowering, "Al and Me," in Bowering, *Words, Words, Words*, as above, 183. Originally published in *The Walrus*, April 2010.

"You take so long": Al Purdy, letter to George Bowering, June 22, 1992, LAC, George Bowering fonds (1999–2003), second accession, Box 32.

"reverse gum boil": Purdy letter to Bowering, June 4, 1989, LAC, as above.

"Here we are": George Bowering, letter to George Stanley, May 26, 1980, Special Collections, SFU Library.

talent for friendship: George Stanley interview, July 2, 2013.

"They ... needed a mother": Gill Collins interview, March 20, 2014.

CHAPTER 16: THE NOVELIST

Mirror on the Floor: Toronto: McClelland & Stewart. Vancouver's Anvil Press reissued the novel in 2014.

"a stand-in": The Delsing figure recalls Alfred Hitchcock's "signatory presence in his films," according to Susan MacFarlane in "Measure's Game: The Writing of George Bowering" (master's thesis, Simon Fraser University, 1989), 84.

Lorne Parton: Bowering clipped Parton's The Written Word column and put it in his diary on May 10, 1967.

A Short Sad Book: First published by Talonbooks.

"fool ... with the trappings": Bowering, "The Three-Sided Room," in his essay collection *The Mask in Place* (Winnipeg: Turnstone Press, 1982), 31.

"get back on the A-list": Bowering, *Pinboy*, 243.

Evangeline: Longfellow's poem is "readable, but ... little read," Harold Bloom writes in *The Best Poems of the English Language* (New York: HarperCollins, 2004).

"Google on their wrist watch": New Star Books publisher Rolf Maurer, email to the author, April 28, 2017.

Burning Water: Don Mills, Ontario: General Publishing. New Star Books reissued it in 2007.

"highlight the shakiness": Jessica Langston, "Burning History: George Bowering's Disruption and Demythologizing of the Canadian Exploration Narrative," in *Open Letter*, Fourteenth Series, 4 (Fall 2010), 108.

"short and unhappy life": Andrew Scott, *The Encyclopedia of Raincoast Place Names: A Complete Reference to Coastal British Columbia* (Madeira Park, B.C.: Harbour Publishing, 2009), 617.

"did speak very fondly": Bowering interview, December 9, 2011.

"without a shred": W. Kaye Lamb, "History as She Wasn't," *Vancouver Sun*, May 29, 1981, 5.

historiographic metafiction: In her book *The Canadian Postmodern: A Study of Contemporary English-Canadian Fiction* (Toronto: Oxford University Press, 1988), 61–77, Linda Hutcheon uses this term to mean telling a historical story in a self-consciously fictive way with the understanding that history, like fiction, is a construct.

still felt queasy: Marcia Crosby, "Construction of the Imaginary Indian," in *Vancouver Anthology*, second edition, ed. Stan Douglas (Vancouver: Talonbooks and Or Gallery, 2011), 280–81.

"Somewhere in the wings": Chris Scott, "A Bum Rap for Poor George Vancouver," *Books in Canada* 9, 9 (November 1980), 9.

"a blast": John Moss, *A Reader's Guide to the Canadian Novel* (Toronto: McClelland & Stewart, 1981), 24.

"does not like … resents": Bowering diary, April 13, 1981.

"overly po-mo": Rolf Maurer, interviewed by the author, Vancouver, January 19, 2012.

offering … a $5,000 advance: Cynthia Good, letter to George Bowering, October 3, 1985, LAC, as above, Box 32.

"You are wonderful": George Bowering, letter to Cynthia Good, October 9, 1985, LAC.

"turn over … furniture": Bowering, *How I Wrote Certain of My Books*, 101.

"Couldn't resist": Bowering interview, May 27, 2016.

four pages: Bowering interview, December 11, 2012.

"reminiscent of … Vonnegut's": Ed Starkins, "Witty, Gripping Novel from Poet Bowering," *Vancouver Sun*, May 23, 1987, G5.

"probably … feminist novel": Frank Davey interview, July 31, 2013.

"None of them were!": Bowering interview, November 9, 2012.

he shivered: Bowering, *How I Wrote Certain of My Books*, 108.

"ahead of his time": Cynthia Good, interviewed by the author, Toronto, May 28, 2014. At the time, she was head of the Creative Book Publishing program at Humber College.

"Why in blazes?": Denise Bukowski, letter to George Bowering, September 8, 1987, LAC, as above, Box 7.

"Greg looks like Gzowski": George Bowering, *The Moustache*, as above, 119.

"Archibald Minjus": That name is his invention, the surname a variant of "Menzies." Bowering had heard that in Scotland "Menzies" is pronounced "Minjus."

Sherrill Grace … afterword: Pages 254 to 260 in the 2008 New Star Books edition.

"without any yuks": Bowering diary, November 4, 1992.

"a poet's novel": Don Gillmor, "Sons of Canada's West Not the Stuff of Myth," *Globe and Mail*, November 26, 1994, E3.

"too many flash-forwards": Letter from Richard Beswick, of Little, Brown and Company, to Elizabeth Van Lear in London, England, May 31, photocopied by Denise Bukowski and sent to George Bowering on September 9, 1994, LAC, as above, Box 7.

"a brilliant work": Hope Dellon, fax to Denise Bukowski, March 14, 1995, LAC.

"intricately plotted": Liam Callahan, "Once Upon a Time in the Northwest," *New York Times Book Review*, February 4, 1996.

CHAPTER 17: THE CRITIC

survival ... brutal winters: In *Survival* (1972), Atwood writes, "Our stories are likely to be tales ... of those who made it back, from the awful experience – the North, the snowstorm, the sinking ship – that killed everybody else."

"garrison mentality": Northrop Frye, "Conclusion" to *Literary History of Canada: Canadian Literature in English, Volume II*, ed. Carl F. Klinck et al. (Toronto: University of Toronto Press, 1965), 342.

"Laughing and guffawing": Bowering interview, March 29, 2013.

Home Truths: Madeira Park, B.C.: Harbour Publishing, 2012.

"pointed out things": Margaret Laurence, letter to George Bowering, November 13, 1974, LAC, George Bowering fonds (1985–2004), first accession, Series A.

Al Purdy Was Here: Dir. Brian D. Johnson, Purdy Pictures, 2015.

five thousand copies: Copp Clark prospectus, enclosed in a letter from Gary Geddes to George Bowering, July 23, 1967, LAC, as above.

unlike ... other criticism: Conversation with Jean Baird, Vancouver, May 27, 2016.

favourite kind of prose: Reviewing a book of Bowering's in the *Globe and Mail* on May 8, 2004, Darryl Whetter wrote that metafiction – "writing that, at least partially, takes writing as its subject – is the writer's cilantro: striking, unmistakable and loved or hated, no middle ground."

"Sheila Watson, Trickster": Bowering made this essay the afterword in *Sheila Watson and "The Double Hook,"* which he edited for Ottawa's Golden Dog Press in 1985.

Craft Slices: bpNichol wrote *Craft Dinner: Stories and Texts, 1966–1976.* Bowering loved the title, borrowed the first half of it, and dedicated *Craft Slices* to Nichol.

alphabetically arranged: He has also used the alphabet as an organizing principle in *Ear Reach* (1982), "Irritable Reaching" (1987), *Horizontal Surfaces* (2010), and *The Diamond Alphabet: Baseball in Shorts* (2011).

most cantankerous: Russell Brown, "Words, Places, Craft: Bowering's Critical Voice," *Essays on Canadian Writing* 38, Summer 1989.

Errata: Red Deer, AB: Red Deer College Press, 1988.

"I much prefer": David McFadden, *Swift Current* message to George Bowering, October 23, 1986, LAC, George Bowering fonds (1999–2003), second accession, Box 27.

particularly unruly: In *A Record of Writing*, 58, Roy Miki says that *Another Mouth* contains "elements of concrete and sound poems, chants, jokes and other trickster techniques ..."

a dialogue ... Tradition: This also appears, as "Tradition," in *Craft Slices*, 19.

My Body ... *introduction*: "Proofing the World: The Poems of David McFadden," reprinted in Bowering's *A Way With Words*.

end of Imaginary Hand: *Imaginary Hand* is Volume I of NeWest Press's The Writer as Critic series, ed. Smaro Kamboureli. "The End of the Line" also appears at the end of *The Contemporary Canadian Poem Anthology*, a 1984 book Bowering edited for Coach House Press.

"My little dog": Bowering was likely thinking of the well-known line of Gertrude Stein's poetry, "I am I because my little dog knows me even if the little dog is a big one" (from "Identity A Poem," 1935).

highly personal affair: In 1967 he was offended when the McGill University professor and poet Louis Dudek criticized his poems on technical grounds and proposed different line breaks.

"I knew George": Roy Miki, interviewed by the author, Vancouver, January 24, 2012.

A reviewer: John Moore, "Bowering Never Looks Back from Postmodern Edge," *Vancouver Sun*, September 12, 1992, D15.

"Alphabiography": Pages 9 to 40 in his 2001 memoir, *A Magpie Life: Growing a Writer*. It had earlier appeared in *Essays on Canadian Writing* 51/52, Winter 1994 / Spring 1994, 21–38.

CHAPTER 18: THE AMATEUR HISTORIAN

Mourning Dove: She was also known as Christine Quintasket, Humishuma, and Mrs. Fred Galler.

"I have a proposition": Cynthia Good, letter to George Bowering, August 31, 1993, LAC, George Bowering fonds (1999–2003), second accession, Series A, Box 32.

payable in ... thirds: Cynthia Good, letter to Denise Bukowski, November 1, 1993, LAC, as above.

"a bullshitter": Good, letter to Bowering, June 2, 1994, LAC.

"might not be as droll": Bowering, letter to Good, September 9, 1994, LAC.

"it's brilliant": Good, fax to Bowering, October 23, 1995, LAC.

"people like my mother": Bruce Mason, "A Swashbuckling History: SFU English Professor George Bowering Reveals the Real B.C.," *Simon Fraser News*, October 3, 1996.

"enough ... about politicians": Bruce Mason, "A Swashbuckling History," as above. With "lifeguards," Bowering had in mind Serafim "Joe" Fortes, the barrel-chested Trinidadian-born man who

taught Vancouver children to swim in English Bay in the early twentieth century.

tone ... is chatty: "Crackerbarrel Tales" was the headline on Stan Persky's review in the *Vancouver Sun*, October 12, 1996, D12.

"small owls burrow": Hence the name of Burrowing Owl Estate Winery, established in Oliver in 1998.

"why not be up-front?": Cynthia Good interview, May 28, 2014.

the Canadian canon: Rolf Maurer email, April 28, 2017.

"swashbuckles ... through": Jean Barman, "B.C. Storyteller Lives Up to Ego," *Globe and Mail*, October 12, 1996, D10.

"so thrilled": Cynthia Good, fax to George Bowering, February 3, 1997, LAC.

"dear familiar face": Bowering diary, March 6, 1997.

Louis St. Laurent: In 1979, Bowering had challenged himself to write a long poem on an inherently dull subject. He wrote one about Louis St. Laurent. Called *Uncle Louis*, it was published in 1980 by Coach House.

"Bowering's PMS": Bowering, letter to Good, March 28, 1998, LAC.

journalist's modus operandi: Bowering was a sportswriter in high school. As a young professor, he interviewed John Lennon and Yoko Ono during their June 1969 bed-in for peace in Montreal, writing an article about it for Vancouver's *Georgia Straight*.

"a cottage industry": Charles Gordon, "Canadian History a Real Hoot," *Edmonton Journal*, September 19, 1999, F6.

"hot-doggers": James Stewart, "Our Flawed, Fascinating Heads," *Montreal Gazette*, October 30, 1999, J1.

"a mission statement": Rex Murphy, "Lectures and Lists on Leaders and Louts," *Globe and Mail*, October 18, 1999, D10–D11.

"economical author intrusion": Verne McDonald, "Putting a Satirical Spin on Canadian History," *Georgia Straight*, September 30–October 7, 1999, 27.

"Once would be cute": J.M. Sullivan, "A New Look at Canadian PMs," *St. John's Telegram*, October 31, 1999, 19.

"Finnish genealogists": George Stanley writes of this in *Vancouver: A Poem* (Vancouver: New Star Books, 2008).

His poem, "Death": In Bowering's *Urban Snow*.

"Imaginary Poems for AMB": In Bowering's *Vermeer's Light: Poems, 1996–2006*. Douglas Barbour, reviewing the book in *Canadian Literature* 194, Autumn 2007, 186, praised these poems for their subtlety and called them "the true elegy for Angela Bowering."

"told so bass-ackwards": Ryan Knighton interview, January 10, 2012.

"Bomber" Lacy: Bowering interview, November 9, 2012.

"unorthodox work": Naomi Brun, "An Amazing History – Perhaps Our Best Ever," *Hamilton Spectator* magazine, May 17, 2003, M9.

"blending the ... àrchitecture": Don Gillmor, "Hipster History Surprisingly Straight," *Globe and Mail*, May 17, 2003, D11.

Kurt Vonnegut: In July 1993, Bowering had written to Vonnegut, with the salutation "Dear Boss," telling him he'd read and enjoyed nineteen of his books. Vonnegut sent him a short, hand-printed note a year later. Library and Archives Canada, George Bowering fonds (1999–2003), second accession, Box 37.

a little too cute: Alex Good, "Breezy 'History' Misses the Mark," *The Record* (Waterloo Region), June 14, 2003, 33.

"gobs of praise": George Fetherling, "The Unexpected Poet Laureate," *Vancouver Sun*, June 7, 2003, D16.

Patricia Roy: University of Victoria professor emerita and co-author of *British Columbia: Land of Promises* (Don Mills, ON: Oxford University Press, 2005).

a journal article: Patricia Roy, "Bowering as Historian," *Open Letter*, Fourteenth Series, 4, Fall 2010, 90–104.

made the idea a reality: Jerahmiel S. Grafstein, "The Making of the Parliamentary Poet Laureate," *Canadian Notes & Queries* 62, 2002, 2.

"Three out of four": "What Rhymes with Prorogue?," *Globe and Mail*, December 15, 2011, A20.

"why I was a good choice": Bowering interview, June 29, 2017.

laureate's web page: https://lop.parl.ca/About/Parliament/Poet/current-poet-laureate-e.html.

"creativity ... quantified": Those words appeared on an earlier version of the laureate's web page, Murray Whyte wrote in "Wanted: A Rhymer for Our Country," *Toronto Star*, March 25, 2004, A23.

"considered solid candidates": "Bowering, 65, was selected over 34 other nominees to be the new poet laureate," Mike Youds wrote in "Unhitching the High Horse," *Kamloops Daily News*, LAC, George Bowering fonds (2006 accession), press clippings from November 2–March 3, Volume 4.

like Robert Pinsky: Grafstein said this to Parliament's Standing Committee on Procedure and House Affairs on June 6, 2001, according to Hansard. See Grafstein, "The Making of the Parliamentary Poet Laureate," as above, 36.

"Predicting who": John Moore, "And the Starter Has the Poets ..." *Ottawa Citizen*, December 27, 2001, A17.

"hardly the mainstream": John Moore, "Against All Odds," *Vancouver Sun*, November 16, 2002, D5.

he isn't embedded: That's debatable. "Isn't it time we declared him a National Treasure?" R.M. Vaughan asked in August 2000 when reviewing Bowering's *His Life: A Poem*.

not ... "a smarmy ... laureate": Susan McMaster, email to Vancouver poet Mark Cochrane (forwarded to Jean Baird and George Bowering), January 3, 2003, LAC, George Bowering fonds (2006–01), Volume 3.

"never felt ... compulsion": Philip Marchand, "Poet Laureate Re-enters Stone Country," *Toronto Star*, July 1, 2003, D4.

"like starting a poem": Helen Buttery, "George Bowering Is Canada's New Court Jester," *Maclean's*, November 25, 2002, 75.

"Lake Erie fury": George Bowering, letter to Mike Matthews, November 11, 2004, lent to the author by Carol Matthews.

Parents from Space: Ottawa: Roussan Publishers, 1994, 1996; Toronto: Scholastic, 1996.

"Horseshit!": Alexandra Gill, "A Little the Verse for Wear," *Globe and Mail*, January 1, 2003, R1.

Johnsonian simile: "Sir, a woman's preaching is like a dog's walking on his hind legs. It is not done well; but you are surprised to find it done at all." Samuel Johnson's biographer, James Boswell, recorded this quotation in 1763.

"suck[ing] up clapping": Vivian Moreau, "Portrait of a Poet," *Times Colonist* (Victoria, B.C.), April 27, 2003, 8.

"Don't get me wrong": T. Paul Ste. Marie, email sent to canadian poetryassociation@yahoogroups.com, January 2, 2003.

"infantile vulgarities": Mark Cochrane, "War of the Poets," *Vancouver Sun*, January 18, 2003, D15–D16.

"Try not to hurt him": Jamie Reid, email to T. Paul Ste. Marie, January 6, 2003, LAC, as above.

"gave me a cake": Bowering interview, March 29, 2013.

"a bore ... more ink": James Hörner, "George Bowering: Vocal Laureate," *Canadian Content*, April 1, 2003, http://www.canadiancontent.ca/interviews/040103bowering.html.

"an excellent ambassador": Terry Schafer, quoted in a *Chronicle* article on February 24, 2004.

"cook up ... plan": Denise Hart, "The United State of Poets Laureate," *Poets & Writers*, March/April 2003, https://www.pw.org/content/united_state_poets_laureate.

"Poetry encapsulates ... history": Debates of the Senate (Hansard), quoted in Grafstein, "The Making of the Parliamentary Poet Laureate," 5.

Lost in the Library: Dir. Elvis Prusic. George Bowering with the Duncan Hopkins jazz trio. Made for Blink Pictures and Bravo!FACT, 2005. See https://vimeo.com/6359731.

circumstances tied his hands: Gordon Phinn, "History's Dirty Laundry Hooks Readers" (primarily an interview about *Stone Country*), *Books in Canada* 32, 8 (November 2003), 12–14.

Grafstein sympathizes: Retired Senator Jerry Grafstein, reached by telephone in Toronto, August 18, 2017.

report to Parliament: George Bowering, "A Report on My Tenure as Parliamentary Poet Laureate, and Some Recommendations," LAC, as above, Box 6b.

a funny story: Bowering diary, June 7, 2004.

CHAPTER 20: THE OLD GINK

"blessed order": "Cates Park and Later That Night," in *Vermeer's Light*, 2006.

"first reader": Dedication in *The World, I Guess*.

"that's the gink": Bowering interview, November 9, 2012.

"I was kinda hoping": Bowering interview, November 9, 2012.

"beyond prolific": Stan Persky interview, August 13, 2012.

Jack David: Telephone conversation with the author, June 14, 2018.

contemplated ... chapbook: Bowering diary, February 3, 2008.

"Say Live": In Bowering's *Craft Slices* (1985).

brainwave of Jean's: "These two gifted writers ... decided at the urging of Bowering's wife, Jean Baird, to put on paper their conversation about fathering daughters ..." – from Tom Sandborn's review of the book, "Diapers, Housework and Fathering Girls," *Vancouver Sun*, October 29, 2016, E6.

"At first, I thought": Kim Pemberton, "Vancouver 'Heroes' Honoured for Saving Lives," *Vancouver Sun*, October 19, 2015.

"cognition is huge": Jean Baird, group email to friends, April 28, 2015.

asked … if he could jump: "George Bowering: Recovering Write-aholic," *BC BookWorld* 29, 3, Autumn 2015, 5.

Sitting in Jalisco: From Nose in Book Publishing, of Castlegar, B.C. This is the micro-press of Linda Crosfield, one of the Georgettes.

asked what legacy: Andrew Bennett, "A Conversation with George Bowering," *Rossland* (B.C.) *News,* September 16, 2010.

valley really was hushed: Bowering interview, March 18, 2017.

Books by George Bowering

Courtesy of abcbookworld.com.

NOVELS

Mirror on the Floor. Toronto: McClelland & Stewart, 1967. Reprinted by Anvil Press, 2014.

A Short Sad Book: A Novel. Vancouver: Talonbooks, 1977. Reprinted by New Star Books, 2017.

Burning Water. Toronto and New York: General Publishing, 1980, 1983. Reissued by Penguin, 1994.

En eaux troubles: Vancouver découvre la côte Ouest, l'amour, la mort. Translated by L.-Philippe Hébert. Montréal: Éditions Quinze, 1982.

Caprice. Toronto and New York: Viking/Penguin, 1987, 1988. 2nd ed., 1994. Reissued by New Star, 2010.

Harry's Fragments: A Novel of International Puzzlement. Toronto: Coach House Press, 1990.

Shoot! Toronto: Key Porter, 1994. Vancouver: New Star, 2009.

Parents from Space. Montreal: Roussan, 1994. 2nd ed., 1996. Toronto: Scholastic, 1996.

Piccolo Mondo: A Novel of Youth in 1961 as Seen Somewhat Later by George Bowering, Angela Bowering, Michael Matthews, and David Bromige. Co-written with Angela Bowering, Michael Matthews, and David Bromige. Toronto: Coach House, 1998.

Diamondback Dog. Montreal: Roussan, 1998.

Pinboy. Toronto: Cormorant Books, 2012.

Attack of the Toga Gang. Toronto: Cormorant, 2015.

No One. Toronto: ECW Press, 2018.

STORIES

Flycatcher & Other Stories. Ottawa: Oberon, 1974.

Concentric Circles. Windsor: Black Moss Press, 1977.

Protective Footwear: Stories and Fables by George Bowering. Toronto: McClelland & Stewart, 1978.

A Place to Die. Ottawa: Oberon, 1983.

The Rain Barrel and Other Stories. Vancouver: Talonbooks, 1994.

Standing on Richards. Toronto: Viking Canada, 2004.

The Box. Vancouver: New Star Books, 2009.

10 Women: Stories. Vancouver: Anvil, 2015.

BOOK-LENGTH POEMS

Sitting in Mexico. Calgary: Beaver Kosmos, 1965.

Baseball. Toronto: Coach House Press, 1967.

George, Vancouver. Kitchener: Weed/Flower, 1970.

Genève. Toronto: Coach House, 1971.

Autobiology. Vancouver: *Georgia Straight* Writing Supplement, Vancouver Series #7, 1972.

Curious. Toronto: Coach House, 1973.

At War with the U.S. Vancouver: Talonbooks, 1974.

Allophanes. Toronto: Coach House, 1976.

Ear Reach. Vancouver: Alcuin, 1982,

Kerrisdale Elegies. Toronto: Coach House, 1984. Reissued by Talonbooks, 2008.

Elegie di Kerrisdale. Translated by Annalisa Goldoni. Rome: Edizioni Empiria, 1996.

His Life: A Poem. Toronto: ECW Press, 2000.

My Darling Nellie Grey. Vancouver: Talonbooks, 2010.

Sticks & Stones. Vancouver: self-published, 1962; Tishbooks, 1963; Talonbooks, 1989.

Points on the Grid. Toronto: Contact Press, 1964.

The Man in Yellow Boots / El hombre de las botas amarillas. Translated by Sergio Mondragón, with collages by Roy Kiyooka. Mexico: Ediciones El corno emplumado, 1965.

The Silver Wire. Kingston: Quarry Press, 1966.

Rocky Mountain Foot: A Lyric, a Memoir. Toronto: McClelland & Stewart, 1969.

The Gangs of Kosmos. Toronto: House of Anansi, 1969.

Touch: Selected Poems, 1960–1969. Toronto: McClelland & Stewart, 1971.

In the Flesh. Toronto: McClelland & Stewart, 1974.

The Catch. Toronto: McClelland & Stewart, 1976.

Poem and Other Baseballs. Windsor: Black Moss, 1976.

The Concrete Island: Montreal Poems, 1967–71. Montreal: Véhicule Press, 1977.

Another Mouth. Toronto: McClelland & Stewart, 1979.

Particular Accidents: Selected Poems. Edited by Robin Blaser. Vancouver: Talonbooks, 1980.

West Window: The Selected Poetry of George Bowering. Toronto: General, 1982.

Smoking Mirror. Edmonton: Longspoon Press, 1982.

Seventy-One Poems for People. Red Deer: RDC Press, 1985.

Delayed Mercy and Other Poems. Toronto: Coach House, 1987.

Urban Snow. Vancouver: Talonbooks, 1992.

George Bowering Selected: Poems, 1961–1992. Toronto: McClelland & Stewart, 1993.

Blonds on Bikes. Vancouver: Talonbooks, 1997.

Poèmes et autres baseballs. Co-written with David McFadden and Michel Albert. Translated by Michel Albert. Montréal: Triptyque, 1999.

Changing on the Fly: The Best Lyric Poems of George Bowering. Vancouver: Polestar Books, 2004.

Vermeer's Light: Poems, 1996–2006. Vancouver: Talonbooks, 2006.

Teeth: Poems, 2006–2011. Toronto: Mansfield Press, 2013.

The World, I Guess: Poems. Vancouver: New Star, 2015.

Some End / West Broadway. Co-written with George Stanley. Vancouver: New Star, 2018.

CRITICISM

Al Purdy. Toronto: Copp Clark, 1970.

Robert Duncan: An Interview. Toronto: Coach House / Beaver Kosmos, 1971.

Three Vancouver Writers. Toronto: Open Letter / Coach House, 1979.

A Way with Words. Ottawa: Oberon, 1982.

The Mask in Place. Winnipeg: Turnstone Press, 1983.

Craft Slices. Ottawa: Oberon, 1985.

Errata. Red Deer: RDC Press, 1988.

Imaginary Hand. Edmonton: NeWest Press, 1988.

Left Hook: A Sideways Look at Canadian Writing. Vancouver: Raincoast, 2005.

Horizontal Surfaces. Toronto: BookThug, 2010.

Words, Words, Words: Essays and Memoirs. Vancouver: New Star, 2012.

Writing the Okanagan. Vancouver: Talonbooks, 2015.

CHAPBOOKS

How I Hear Howl. Montreal: Beaver Kosmos, 1967.

Two Police Poems. Vancouver: Talon, 1969.

The Sensible. Toronto: Massasauga Editions, 1972.

Layers 1–13. Kitchener: Weed/Flower, 1973.

In Answer. Vancouver: William Hoffer, 1977.

Uncle Louis. Toronto: Coach House, 1980.

Spencer and Groulx. Vancouver: William Hoffer, 1985.

Quarters. Prince George: Gorse Press, 1991. Winner, bpNichol Chapbook Award, 1991.

Do Sink. Vancouver: Pomflit, 1992. Winner, bpNichol Chapbook Award, 1992.

Sweetly. Vancouver: Wuz, 1992.

Blondes on Bikes. Ottawa: above / ground press, 1997.

A, You're Adorable. Ottawa: above / ground, 1998, 2004.

6 Little Poems in Alphabetical Order. Calgary: House Press, 2000.

Some Writers. Calgary: House Press, 2001.

Joining the Lost Generation. Calgary: House Press, 2002.

Lost in the Library. Ellsworth, ME: Backwoods Broadsides, 2004.

Rewriting my Grandfather. Vancouver: Nomados, 2005.

Crows in the Wind. Toronto: BookThug, 2006.

A Knot of Light. Calgary: No Press. 2006.

Montenegro 1966. Calgary: No Press, 2007.

U.S. Sonnets. Vancouver: Pooka, 2007.

Eggs in There. Edmonton: Rubicon, 2007.

Some Answers. Mount Pleasant, ON: Laurel Reed Books, 2007.

Horizontal Surfaces. Edmonton: Olive Collective, 2007.

Tocking Heads. Edmonton: above/ground, 2007.

There Then. Prince George: Gorse Press, 2008.

Animals, Beasts, Critters. Vancouver: JB Objects, 2008.

Valley. Calgary: No Press, 2008.

Fulgencio. Vancouver: Nomados, 2008.

According to Brueghel. North Vancouver: Capilano University Editions, 2008.

Shall I Compare. Penticton: Beaver Kosmos, 2008.

A Little Black Strap. St. Paul, MN: Unarmed, 2009.

Los Pájaros de Tenacatita: Poems of la Manzanilla del Mar. Castlegar, B.C.: Nose-in-Book Publishing, 2013.

Sitting in Jalisco. Castlegar: Nose-in-Book, 2016.

MEMOIRS

The Moustache: Memories of Greg Curnoe. Toronto: Coach House, 1993.

A Magpie Life: Growing a Writer. Toronto: Key Porter, 2001.

Cars. Co-written with Ryan Knighton. Toronto: Coach House Books, 2002.

Baseball Love. Vancouver: Talonbooks, 2006.

How I Wrote Certain of My Books. Toronto: Mansfield Press, 2011.

The Diamond Alphabet: Baseball in Shorts. Toronto: BookThug, 2011.

The Hockey Scribbler. Toronto: ECW, 2016.

HISTORY AND NON-FICTION

Bowering's B.C.: A Swashbuckling History. Toronto: Viking, 1996. Penguin, 1997.

Egotists and Autocrats: The Prime Ministers of Canada. Toronto: Viking, 1999. Penguin, 2000.

Stone Country: An Unauthorized History of Canada. Toronto: Viking, 2003.

The Dad Dialogues: A Correspondence on Fatherhood (and the Universe). Co-written with Charles Demers. Vancouver: Arsenal Pulp Press, 2016.

PLAYS

The Home for Heroes. Vancouver: Prism, 1962.

What Does Eddie Williams Want? Montreal: CBC Television, 1966.

George, Vancouver. Vancouver: CBC Radio, 1972.

Sitting in Mexico. Vancouver: CBC Radio, 1973.

Music in the Park. Vancouver: CBC Radio, 1986.

The Great Grandchildren of Bill Bissett's Mice. Vancouver: CBC Radio, 1989.

AS EDITOR (BOOKS)

The 1962 Poems of R.S. Lane. Toronto: Ganglia Press, 1965.

Vibrations: Poems of Youth. Toronto: Gage, 1970.

The Story So Far. Toronto: Coach House, 1972.

Imago (Twenty). Vancouver: Talonbooks, 1974.

cityflowers, by Artie Gold. Montreal: Delta Canada, 1974.

Letters from Geeksville: Red Lane to George Bowering, 1960–1964. Prince George: Caledonia Writing Series, 1976.

Great Canadian Sports Stories. Ottawa: Oberon, 1979.

Fiction of Contemporary Canada. Toronto: Coach House, 1980.

Selected Poems: Loki Is Buried at Smoky Creek, by Fred Wah. Vancouver: Talonbooks, 1981.

My Body Was Eaten by Dogs: Selected Poems of David McFadden. Toronto: McClelland & Stewart, 1981. New York: Cross Country, 1981.

"1945–1980." In *Introduction to Poetry: British, American, Canadian*, edited by
 Jack David and Robert Lecker. Toronto: Holt, Rinehart and Winston
 of Canada, 1981.

The Contemporary Canadian Poem Anthology. Toronto: Coach House, 1983.

Sheila Watson and "The Double Hook": The Artist and Her Critics. Ottawa:
 Golden Dog Press, 1984.

Taking the Field: The Best of Baseball Fiction. Red Deer: RDC Press, 1990.

Likely Stories: A Postmodern Sampler. With Linda Hutcheon. Toronto: Coach
 House, 1992.

An H in the Heart: A Reader. With Michael Ondaatje. Toronto: McClelland
 & Stewart, 1994.

And Other Stories. Vancouver: Talonbooks, 2001.

The 2008 Griffin Poetry Prize Anthology. Toronto: House of Anansi, 2008.

The Heart Does Break: Canadian Writers on Grief and Mourning. With Jean
 Baird. Toronto: Vintage Canada, 2009.

AS EDITOR OR CO-EDITOR (PERIODICALS)

TISH. Vancouver: 1961–63.

Imago. Calgary, London, Montreal, and Vancouver: 1964–74.

Beaver Kosmos Folios. Calgary, London, Montreal, and Vancouver: 1966–75.

Acknowledgments

Thank you to the British Columbia Arts Council for having enough faith in me, a first-time author, to give me a grant. It covered two trips to Ottawa, where I consulted parts of Library and Archives Canada's dauntingly large George Bowering archive.

Bowering and Jean Baird kindly received me at their home many times, answered my questions, and lent me fifty volumes of George's long-running diary. Without it, my comprehension of his life story would have been much spottier. The loan of this supremely personal document was a real act of trust on Bowering's part.

I owe a debt to Roy Miki, whose prize-winning book, *A Record of Writing: An Annotated and Illustrated Bibliography of George Bowering*, is a meticulously detailed record of George's literary career up to 1989. It's where every Bowering scholar needs to start.

Thanks to everyone in George's life who bolstered my understanding by speaking with me, sometimes more than once. These informants include:

– his mother, Pearl Bowering, his brother Roger Bowering, and his daughter, Thea Bowering;

– childhood and family friends Tony Bellette, Dr. John Boone, Lynn Spink, and Will Thornton-Trump;

– literary friends and approximate contemporaries Douglas Barbour, Pauline Butling, Victor Coleman, Pierre Coupey, Frank Davey, Brian Fawcett, Maria Hindmarch, Robert Hogg, Smaro Kamboureli, Lionel Kearns, Daphne Marlatt, Carol Matthews, Dan McLeod, Roy Miki, W.H. New, Stan Persky, Carol Reid and Jamie Reid, George Stanley, Sharon Thesen, and Fred Wah;

– publishers Stan Bevington, Cynthia Good, Rolf Maurer, rob mclennan, and Karl Siegler;

– former academic colleagues and/or bosses Sandra Djwa, Kathy Mezei, David and Mary-Ann Stouck, and Jerry Zaslove;

– former students and/or younger literary friends Colin Browne, Stephen Collis, Wayde Compton, Roger Farr, Dwight Gardiner, Reg Johanson, Ryan Knighton, Miriam Nichols, Carl Peters, and Chris Turnbull; and

– Jim Allan, Marke Andrews, and Gill Collins, who played ball with Bowering.

As well, I appreciate the time and thoughts of Karen Tallman and retired Senator Jerry Grafstein.

An earlier version of the first paragraphs of Chapter 6 appeared in *The Capilano Review* 3.24 (Fall 2014). Thanks to the editors.

The librarians and archivists who helped me were Catherine Hobbs, Lynn Lafontaine, and Sara Viinalass-Smith at Library and Archives Canada, and Tony Power, Simon Fraser University's Contemporary Literature Collection librarian. John Mackie, of the *Vancouver Sun*, and Carolyn Soltau, of Postmedia Network, helped track down archived newspaper photos.

The professional rigour with which Talonbooks editors Catriona Strang, andrea bennett, and Charles Simard handled my manuscript impressed me. There are thousands of facts in this book and, while I've done my level best to keep them straight, any errors or infelicities are mine. With luck, there won't be many *errata*.

Publisher's Acknowledgments

Talonbooks would like to thank Tony Power, Ewa Delanowski, and Judith Polson from the Simon Fraser University Library's Contemporary Literature Collection for their help with the images inserted in *He Speaks Volumes*.

Index